Astrology for Career Success

How to Analyze Career Choices and Timing

by Gayle Geffner

Astrology for Career Success
How to Analyze Career Choices and Timing

by Gayle Geffner

A first edition including substantial portions of this book
was published in 2003 with the title Pathways to Success.
This book is a revised and expanded version.

Cover and book design by Maria Kay Simms

Library of Congress Control Number 2012934709

International Standard Book Number: 978-1-934976-30-2

Published by ACS Publications, an imprint of Starcrafts LLC
334-A Calef Highway, Epping, NH 03042
http://www.starcraftspublishing.com
http://www.astrocom.com
http://www.acspublications.com

Printed in the United States of America

Dedication

This book is for my husband,
James Geffner,
without whose support it
would not have been possible.

Acknowledgements

Thank you to my friend, Barbara Hawkins
for contributions to Chapter One, as well
as for her many helpful suggestions.

Thanks also to Maria Kay Simms
for her editorial assistance.

I am especially grateful to my clients
(whose names were changed in the text,
but whose birth data and experiences are
quite real), for permitting me to include
their charts in this book, and to relate
their stories and and their consulting
experiences with me.

Table of Contents

Tables & Chart Illustrations

Introduction

Astrological career counseling is of the utmost importance. Astrologers assume a great responsibility when helping clients with career choices and opportunities. If you choose to help others in connection with career counseling, this book will prove invaluable. The methods discussed will also apply to other facets of life.

If you work full-time, you usually spend more time at work than at home. It is a time when ideally you are fulfilled, are making a contribution, and want to rise in your chosen field, or at the very least be happy most of the time you spend at work. Career choice, timing of career events, change of jobs or pursuing further education for your career are important parts of each of our lives. Feeling confused about our career is common to all of us.

If you are fortunate, you will be happy in your career. If you are lucky, you will find new opportunity even when you are not looking for it. Happenstance is beneficial if you are open to it. Perhaps you may find a new direction that is fulfilling to you. In fact, astrology leads us into directions we may not have thought of in our current life circumstance.

Astrology is a road map for each part of your life, including your career.

When you look at a map, you can go in almost any direction you choose. You can choose the difficult road, what appears to be the easy road, the road untraveled, the road with many sites, the road with many road blocks that may not lead you where you want to go, or just stay put.

Astrology can be your guide no matter what you choose to do. Astrology can show you the best times to make a change, the best times to pursue further education or the best times to start a new business. However, and more importantly, astrology offers insight into your deepest desires and even your subconscious needs. Astrology helps bring forth what may be truly fulfilling as well as lucrative for you. Let's face it, we all want to be compensated well for what we do. But, we also want our desires and our personal values to be fulfilled, not just monetarily rewarded. WE WANT IT ALL. It is the meshing of these two things and a way to get there that astrology brings to the table.

Although I begin with very basic astrology applicable to career direction and potential, this book will quickly progress into the use of intermediate to advanced techniques. Some of the key methods that I use for career counseling, as presented here, assume prior knowledge of astrology on an intermediate to advanced level. For readers who may not yet be familiar with some of the techniques I'm using, please consult my bibliography where I have recommended books that I've used to help myself learn them. Using the full range of the key methods that I am demonstrating in this book can help you gain deeper insight into yourself and your career potential.

If you are already a consulting astrologer, may my method assist you in guiding your clients to achieve deeper insight into themselves, their career direction and success potential.

This book contains comprehensive definitions, astrological patterns and an emphasis on certain planets and their placements. There are many astrological chart examples in the book. **The last chart example, in particular, ties the entire book together.** It is of a Los Angeles police officer who was asked to do something that was probably as difficult as anything he had ever done on a moral level and tested his true character and moral fiber. Yes, he received a salary, but compensation was not what was important here, and he showed courage and demonstrated what his real personal value system was. What went on is outlined in a cohesive and clear astrological manner. It is a true demonstration of **the full scope of** what this book is about.

Chapter One

The "At Least Three Charts" Method

In order to analyze career potential, I use the **"at least three charts"** method. I look at three astrological charts. The three charts I prefer to use are the Natal Chart, the Solar Return Chart[1] (including Solar Return birthday trips) and the Lunar Return[2]. (You should use whichever three charts you are most comfortable with, but they should include, of course, the natal chart plus two other charts that address current patterns.) If I miss something in one of the three charts, I invariably find it in one of the other charts. Also, I use three charts to verify each other. Something may not appear as prominent in one chart as it does in another, thus its importance may not be as easy to spot. Using three charts gives the astrologer a very sound basis for counseling. (In fact, I recommend this method in all astrological counseling.) I then interpret each chart completely with a view toward career. The Three Charts Method allows you to ascertain clear patterns upon which to act and gives you a complete picture of career potentials for your clients.

---

[1] A Solar Return chart is calculated for the time each year the Sun returns to the exact position it occupied at your birth. Solar Return charts are discussed more fully in Chapter Six.

[2] A Lunar Return occurs about once a month when the Moon returns to the exact position it occupied at your birth. Lunar Returns are discussed more fully in Chapter Seven.

The Natal Chart

A natal chart, calculated for the date, time and place of birth, is your personal guide, but only a guide, offering insight into your personal choices. Rarely, if ever, is anything set in stone. In fact, that is the fun of a natal chart—it can indicate options you may not be aware of, or that you thought were unattainable. In order to interpret an astrological natal chart, there are basic procedures that any good astrologer must follow. The basic techniques listed below may be applied to any type of chart interpretation and work extremely well in career counseling.

Begin with your Sun Sign. It is where your drive and ambition lie and where you will shine. This is the place to start when looking at career potential.

Look up the definition of your Ascendant (the sign on the cusp of the first house) to determine your personality, how you appear to others and your direction in this lifetime. Obviously, your direction in this lifetime will greatly affect your career, and your personality greatly affects the type of career you may choose, although the second, sixth and tenth houses are particularily important.

Go around the astrological wheel and interpret each of the twelve houses. The meanings given for each house and sign are discussed later in this chapter. Any house on a astrological chart may hold clues to the type of career you choose, although the second, sixth and tenth houses should be given extra weight.

Look to the ruler of the sign on the cusp of the house for further help in interpreting that house. For example, the tenth house is the house of career and profession but there may be no planet in that house. Suppose Aries is on the cusp. The ruler of Aries is Mars, so you would look to the house where Mars lies. If Mars lies in your eighth house, you may work in insurance or government or handle other people's money. (These are eighth house areas.)

You must also look at the qualities and elements of the signs. For instance, Aries is a fire sign and you would approach your career with a tremendous amount of fire energy. Aries is a cardinal sign and cardinal signs represent action.

As you go from house to house, look up how the planets in a house add further information to the cusp meaning of the house. Some planets may reinforce the motifs of the astrological sign on the cusp, while other planets bring in conflicting themes to be faced. Some planets are more personal and others represent society. Your Mercury is very personal, indicating how you think and communicate. Pluto is slow moving, and often indicates world conditions. If Pluto is in your tenth house, you may work for the good of the community.

A stellium[3] of planets is an obvious indication of where a client's strengths lie. You must always look at a stellium with a view toward how such a concentration of planets can help your client choose a career, and show opportune times to act regarding his/her career. Again, this will be repeated in the chapter, "Advanced Methods," but should be mentioned at this time for initial delineation.

Also consider the aspects the planets make to each other for their further significance throughout the chart. This is very important in light of your career. Aspects will give you clearer clues as to your careeer even when there are no planets in your sixth or tenth houses. An **unaspected planet** is quite significant, since its energies are not harnessed in any way. When an unaspected planet is subject to a transit, a tremendous opportunity is created to use this usually non-harassed energy constructively. This will also be discussed with further examples in the chapter on "Advanced Methods."

I also look at certain transits, aspects, the South Node and planets conjunct the South Node, and combinations of planets when advising a client on career matters.

The two transiting planets I emphasize when looking at a client's career are Jupiter and Saturn. Jupiter opens doors. It is the planet of opportunity. Saturn is equated with restrictions or obstacles. Obviously, Jupiter transting the Second, Sixth or Tenth Houses will indicate open doors for work, career and monetary advancement, while Saturn may symbolize limited opportunties or restricted advancement for a time. At the very least, with a Saturn transit, you will have to work very hard to accomplish your goals. I do not necessarily find Saturn restrictions a bad thing, though, since Saturn is a teacher. What you learn with a Saturn transit benefits you throughout your lifetime. A Saturn transit may be a very good time to work toward long-term goals. Jupiter and Saturn transits should not be solely looked at when transiting the Second, Sixth and Tenth Houses. Look at Jupiter and Saturn as timing mechanisms when transiting midpoints or sensitive points that activate any of these three houses. This will be repeated with further examples in the chapter on "Advanced Methods," but should be mentioned at this time, for initial chart interpretation.

You should get a feeling of what each house represents by continually

[3] Stellium usually refers to three or more planets occupying the same sign. (Some refer to a stellium by house as well.)

[4] Transit can refer to a planet's movement through a zodiac sign or house of the horoscope. Transits can also refer to the position of the planets on a specific date—usually compared to a natal chart. Transits are discussed more fully in Chapter Three.

weighing planets, house cusps, rulers and aspects to determine which motifs are repeated by several chart factors and which motifs are minimized.

By using the above method, the houses come alive. There is a constant flux of information until a vivid picture of career potential forms.

It is critical to interpret the entire chart for effective career counseling. There may be certain elements which are not apparent at first glance, but which can greatly enhance your client's career. These need to be emphasized and worked with in order to aid the person in his/her career choices. Although this book is intended for career counseling, it also reveals the method I use to interpret charts in general, and for any other specific area of life in which a client may require counseling.

Critical: Though I have an educational background in psychology and sociology, I refer some of my clients to professional counselors if they are having a terribly difficult time. Throughout the following chapters, I indicate that if you do not have the educational tools and licensing for counseling (as differentiated from astrological guidance only), you should refer your client to a professional counselor.

Definitions
The Twelve Signs of the Zodiac—the "Sun Signs"

There are twelve astrological signs which represent twelve different sets of character traits, commonly called "Sun Signs." They are based on the date of birth and correspond to each of the twelve houses on a solar chart (a chart set up for the date, but not the time of your birth). Most of us relate to our Sun sign type, although due to other factors in our charts, other signs may also be strong. If you choose a career that harmonizes with the traits described for your Sun sign (or perhaps the house your Sun rules, the house of Leo within your chart), you are more likely to feel fulfilled, your self-esteem will rise and you will be proud of what you do. The Sun Signs indicate traits, as described below. However, these traits are just symbols or suggestions (as are my possible career suggestions that demonstrate characteristics of the signs), and are not written in stone. Each individual will determine which of the traits are brought into his/her professional life. They are:

Aries—a cardinal sign, ruled by Mars

Aries suggests a fierce drive. You are a self-starter. You will bring the Aries traits into any career with a tremendous enthusiasm and quick action. You will be the first to try something new and move in a new direction in a fearless manner. You are highly competitive (fiery) and seek attention, which makes you a very good worker—one who tries to outshine others and gain favorable attention from the boss. On the other hand, if you are the boss, you will consistently want to be moving forward and work will not be dull.

You must watch the Mars combativenes when working with others, and use your Mars energy in a positive manner. In order to be fulfilled in your career, you should look for a position with challenge and an opportuntiy to regularly try something new.

For an example of an Aries type, I will use the Sixth House which relates to work routines, colleagues and health matters. How we feel about our work often affects our health and how we work, i.e., working too hard affects our health. If Aries is on the sixth house cusp, or Mars is in the sixth house, you will probably work for others with extreme drive and enthusiasm, and will advance your position while in the employ of others. You are really at your best when there is competition and when working in a busy, often noisy atmosphere—to the point of near chaos.

Aries rules the head and face, so guard against stress headaches in the workplace. Look to the Mars placement in the natal chart for further insight into the cusp and house where Aries is located.

Taurus—a fixed, earth sign ruled by Venus

Taurus suggests a practical, dependable, creative person, a lover of luxury and beauty, and an artistic temperament. Your dependability, as well as your methodical, plodding manner of getting the job done are tremendous career assets. You will create a pleasing work environment and since you love possessions, you will probably work very hard for personal gain. The Venus charm is an asset in dealing with others. Since you are both methodical and charming, such fields as accounting or law where you can use your mental abilities and your charm to obtain new clients are practical potential career choices. Taurus also suggests loyalty, and you are definitely a loyal employee (or employer). Any situation in which you work with others in a structured environment should bring you happiness.

Taurean qualities also indicate that you do not like change. Although you will work very hard and be dependable, you must learn to adapt when your work environment is changed. Taurus' creative side may manifest in an employee artist, but the need for stability would probably eliminate a freelance artist. Music and crafts are also possibilities. Taurus rules the throat and neck. A tension-stiff neck could arise if you are slumped over a desk, or if there is stress at work. Look to the Venus placement in the natal chart for further insight into the cusp and house where Taurus is located.

Gemini—a mutable, air sign ruled by Mercury

Gemini indicates adaptability and the need to have variety when working. Since Gemini is a dual sign, it suggests you will probably work on more than one project or more than one job at a time. Without multiple tasks,you may tend to be highstrung, looking for a place to expend nervous energy.

Gemini also indicates a quick mind and someone who is very verbal. You will be more fulfilled with a career that involves a lot of communication, writing or problem-solving, and one which varies not only from day to day, but hour to hour. One example is a secondary school teacher who teaches English for one period and physical education the next, or perhaps is a speech writer for many different persons. Journalism is also very rewarding to a Gemini.

Gemini rules the hands, arms and nervous system. You must have a physical release, as well as mental release, or you may have problems with your pent-up nerves. Look for the Mercury placement in the natal chart for more insight into the cusp and house where Gemini is located.

Cancer—a cardinal, water sign ruled by the Moon

Cancer indicates a sympathetic person who is emotional, romantic, retentive, sometimes insecure, and above all, a nurturer. Cancer also has a wonderful memory for detail, as well as for people. Here again is a variety of attributes upon which to draw for career potential. You must take care not to crawl back into a shell when facing adversity or as an escape. Fulfilling career choices might include helping others (i.e. day care, nursing, physcial therapy). Or, any career in which you feel like you are doing good would be tremendously rewarding for you.

Another indication of the Cancer personality is the homebody. You may be happy in working from home while raising a family. However, the Cancer memory for people and details can also suggest a good business person. When afflicted in any way, you should be careful not to let insecurity creep in and allow you to become upset while working. Every career has its difficulties—do not take them to heart. Also be careful not to hide too much from the world. I can visualize an energetic Cancerian writing romance novels from his/her home.

Cancer rules the stomach and too much job stress can contribute to digestive problems. Look for the Moon placement in the natal chart for more insight into the cusp and house where Cancer is located.

Leo—a fixed, fire sign, ruled by the Sun

Fire signs are energetic. Leo suggests generosity, confidence, stubbornness—someone who is opinionated, persistent and passionate. These are strong traits to bring to a career. Above all, Leo indicates creativity.

Leo is the actor and the spokesperson of the zodiac. As with everything else, you will gamble and take risks in your profession, especially if it puts you in the limelight. You are fulfilled in a career that affords you lots of attention. If you work for an ad agency, you want your ads to be highly visible. If you work for a hamburger chain, you want to be the one in the hamburger costume calling in business off the street.

You are aided by your extreme confidence, and you are not easily discouraged. You will persist until you achieve your goal. In fact, one of the most important indications of Leo is your ever-optimistic outlook while pursuing your goals. Because another Leo trait is generosity, your co-workers willl put up with your overconfidence and (at times) irritatingly fierce energy. You may not give them a break, but they like you anyway. You are happy on a job that affords you the opportunity to find new and creative ways to accomplish your tasks.

Leo governs the heart, and a lot of heart is what you bring to your career. Look for the Sun placement in the natal chart for more insight into the cusp and house where Leo is located.

Virgo—a mutable, earth sign ruled by Mercury

Virgo suggests a person who is analytical, meticulous, critical, cautious, shy, health-oriented and a linear, step-by-step worker. In order to be fulfilled, you may wish to seek out a career that satisfies the analytical mind, perhaps working alone. You will feel satisfied when you achieve recognition from superiors for your efficiency and organizational skills. You will draw attention to yourself by figuring out the most expeditious ways to accomplish any task, and this is an area of satisfaction for you.

Although Virgo shyness may put you in the background while your boss received the accolades, you will probably be quite happy. What boss wouldn't want an employee like you? If you work for yourself, you will be productive and happy. If you are high up on the chain of command, you will be happy and fulfilled when allowed to work on your own, contributing your individual expertise to the company.

Your analytical mind is good for business and accounting, and you will probably be contented in any job tht uses analysis of numbers, issues or economic schemes. You would be a good code breaker or statistician. Mercury rules the solar plexus and intestines, and these are areas to watch when you are under work stress. Look for the Mercury placement in the natal chart for more insight into the cusp and house where Virgo is located.

Libra—a cardinal, air sign ruled by Venus

Libra indicates you may be indecisive, nonagressive, artistic, adaptable, temperatmental, just and charming. Libra is a dual sign, and just as Gemini, may have more than one job or will at least be doing more than one thing on the job. There is an indication of working with a partner. Since seeing both sides of an issue is a strong Libra trait, you are adaptable when necessary. This is a very good trait when working with others, and a very big asset as an employee or employer. However, Libra tends to weigh one side against the other over and over again, and may be too slow in making decisions. Because of this trait, you must guard against seeming indecisive to your employer. On the other hand, your decisions are well thought out and viewed from all sides, since this is your nature. Such jobs as an arbitrator or perhaps a dipomat would intrigue you. You will also be satisfied if you lean toward your artistic side and work in any field having to do with beauty, luxury or design. Libra is a charming sign, and this trait is essential in working with others.

On the other hand, you may be non-agressive, and your kindness may create an environment within which you are too accommodating. It is important for you to look for a balance, since you must meet your own needs just as you meet the needs of others. Libra rules the kidneys, loins and lower back. Take care against mild kidney infections and lower back pain when under any stress on the job. Look for the Venus placement in the natal chart for more insight into the cusp and house where Libra is located.

Scorpio—a fixed, water sign ruled by Mars and Pluto

Scorpio suggests one who is suspicious, penetrating, magnetic, sarcastic, jealous, domineering, intuitive, persevering, loyal and powerful. As with all fixed signs, you will work doggedly, determined to finish a project. Nothing makes you happier than ferreting out that which is hidden, solving the puzzle. You are indeed the natural detective of the zodiac.

An intense, darker side is also indicated with Scorpio, and there is a temptation to misuse power. You must take care to control this impulse and use power for the good of humankind. One good example of using a dark side to positive advantage is crime solving. You would be a good police detective or forensic scientist, using your skills to seek the truth.

You are intuitive and this is a key to your ability to go beyond the surface, to look until you see the whole picture. For example, if you work in a large corporation, you are able to determine the motives and agendas of the executives in a corporate takeover. You are fulfilled by work which allows you to get to the bottom of things. Psychiatry is a Scorpio interest. Other areas of interest might be a minister, psychic or anything in the occult field. You are very determined, and this is a good trait if you do not let it turn into an obsession.

Scorpio rules the bladder and sex organs. Drink lots of water under stress. Look for the Mars or Pluto placements in the natal chart for more insight into the cusp and house where Scorpio is located.

Sagittarius—a mutable, fire sign ruled by Jupiter

The sign of Sagittarius suggests you may be self-righteous, blunt, dogmatic, restless, scattered, hopeful, optimistic, giving, idealistic and desire freedom. In fact, the strongest Sagittarian trait is the desire for independence and freedom, and your career must reflect this trait.

Your ideals should also be reflected in your career if you are to be fulfilled and proud of what you do. You cannot do a job in which you feel your values are compromised.

You work with fiery energy and, being ruled by Jupiter, you are open to just about anything. You are the one that other people follow. You could easily come up with a life philosophy for the 21st century, or work for the good of others in an organizations such as Amnesty International promoting human ideas, just as long as you keep moving and communcating with others. Traveling and lecturing are perfect for you. You will open up possibilities to the world. However, you do need to watch for a self-righteous attitude.

Sagittarius rules the liver, hips, thighs and blood. Watch hurting hips and thighs through over-extended activity or rushing around and not being careful; monitor your blood pressure when under work-related stress. Look for the Jupiter placement in the natal chart for more insight into the cusp and house where Sagittarius is located.

Capricorn—a cardinal, earth sign ruled by Saturn

The sign of Capricorn indicates self-discipline, seriousness, rigidity, secretiveness, caution, responsibility and cynicism. You will be fulfilled in a career which incorporates discipline and rules, such as accounting. Your approach is very cautious and you act with great responsibility. A career which enables you to act in a disciplined manner and show the world how responsible you are will make you proud.

You may be rigid, so don't like to change careers, but if you are not proud of what you are doing, you will reluctantly change. Working with taxes or a tax attorney would be ideal as you would be cautious with your client's finances. An architect, engineer or surveyor are also possibilities.

With Saturn as a ruler, you will work very hard. Although you may encounter obstacles in your career path, you will work through them tenaciously. Obstacles will only make you more determined and an even better worker when you achieve your goals. Sometimes, however, you get insecure and give up after a failure. Beware of cynicism which could turn to chronic pessimism if you are not careful.

Capricorn rules the knees and spleen. Get up from your desk and swing your legs. Keep your knees flexible. Look for the Saturn placement in the natal chart for more insight into the cusp and house where Capricorn is located.

Aquarius—a fixed, air sign ruled by Uranus.

Aquarius suggests that you are self-suffcient and a visionary in respect to ideals rather than "seeing a vision," reformer, rebellious, impersonal. Since Aquarius is ruled by Uranus, if you are to be happy you must have a career that is unpredictable and goes beyond the bounds of the field within which you work. You are the rebel (with a cause) and do not work using traditional methods.

Even if you are stuck in a seemingly mundane job, you will find a new approach. You are the inventor. Your ideas are far reaching. Your thinking may be detached. If you combine your far-reaching ideals with a scientific detachment, you will be the person with the new invention, unusual economic approaches to trade which benefit the entire world, new ways of space exploration, or a really innovative teaching style.

Aquarius-based careers lean toward benefiting humanity. You will look for the 21st-century career. If you are in a career which lets you be wild, benefits the world and uses your far-reaching ideas, you will be a very happy camper. Aquarius rules calves, ankles, bodily fluids and circulation. Drink lots of water and watch for turned ankles while you are traveling at your lightning-speed pace. Look for the Uranus placement in the natal chart for more insight into the cusp and house where Aquarius is located.

Pisces—a mutable, water sign ruled by Neptune

Pisces suggests one who is trusting, humble, impractical, adaptable, empathic, moody, easily influenced, artistic and psychic. Pisceans have a great empathy for the plight of others and are highly intuitive. You are content when helping others with their problems, and may have insight into their situations even before they express themselves. You are very happy and fulfilled in helping professions such as social work and counseling. The one caveat is that you must take care not to absorb the hurt of others or their negativity and become distraught or depressed yourself.

It can be hard for a Piscean to separate other people's negative feelings from their own. Your intuition absorbs what is around it, and your own feelings can become clouded. A good use of your empathy would be to create an artistic outlet (using your artistic talent) within which others could express their feelings, rather than doing actual counseling (i.e., plays in which the characters act out their problems). You would both benefit. You may be drawn to helping professions but they may be rougher on you than any other sign of the zodiac.

Mediumistic and psychic fields are also attractive to Pisceans, but again you must take care not to take on the burden of others. Creating plays or writing romance novels are healthy career outlets—you can let your imagination run wild. Pisces rules the feet and psychic faculties, which is rather ironic since it is Piscean psychic ability which makes it hard for Pisceans to keep their feet on the ground.

The Four Elements

The signs of the zodiac are each one of four elemental types. They are:

FIRE signs. Aries, Leo and Sagittarius. Fire signs are the ones with drive, ambition and action. They are the go-getters.

EARTH signs. Taurus, Virgo and Capricorn. The earth signs are the practical ones—the ones who work and cope on a day to day basis. They are the steady plodders.

AIR signs. Gemini, Libra and Aquarius. The air signs are the thinkers and the communicators.

WATER signs. Cancer, Scorpio and Pisces. The water signs are the emotional ones. They are empathetic and often deal on intuitive or subconscious levels.

The Houses

The natal chart, or any other astrological chart, such as a solar return chart is a circle which is divided into twelve segments. Each segment is a house and each house represents facets of your life, which may or may not be interrelated. Each house may be tied to your career at some point in time either directly by the sign that occupies that house, its planetary ruler, by aspect of the planets in the house, or by planets that are in it by transit.

However, the emphasis on houses with regard to career should be placed on the second, sixth and tenth houses. Each house is described below in terms of career potential.

First House

The first house represents you personally—your nature, diposition and the face you show to the world. It represents your individuality. This individuality is what you bring to your career, whether in your choice of career or the way you do your job. The first house also suggests the way those around your work perceive you. This house is especially important in looking for motivation in the choice of a career that is fulfilling to you. Planets in this house are very important and you need to look very thoroughly at this house when doing career counseling.

Second House

This is the third most important house of career—after the tenth and sixth houses. The second house represents your money, financial affairs, possessions, financial prospects, and your personal value system. This house indicates ways in which you might best be able to make money. Even more importantly, this house indicates what you value and enjoy. These values help you choose a career that will give your life comfort and pleasure in addition to accumulating money and possessions. This is very important to your happiness.

Third House

The third house indicates your conscious mind and mental activity, communication and writing, brothers and sisters, elementary education and short-distance travel. And yes, there is a lot of career potential here. This house can indicate whether or not communications is a good career choice, and your ability to communicate with others professionally. It also indicates whether you may go into business with your siblings, whether you may travel (at least short distances) for your job, whether you may teach elementary school or write children's books. Since communication is the key to dealing with others, this house will indicate how well you communicate with your co-workers and how well you will get along on the job. It is essential to find a career within which you are comfortable and this house is crucial to your choice.

Fourth House

This house indicates your home and your foundation. It also indicates the influence of your father with regard to career (some astrologers say the mother, but I find it more the father when looking at career), and end-of-life conditions. With today's marketplace, many people are choosing home offices on an independent contractor basis, and this house can suggest if work at home is a viable option. The fourth house will indicate whether there will be a conflict between home and family and your career (as is often the case in modern society). Your emotional foundation is also as critical a factor in your choice of career as your second house personal value system. Did a dominating father influence and push you in a direction that is in conflict with your second house personal value system, or in a direction you do not really want to go? The second and fourth houses are very good places to look for career motivation.

Fifth House

This house indicates romance, creativity, speculation and children. This house can suggest whether a creative, artistic career is a good possibility, whether you can gamble and take chances with your career, or whether your preference would be to stay home and care for children. You may consider your children your career.

Sixth House

This is the second most important house to consider in terms of career potential. The sixth house indicates work, service, health and small animals. Look to this house for suggestions about whether you will be the "worker bee," a hard worker (often behind the scenes), if your health will be a factor in your ability to work, or if work will create health problems. Perhaps you could work in health-related fields. Your methodology or how you work is also exhibited by the sixth house. How you relate to co-workers is indicated here. If you have a stronger emphasis in this house than the tenth house, you are probably going to be a hard worker and may not necessarily want to be in the limelight. You may not be as prominent as your employer, but may work for someone who gets exposure. This does not mean you are not successful—you just may not want to be as prominent as you would with a heavier focus on the tenth house.

Seventh House

The seventh house indicates partnerships, contracts, marriages, dealing with the public in general and open enemies. This house suggests whether you will work with a partner, how you will deal with the public and whether it is a good idea for you to work with the public. It will caution you as to work-related enemies (i.e., whether a potential partner would take advantage of you) and whether it would be a good idea to work with your spouse. It may indicate the financial condition of your employer.

Eighth House

This house points to legacies, death, taxes, insurance, government and other people's money, as well as the money of your spouse or partner. It indicates potential to work for the government or advising others how to invest their money—perhaps dealing with probate and estate planning. It indicates how you will handle investments or advise others in matters such as retirement plans, insurance policies, stocks and bonds. It is also the house of crime and may indicate criminal tendencies. It may point to underworld depth, psychology, occult studies, research and investigation.

Ninth House

The ninth house points to foreign affairs and places, long journeys, philosophy, higher education, and spiritual and intuitive matters. A look at the ninth house suggests whether your career potential will involve foreign places or matters (i.e., trade and commerce or for the State Department), or higher education (i.e., teaching in a foreign university or teaching foreign languages). It also points to courts and judges, expansive occupations such as development and the spiritual field.

Tenth House

This is the most important house to look at in terms of career potential. This is the house which specifically points to career, profession, fame, honors and dishonor, and authority (either yours or someone over you). It will suggest how you make your mark in this world, how responsible or irresponsible you are, and any contributions you may make to society. Areas within which you can excel are also suggested. Will you be in a position of authority? How well do you handle authority? This is the house of social standing as influenced by your career and profession. It is important to note that if there are no planets in your tenth house, it will draw upon other houses through rulership and aspects to transits to the tenth house. This is the very reason why you must look at the entire chart as one big picture to determine important career potentials. Even if there are planets here, you cannot get the whole picture from this one house. If you have an emphasis on this house (more so than the sixth house), you may tend to be more prominent and your work may be more open to the public. This is the house that indicates the honors you may receive.

Eleventh House

This is the house pointing to friends, your hopes and wishes, where you will push beyond limits to achieve for the greater good of society, and organizations. This house holds many clues to your career. It will indicate how stable the financial foundation of your career is. This house will suggest how friends may help you achieve your goals, how far you will push yourself and in what manner you will push yourself to make your dreams come true—including career hopes. It also suggests whether you will work toward a more enlightened and productive society or for more personal rewards.

Twelfth House

This house illustrates the subconscious, things hidden (unknown to you), secret enemies, hospitals or institutions, jails and restraint, large animals, motivations you do not understand (both positive and negative), mysticism, imagination, escapism and compassion. The key to the twelfth house in light of your career is the fact that your unconscious often directs your conscious choices. It may be your motivation although you do not realize it. This is the place to look to determine why you may or may not choose a career that is of benefit to you. For example, if an idealistic planet is located in the twelfth house, you may choose work that is rewarding to you and compassionate toward others. You may choose to work in a hospital helping others and feeling very good about yourself in the process. Perhaps satisfaction would come from being a veterinarian working with large animals. If you have planets with challenging aspects or whose motifs do not blend well with the twelfth house, you may yearn for unattainable perfection or you may choose jobs from which you receive no personal satisfaction. Also, you surely do not want to do anything wrong that could land you in jail. You must look at the cusp of this house, find its ruler in your chart and look at the planets in this house to find your true motives. This house is very helpful to those who really do not know what they want to do, but continue to make choices wherein they find no satisfaction.

The Three Qualities

The qualities of the twelve houses may also be considered when career counseling. They are:

Angular or Cardinal Houses (1, 4, 7 and 10)

These houses represent action. This is where you will find your ability to move forward and take decisive action with whatever career you choose. If there are no planets in a house, again look to the ruler of the sign on the cusp for help in determining what action is likely to advance your career.

Succedent or Fixed Houses (2, 5, 8, 11)

These houses represent stability. Look to these houses to determine how to make your career choices more stable so that you will not go from one thing to another with no real direction. Again, if there are no planets in a house, look to the ruler of the sign on the cusp for help in determining what action is likely to stabilize your career.

Cadent or Mutable Houses (3, 6, 9, 12)

These houses represent the mental and belief systems. Look to these houses for motivation and ability to communicate. Again, if there are no planets in a house, look to the ruler of the sign on the cusp for help in determining what action is likely to motivate you with regard to your career.

The Planets

The Sun

The Sun is your ambition and drive. The Sun is where you need to shine. It has both positive and negative qualities and if you use your solar energy positively, you will be proud of what you do. Your Sun is where you can achieve recognition with regard to your career. It is where you will be honored by society for career contributions. It denotes your position in your career, your rank or title, publicity, government officers or officials, whether you are a boss or worker, and how you relate as either. It is also where you may dishonor yourself if your solar energy is used in a negative manner, i.e., some act of pride which would hurt a co-worker. The Sun is one of the places in your chart which indicates the mark you make in this lifetime.

The Moon

The Moon is the planet that can symbolize changes in your career. It represents fluctuation. In fact, if the Moon actually sits in your sixth or tenth houses, you will probably have many jobs. The Moon also indicates emotions and thus relates to the emotional side of your career, or your career as a security blanket so to speak. The Moon suggests sensitivity in dealing with others. It is an indicator of how you will deal with the public in general and whether you are sensitive to your co-workers. It demonstrates whether you are the nurturer or the needy worker fishing for compliments and support from those around you. If the Moon is in your second house of money, your finances will often fluctuate—no matter what your career. The Moon suggests motherly or caretaking traits, and you would probably be happy where employees come to you for help, or as a day care owner/worker, a nurse, or something along those lines. I look at the Moon when in transit to set off career opportunity (transits will be discussed at the end of this chapter and in chapter 3). It is fast-moving and can set off points in your chart over and over during a one-year period. Moon career placements include nursing, fishing, sailing and working with the public.

Mercury

Mercury suggests your ability to think and communicate with others. I view Mercury as almost as important as the Sun when looking at career potential. After all, cognitive thinking and communication are essential in almost every profession. It indicates whether you can speak or write with authority. Mercury is associated with literature, publishing, writing, teaching, clerks, secretaries, bookkeepers. It is information-oriented. In other words, Mercury is involved in almost every facet of every career. Mercury also symbolizes criticism, whether self-criticism or criticism of others. Criticism is one area within which you must take extreme care and offer positive suggestions rather than criticizing others. Mercury shows how you deal with and assimilate facts. As you mature, your ability to place facts in a perceptible order, write, speak and communicate clearly should become an essential part of who you are, and an essential part of your contribution to your career of choice. You can then better shine through your Sun. Traditional interpretation suggests that teachers, clerks, writers, publishers, secretaries and bookkeepers are associated with a strong Mercury career placement.

Venus

Venus is your desire for pleasure and luxury. When relating Venus to your career, it shows a desire for comfort in your work surroundings, wanting to work in a beautiful environment or with something of beauty, and possibly musical or artistic endeavors. You seek security, both financial and mental, through your work environment. Venus suggests that you may tend to seek the easy way in work projects and should guard against this trait. Venus implies an even temperament with others in your work environment. You are possibly charming and easy to get along with. Traditional interpretation connects careers in the arts or literature with a Venus career placement.

Mars

Mars indicates drive, independence, doing one's own thing, seeking adventure, and an inner core need to be self-reliant. A prominent Mars suggests you will work very hard and strive for personal power and control. Mars motifs imply that you do not take orders well. You will definitely work in your own way despite any obstacles. With Mars spirit, you are the person who volunteers for projects and likes workplace competition. Harness Mars energy, direct it in a positive manner, and it will be a tremendous asset. Mars anger and argumentative tendencies should be checked. Traditional interpretation indicates that the military, police, surgeons and chemists reflect a Mars career placement.

Jupiter

Jupiter represents opportunity, idealism and optimism, or faith in a higher order. Jupiter symbolizes open doors to your future. Jupiter symbolizes expansion. When Jupiter is prominent in your career, it brings ideals and moral values into play. You will not be satisfied unless your career meets your expectations and lives up to your ideals. If Jupiter happens to be in your sixth or tenth houses, you will probably always find a job, even in hard times. I view a Jupiter transit as one of the most important transits in dealing with career opportunity because it does suggest expansion and growth. A Jupiter transit or an aspect created by the Jupiter transit to your sixth or tenth house is highly beneficial and a time to act. You should find what you are seeking with your career at this time. Even a career opportunity that seems unattainable may open to you with this transit. Traditional interpretation indicates that science, law, and theology are associated with a Jupiter career placement.

Saturn

Saturn is the tough planet suggesting potential obstacles, limits and life lessons. Saturn is the planet of Karma. On the other hand, Saturn is where you work hard and steadily build your career. It is your career drive and where your sense of responsibility lies. It is Saturn lessons which allow you to grow and find a fulfilling career. I look very closely at the Saturn transits when dealing with careers. Saturn symbolizes the harsh reality from which we grow. If Saturn is transiting or its transit makes an aspect to your sixth or tenth houses, this is the time to buckle down and lay a foundation for your career and future. Saturn represents a desire for stability and tangible, measurable achievements. A Saturn career placement traditionally suggests working with land, the environment, executives, the corporate structure, scientists, or the elderly.

Uranus

Uranus' motifs are unconventional. Uranus suggests a desire for freedom in your career, perhaps a humanitarian effort, but above all variety. Expect the unexpected in your career opportunity. Careers may be unusual. Your work methods will be unusual, and work must not be structured. Since freedom in your career is very important, you may be better off working for yourself. Traditional interpretation suggests electronics, cars, airplanes or space exploration with a Uranus career placement.

Neptune

Neptune suggests intuitiveness which can be directed toward concrete achievement. Use Neptune energy positively rather than daydreaming about what could be. Use Neptune inspiration to find a career which makes you proud. Take care to avoid the confusion symbolized by Neptune in your search for something ideal. Nothing is perfect and a continual search can become confusing. Neptunian careers tend to help others, but you must take care not to let others' troubles become your own. Do not carry the world on your shoulders. Creative and imaginative career choices fulfill Neptune's desires. Traditional interpretation suggests careers involving water (such as marine biology), investigation, film, aesthetics or healing with a Neptune career placement.

Pluto

Pluto suggests reform, transformation, reorganization and upheaval. Pluto's prominence may suggest you will try to reform or change your work environment or the way work is done (perhaps to the point of power plays). Career control is important. Pluto indicates the ability to organize, suggesting successful managers or any career that calls for organization such as an actuary, historian or investigator. Pluto represents tenacity, do-or-die determination. Traditional interpretations (since Pluto rules the subconscious) suggest a career as a therapist, detective, occultist, emergency room worker, hospice worker, or a participant in brutal sports.

The Signs as Applied to the Planets

The Sun sign traits described earlier in this chapter may be applied to the other planets as well and are not just career indicators. The key words indicate where to look for a sign's significance with regard to a planet. The planets themselves will either reinforce or contradict the traits of the astrological signs within which the planets sit. Some planets are personal and some are generational.

The Personal Planets

The **Sun** is obviously the most personal "planet." It symbolizes your personal drive and where you shine. It takes the Sun one year to move around the zodiac (one month in each sign).

The **Moon** is very personal as well since it represents your emotions. However, the Moon moves from sign to sign every two and one half days. When transits (current positions of the planets) are discussed, you will see how crucial the Moon is as a tool to see the timing of changes in your career.

Mercury is also very personal. It indicates your thoughts, communication skills and style. Mercury stays in an astrological sign about two and a half weeks (up to two and one half months when retrograde).

Venus is also a personal planet representing your emotional nature and creative nature. It takes one year to thirteen months for Venus to move around the zodiac.

Mars is also personal since it symbolizes your drive, personal and sexual desires, and combativeness. It takes almost two years to move around the zodiac.

The Transitional Planets

Jupiter is a transitional planet, from the personal to the outer planets. It spends about one year in an astrological sign. During the time it is in a sign, it offers great benefit and opportunity personally. (Again this will be discussed with transits in chapter 3.) Where Jupiter sits in your chart is personal as to your philosophy of life and your belief system, but because it is a year in a sign, your peers will tend to agree with you. Jupiter takes twelve years to move around the zodiac.

Saturn is also transitional between personal and outer planets. It is personal as far as indicating Karmic issues and areas of hard work in your chart. Because Saturn takes 28 to $29\,^1/_2$ years to travel around the zodiac, you also share common issues with those close to your age.

The Outer Planets

Uranus is an outer planet. It takes 84 years to travel around the zodiac, spending about seven years in each sign. Thus, you share the eccentricities of your age cohorts. House positions will give some individuality to your Uranus.

Neptune is an outer planet. It takes 165 years to travel around the zodiac or about 13 $^3/_4$ years in one sign. Again, it is a generational planet. The house within which Neptune sits will indicate your personal reaction to generational issues.

Pluto is an outer planet. It takes 245 to 250 years to travel through the zodiac. It marks generational issues. Pluto was in Cancer from 1913 to 1938, including World War I. Pluto was in Leo for those born in the 1940's (World War II) and early 1950's (the Korean War). It is easy to see how those born in the late 1940's and early 1950's became the "flower children" of the 1960's since the recent history of war was a powerful lesson. This generation also saw the onset of the United Nations to avert further world wars. Again, the house occupied by Pluto will suggest how you will personally deal with generational issues.

The Planets/Qualities/House Placement

Any planet may lend its symbolism to your career. The placement of the planet by house determines what potentials are available in your career and how important that planet's motifs may be toward your career. If a planet is located in an **angular house** (1, 4, 7 or 10), its themes will be central in the decisive action you take. It is a very strong placement, indicating lots of action. Your tenth house (of career) is an angular house, so any planet there will be particularly significant to your career. Any planet aspecting the cusp of the tenth house will be a major key to your career.

Planets in and conjunct the cusp of a **succedent house** (houses 2, 5, 8 and 11) indicate stability. A planet in the second house of money and personal values may help to stabilize this house (unless, of course, it is the Moon that indicates fluctuation or Uranus that symbolizes chaos). Look for planets in the second house or aspecting the cusp of the second house for help in stabilizing income and developing your personal value system.

The **cadent houses** (3, 6, 9 and 12) are houses that reflect mental and belief systems. The sixth house is the house of work and service. Look to planets in this house, or in aspect to the cusp or the ruler of the cusp, for career motivation.

Planets do not have to be in the second house (money and possessions), the sixth house (work and service) or the tenth house (career and honors) to be a profoundly important influence in your career. A planet may be the ruler of the sign on the cusp of your second, sixth or tenth house, or it may aspect the cusp, or it may aspect a planet in one of these houses. Thus, a planet's placement may give you many more areas from which to analyze potentials and options within your career. Aspects (discussed later in this chapter) from planet to planet are also very significant in career opportunity and career choices.

The planet that rules your Ascendant can also be a major key to your career choice as the chart ruler. Look at the chart ruler's house placement and any aspects it makes. The Ascendant, which symbolizes your personality, influences your career choice. The house within which the ruler of the Ascendant is located adds further information. Any aspect that the ruler makes to another planet needs to be factored in as well. It is like a chain of repeating and/or conflicting themes. Give extra emphasis if the ruler is in the second, sixth or tenth houses, or if it makes an aspect to a planet in one of these houses.

Aspects

Finally, the aspects the planets make to each other, or perhaps to the Ascendant (the cusp between the 12th and 1st houses) or the Midheaven (MC, the cusp of the 10th House), play a very important role in delineation. An aspect is the angle between two planets or two points in a horoscope. Aspects are considered when they are within a given orb. An Orb is defined below.

The major aspects are:

Conjunction. The planets are next to each other (within about 9 or 10 degrees at the very most).

Opposition. 180 degree aspect (5 degree orb or from 175-185°).

Square. 90 degree aspect (5 degree orb or from 85-95°).

Sextile. 60 degree aspect (3 or 4 degree orb or from 56-64°).

Trine. 120 degree aspect (5 degree orb or from 115-125°).

Inconjunct or Quincunx. 150 degree aspect (5 degree orb or from 145-155°).

Semi-square. 45 degree aspect (3 degree orb or from 42-48°).

Sesqui-quadrate or sesqui-square. 135 degree aspect (3 degree orb or from 132-138°).

The number of degrees on either side of an aspect is called an "orb." For example, an opposition is 180 degrees. If a 5 degree orb is used, there is a 10 degree range for the aspect from 175 to 185 degrees. As a general rule, I use a 5 degree orb but the closer to the exact degree, the more powerful the aspect. I may narrow or slightly expand the orb depending on other indications in the chart. For a sextile I usually use a 3 or 4 degree orb. The more you delineate charts, the more you are able to determine whether you want to use a lesser or greater orb, but to start, use 5 degrees.

Aspects are mutual and work both ways. For example, Venus opposite Neptune is tantamount to Neptune opposite Venus.

Conjunctions, sextiles and trines are considered harmonious aspects where the drives and desires indicated reinforce each other and egg each other on (perhaps too much).

Oppositions, squares and quincunxes are more difficult aspects to deal with because they point to inner conflicts or drives that compete with one another but are beneficial to you as you work your way through them. In fact, the easier aspects are sometimes too easy and you miss opportunities just drifting through. The more difficult aspects can indicate areas where we develop strength through challenges, like resistance training when building the muscles.

On the next two pages you'll find two list format outlines: **Astrological Outline (Figure 1)** and **Major Aspects Outline (Figure 2)**, followed by a **Solar Wheel (Figure 3)**. Together they demonstate the key concepts from this chapter.

ASTROLOGICAL OUTLINE
(Figure 1)

SIGN	SYMBOL	RULER	SYMBOL	ELEMENT	QUALITY
Aries	♈	Mars	♂	Fire	Cardinal
Taurus	♉	Venus	♀	Earth	Fixed
Gemini	♊	Mercury	☿	Air	Mutable
Cancer	♋	Moon	☽	Water	Cardinal
Leo	♌	Sun	☉	Fire	Fixed
Virgo	♍	Mercury	☿	Earth	Mutable
Libra	♎	Venus	♀	Air	Cardinal
Scorpio	♏	Pluto	♇	Water	Fixed
Sagittarius	♐	Jupiter	♃	Fire	Mutable
Capricorn	♑	Saturn	♄	Earth	Cardinal
Aquarius	♒	Uranus	♅	Air	Fixed
Pisces	♓	Neptune	♆	Water	Mutable

MAJOR ASPECTS OUTLINE
(Figure 2)

ASPECT	DEGREE	SYMBOL	PROPERTY
Conjunction	0	☌	Planet motifs enhanced/harmony
Opposition	180	☍	Planet motifs inhibited/challenging
Square	90	□	Planet motifs inhibited/challenging
Sextile	60	⚹	Planet motifs enhanced/harmony
Trine	120	△	Planet motifs enhanced/harmony
Inconjunct or Quincunx	150	⚻	Planet motifs inhibited/challenging
Semi-square	45	∠	Planet motifs challenging
Sesqui-quadrate	135	⚼	Planet motifs challenging

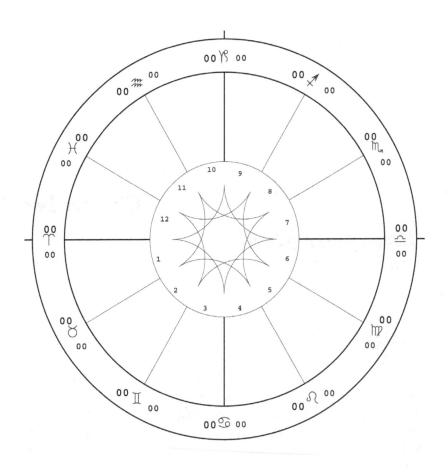

SOLAR CHART
INDICATING HOUSES AND SIGNS
ON THE CUSP OF EACH HOUSE
(Figure 3)

Chapter Two

Three Case Studies

Case Study No. 1 Sarah
Background

At the time Sarah began her job she had two small children, one in pre-school and one in grade school. She had an agreement with her husband not to work until her children were older. Although her husband agreed that she should not work while the children were small, he resented the fact that she was not working. Her marriage was never smooth and became increasingly difficult during the years she stayed at home with her young children. Her husband became very verbally abusive, irrational, and difficult to live with for long periods of time. Sarah always felt he was hiding assets from her. When her husband finally pushed Sarah into working prior to their agreed-upon time for her to return to work, and she started her job, he ended his law partnership. He was out of work for approximately one year. Although she earned much less than her husband had earned, they were able to pay all their bills and live on her salary (which barely covered a very large house payment). Sarah was now positive that he had indeed hidden assets from her. At the time Sarah went back to work, she was seriously considering divorce and the only reason she did not leave the marriage was because of her children. Going back to work, which should have been Sarah's biggest problem, was greatly overshadowed by her personal turmoil.

Although the description of her circumstances and the delineation of her natal chart (below) indicate a very difficult time for Sarah, her life was not all terrible, nor did she consider her marriage a failure. Over the early years, the good in the relationship outweighed the problems. The marital problems I have described were a part of her life at the specific time dealt with here, as was her difficult adjustment to a new job. Her family and her return to work were the conflicts in her life. Sarah began her job on November 30, 1994.

Sarah's Natal Chart
See Figure 4 below.

The first thing I look at in initial chart analysis is the Sun sign. Sarah's Sun is in Libra in the fifth house. Remember, the Sun symbolizes energy, drive and where you will shine. The fifth house represents creativity, speculation and children. This is the first suggestion that Sarah's goal, priority and where her strengths lie is with her children or pursuing a creative outlet. She

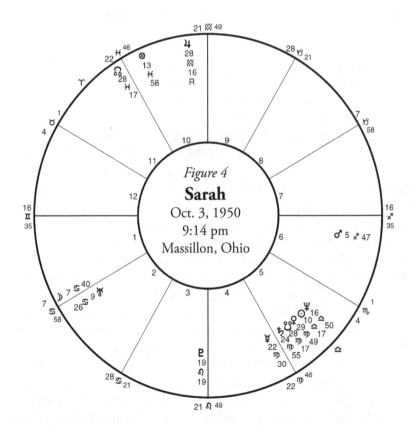

Figure 4
Sarah
Oct. 3, 1950
9:14 pm
Massillon, Ohio

will be happy and fulfilled in any creative environment, teaching or actively creating works of art or design, or where she takes calculated risks, or with children. This is where her self-esteem will advance. Virgo is on the cusp of the fifth house indicating that Sarah has practicality, dependability and a steady nature, but Libra is intercepted in the Fifth House. (Interception occurs when no degree of a sign appears on the house cusp within which it is located.)

The Sun in Libra implies that it may be difficult for Sarah to decide what to do. She constantly weighs her options. She could also be a good mediator or diplomat—seeing more than one side of an issue. There is a lot of career potential in her fifth house.

Next, look at Sarah's Ascendant for her individuality, her personality and how she is perceived. Sarah has Gemini on her Ascendant suggesting a quick mind and good communication skills. Anything verbal, written, in the line of communications or helping others communicate will be very fulfilling. Sarah will be happy when doing more than one task at a time. In fact, with Gemini's dual nature, she will be bored if not constantly busy. The Ascendant trines her natal Sun (stretching the orb a bit), again tying her personal drive to her children and creativity.

Sarah's Moon is in Cancer conjunct the second house cusp. This suggests Sarah is very intuitive. She can usually tell during an interview if she will get the job. Sarah's intuition is great when paired with the Gemini Ascendant and strengthens Sarah's communication skills. The Moon also relates to her ties with children and family. Sarah is one who will be fulfilled in a nurturing role, or a helping role. The Moon also implies fluctuation and it squares her natal Sun in Libra suggesting it may be difficult for Sarah to make a decision to act. Her children (her priority) may be a conflict for Sarah in making personal choices. Since the Moon suggests family ties, I suspect that going back to work away from her children may be difficult for Sarah. This may seem obvious since it is natural for any mother of young children to feel stress in leaving them and going to work, but Sarah's placements bring these feelings very much to the forefront. The Moon rules Cancer, so is "at home" and especially strong in this sign.

Sarah's **second house** cusp is also Cancer. Since the second house is one's personal value system, Cancerian values of home, family and being a nurturer should be extremely important. Again, career choices that help others will be extremely fulfilling. Sarah will also be very good in business since a Cancerian memory is excellent when dealing with details. With Cancer, Sarah needs a job that does not conflict with her personal values of home and family, and in her present situation she is doing pretty well. Because she has a job with the school system, her hours are approximately the same as her childrens' hours and they also have the same vacation time. Her children spend much less time in daycare than they would if she had a different position (which may pay more than the school system but is not worth it to Sarah). She does not feel her job is taking her completely away from her children.

Uranus' placement in House 2, relating to her personal values, suggests Sarah would prefer a job which requires a humanitarian effort, something unconventional and without structure. Freedom is very important. Although she has not quite found the perfect career, in her current job she is left to work on her own, using her own methods. Uranus rules Aquarius which is on the cusp of her tenth house of career and status.

The third house represents your conscious mind, how you think and communicate. This house is quite important to your career potential, since almost every job involves communication. Sarah has Cancer on the cusp of this house—her thoughts go to home and family. Again, she is very intuitive. She is a conscious nurturer.

Pluto is conjunct Sarah's IC, the fourth house cusp, suggesting on a conscious level that career control is very important. Sarah will work very hard to reform her work environment so that it is fulfilling and so that she is in control of her circumstances. On a larger scale, Pluto here suggests a strong social conscience, i.e., someone who would be fulfilled when working for the good of humanity in such areas as communication, teaching, or writing. Pluto here opposes her MC (Midheaven—the tenth house career cusp) which suggests mental conflict in coping with career, but it can be overcome.

The fourth house cusp is Leo which is ruled by the Sun in the fifth house. Again, the strong link from home to children to creativity is emphasized. The more I look at Sarah's chart, the more likely it seems she will find a way to work in a creative way, a nurturing or helping way, and possibly from her home. This will make her most happy.

Mercury in Virgo suggests a very logical mind, working step by step. Sarah is quite able to speak, write, assimilate facts and figures, and communicate methodically and clearly. This is very important in her position as an accounting clerk for the school system. This placement suggests a natural ability to work with figures. The fourth house Mercury is quincunx the cusp of the tenth house of career—suggesting conflict between Sarah's desire to be home and her career.

Virgo is on the cusp of the fifth house suggesting a great dedication to love life and children. Virgo is ruled by Mercury which is in the fourth house and again concern with home is emphasized. The fifth house is where

Sarah's largest concentration of planets lie, including the Sun as previously discussed. One of the first things I noticed in Sarah's chart is her Saturn-Mercury conjunction (Mercury in the fourth house). This is an aspect suggesting intellectual ability and reasoning, pragmatism, common sense, and a businesslike and factual manner. Obviously this is a good placement for success in business.

Libra is intercepted in Sarah's fifth house, suggesting she also has strong diplomatic tendencies. Venus is also conjunct Saturn suggesting tact, good methodology in tasks, an ability to take opportunity to its utmost, and, above all, family attachment. With Venus here, Sarah will be fulfilled in a career dealing with arts, design or fashion, entertainment, or working with children. Romance is a source of self-fulfillment as well. The Sun is conjunct Neptune, again suggesting creativity, and this conjunction is in the house of creativity. Thus, a profession in the arts or dealing with art and working in the home would be ideal, as would a more practical or business type endeavor with the Saturn conjunct Mercury in the fourth house.

Neptune in Libra suggests Sarah will seek whatever is perfect and ideal in life, so she must try to see the true reality of any job, since nothing is perfect. Neptune is sextile to Pluto in Sarah's third house of conscious mind and this also brings a desire to identify with her generation and a desire to work for the good of humanity. Again, she may over-idealize her mission in her work. With the largest concentration of planets in the fifth house, Sarah's preference that her children be her main career is apparent. No wonder it is difficult for Sarah to go back to work, no matter how good she is with numbers and her new accounting job.

Scorpio is on the cusp of the **sixth house**. This is a house to look at very carefully, since it is the house from which work and service are read. Scorpio is ruled by Pluto in the third house of communication in Leo. This Pluto placement, considered with Mars in Sagittarius, suggests that Sarah will work very hard, and that she would find work involving communications, and with issues relating to themes of significance to her generation to be very fulfilling. These attributes are along the lines of her current ambition and training.

Since I first analyzed Sarah's chart at the time she started her accounting job for the school system, she has recently gone back to college to find a career within which she can work out of her home (fourth and fifth house emphasis). She is studying speech therapy with a view toward helping stroke victims regain their speech since, "my generation is getting to an age where strokes will begin to occur." Her business and accounting background (and natural ability with facts and figures) would enable her to run her own business quite well. She has done a great deal of research into her area of interest, and her services are very needed. With her Gemini Ascendant, anything in communications or speech would be very satisfying.

This new plan is a very personal choice for Sarah. She was passed over for a promotion because she needed a college degree in her initial job with the school system, and this pushed her to go back to school. Thus, her initial job was a stepping stone which led her to her current career plans, helping others (a Libra nurturer) while working from home (the Cancer traits) and dealing with a specific problem that will affect members of her generation within the next 10 years or so (the Pluto generational motif). Her job as an accountant will be discussed further in the chapter on transits.

Sarah has Sagittarius on the cusp of her seventh house. Sagittarius is ruled by Jupiter in the tenth house suggesting working with a partner is another viable option for Sarah. Jupiter is in Aquarius ruled by Uranus, which is in the second house of money so a partnership would probably be lucrative.

The eighth house has Capricorn on the cusp ruled by Saturn in the fifth house. The eighth house represents taxes, insurance, government and other people's money and since the fifth house represents speculation, there is a slight suggestion of investment for other persons, however there is not a great deal of 7th or 8th house activity in her chart with regard to career.

Sarah has Capricorn on the cusp of her ninth house. Capricorn is ruled by Saturn, which is in her fifth house of creativity, romance and children. The ninth house of higher philosophy, foreign matters/places and higher education, with a fifth house ruler, once again brings Sarah's thoughts of children and creativity into her higher consciousness. Philosophy, creativity, children and foreign travel or dealing with foreign matters would all be fulfilling for Sarah.

Sarah has Aquarius on the cusp of her **tenth house**. Aquarius is ruled by Uranus in the second house. This suggests that Sarah must have a career which aligns with her personal value system, and her career should be lucrative. Uranus is in Cancer, the nurturer—i.e., helping others. Jupiter in Aquarius represents the idealist. Jupiter in the tenth house is a very fortuitous placement as Jupiter represents open doors; Sarah will have career opportunities throughout her life. Jupiter conjunct the Midheaven is very significant. She is one person who will find work even when others cannot. Aquarius in this house suggests Sarah will seek a career based on strong ideals. She will work independently and on the cutting edge of new technology in her field. If she is pioneering something new in her field, she will be quite fulfilled.

The eleventh house of dreams and wishes has Pisces on the cusp and is ruled by Neptune again in the fifth house of creativity and children. This repeats the theme that her family is really her hope for the future. But, she may daydream too much, vacillating with her Libra Sun and Cancer Moon, rather than pushing forward to achieve her dreams. She needs an outside push to get her started. Her husband first pushed her to go to work, but she could not receive a promotion in her accounting job because the next level required a college degree. This fact pushed Sarah to go back to school, and she is now seeking a career she really wants.

The twelfth house of unconscious motivation has Taurus on the cusp. Taurus is ruled by Venus which is also in her fifth house. Sarah's primary motivations are her children and creative endeavors.

As you can see, there are four strong themes emerging within this chart analysis: 1.) a good business sense and analytical mind; 2.) something in a creative field as a strong career option; 3.) the strongest emphasis is on Sarah's children and her home; and 4.) any career must align with Sarah's personal value system which is strongly tied to **generational** issues.

All four of these themes were carried out beginning in November 1994. Sarah started back into the work-force as an accountant (the business, analytical mind) for the school system. Her hours did not conflict with her children and home. She had a desire for a more peaceful, nurturing field by helping others with speech therapy. Finally, she went back to college to obtain a degree in speech therapy where she could run her own business from her home. Sarah's career choice reflected the difficulties people of her generation may be facing as potential clients, if for example, they might need speech therapy after a stroke.

Case Study No. 2 John
Background

John has always worked with children. He worked at day camp and as a coach for young children when he was a teenager. He wants to help children and his choice of career reflects this life-long interest. Upon college graduation, John received a fully funded scholarship to a Ph.D. program in psychology at a major university. After a year at the university, John realized the work was all computer entry, theory, reading and writing (information only) such that he feared he would not end up in actual counseling, but instead in esoteric research. It was not the "hands on" work

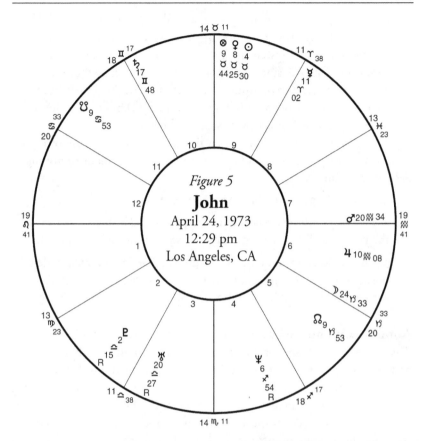

Figure 5
John
April 24, 1973
12:29 pm
Los Angeles, CA

with children that he wanted. He left that very prestigious program to attend another school with a graduate program to become a school counselor. By June 2001, John had been married for three years and received his graduate degree (a Masters). On September 4, 2001, he began his career as a school counselor.

John's Natal Chart
See figure 5.

In looking at John's chart, I immediately noted his **Leo Ascendant.** This suggests that John brings a great deal of enthusiasm to whatever career he chooses. He will be generous to the point of fault, but wants to run the show. Children are a source of fulfillment for John, and with Leo rising, he is charismatic and able to relate to children, sports, acting and teaching. He has been consistently true to his Ascendant since his teenage years when he coached children in sports and worked as a camp counselor. He found coaching very fulfilling and his self-esteem increased as a result of his success with children. Counseling allows him to work on a more independent level than positions in the school system such as teacher or coach. He is also in more of a position of power since he can call his own shots without as much school board interference or input as a teacher or coach might receive. Thus, counseling would satisfy both his desire to work with children and his desire for leadership and self-direction as suggested by Leo.

Leo is ruled by the Sun which sits in John's ninth house of higher education, foreign matters and personal philosophy. This strongly suggests three things to me.

1. John's job must meet his own high expectations;

2. He will continue his education and get a Ph.D. in counseling over the years, possibly teaching college, as well as counseling children;

3. He would enjoy a job having to do with foreign matters, trade or business, or in a foreign country, as well as higher education. All of these options would be fulfilling for John.

John's second house has Virgo on the cusp and Pluto in Libra

This is the house of personal values, and the Virgo-Pluto combination suggests a reformer who may be critical of accepted conventions. In his present job, John may be interested in initiating reform in the school counseling system or at least advancing current methods. The Libra implies he will be very charming in order to push reform and continually weigh all sides of issues for the best outcome for the children. Pluto suggests a need to control and this need is in his house of values. This indicates that John will seek a career which he can control, and which is based on his values. Pluto rules Scorpio which is on the cusp of his fourth house. His foundation and his basic familial values will also influence his choice of career. John is fulfilled if he values what he does, and if he controls his own work. Virgo suggests that John is a steady and plodding worker with good business acumen. It also suggests some sort of healing or service vocation, so counseling would appeal to this facet of Virgo.

The third house is the house of communication and conscious mind and is very, very important to any career.

John has Libra on the cusp of his third house, and Uranus is retrograde there. Venus rules Libra and is in John's ninth house and conjunct his Midheaven, again bringing his personal philosophies into his conscious thoughts and into his actions. With

Libra, he will be satisfied only after he has weighed one concept or perspective against the other to achieve balance. Uranus in this house suggests that he may shake up the school system. Uranus symbolizes the rebel and the revolutionary, and John will be fulfilled if he can revolutionize the methods currently used in counseling. He will only be content if he is sure his counseling is an asset, whether or not his unusual, unconventional (Uranus) methods come to be widely accepted. Libra is people-oriented and John will also be proud and fulfilled when he is recognized for his work with children.

The third house also represents lower education, but if John were to choose another field later on, he still would express the revolutionary and reforming tendencies of Uranus in how he thinks and communicates with co-workers.

The fourth house is John's emotional and domestic foundation.

The Scorpio cusp suggests intense feelings (often around family situations) and a need for security. There is a persistence to get to the bottom of interpersonal issues and to understand the motivations of family members. For John, this need for security translates to a need to help others gain security.

Neptune is in Sagittarius in the fourth house. This suggests someone with Utopian ideals stemming from paternal influence. Scorpio on the cusp is ruled by Pluto in the second house (of personal values). John's parents were divorced when he was quite young. Obviously, this is very traumatic for a child. On the other hand, his father has always been there for John. He saw John all the time, living only ten minutes away. This strong paternal influence (fourth house) coupled with the childhood heartbreak of divorce was one of the foundational issues that contributed to John's wanting to help children with their problems. He could relate to their needs and he has the foundation upon which to help them. This is further explained when looking at the **sixth house** of work and service. The Moon sits in this house and rules Cancer which is on the cusp of the twelfth house (subconscious mind). Any repressed feelings from childhood will come out in work and service. We are now beginning to get a picture of how the counselor in John developed.

The fifth house has Sagittarius on the cusp and suggests that the freedom to create will be fulfilling.

The fifth house represents creativity and children, and the North Node is there in Capricorn. If you look at the South Node as where you came from karmically and the North Node as what you are doing this time around, creativity and children are excellent choices for John in which he can feel proud and fulfilled. Sagittarius on the fifth cusp might represent someone who is an idealist wanting only the best for children. John wants an ideal situation within which children learn, and he has a natural ability to inspire them. The North Node in Capricorn may indicate a role of authority, and suggests John may seek recognition through a career. Also, the Capricorn motif of pragmatism helps John deal with the traditional methods currently used in counseling, while adventurous Sagittarius helps him try to advance these methods.

The sixth house has Capricorn on the cusp and is ruled by Saturn in the tenth house of career and honors. John's work should bring him prominence and honors. Located in the sixth house are the Moon (already discussed) and Jupiter which rules Sagittarius on the fifth house cusp, again bring in the potential of work with children. Fulfillment is indicated by freedom to work in his own way. He has a very creative approach to any job.

Jupiter is in Aquarius , suggesting the worker of the 21st century, and a breaking away from the old order to form something new. The Moon is square Uranus in the third house, suggesting that John will be bucking the system, and that a lot of communication and unusual circumstances can bring about progressive change. This is also evident with the ninth house Sun square Jupiter, which indicates a risk taker, someone who is inspirational, can uplift others, and has a sense of humor. The Moon in the sixth house suggests nurturing work, or that emotions are dealt with during work and service. With Capricorn John uses common sense, but may incline to pessimism, and feel the need to work very hard to overcome barriers or time pressures. With Moon in Capricorn John's emotions may be inhibited by a need to control his situation. This placement deals with what we can do, cannot do and must do, or the "rules of the game." As a career counselor, you might suggest to John that he not become too frustrated when dealing with the system (and trying to reform it), or when dealing with childrens' problems, which may be very emotionally draining. He cannot control everything; he can just do his best. He must recognize the reasonable limits of his own responsibility and power.

Aquarius is on the cusp of the seventh house of partnerships and marriage. Aquarius is ruled by Uranus in the third house of communication and lower education. John's wife is a teacher so this seems to be a very good match, careerwise. Mars in the seventh house trines Saturn in the tenth house of career, profession and honors. Saturn is the planet of ambition and hard work and Mars suggests that John has the drive and energy needed to succeed in his career. Mars here also points to help from his partner (wife) and since she is a teacher, their careers are an asset to each other. Mars is in Aquarius and she will be behind him 100% in his ideas for reform. Mars in the seventh exactly trines Uranus, the ruler of the seventh, again suggesting a very supportive partnership.

The cusp of John's eighth house is Pisces, ruled by Neptune in the fourth house. The eighth house is the house of therapy and understanding hidden motivations, suggesting that his childhood experiences (fourth house) contributed to his choice of a career in counseling. Mercury in this house reinforces the importance of communication, particularly about intense emotional issues. Mercury also suggests a good business sense which, when combined with his communication skills can be used to obtain funding for school counseling (or any type of counseling programs). Mercury here also implies that John is intuitive in his thought processes and seeks to delve deeply into the minds of others. His own emotional experiences lead to exploring the inner psyche, and his interest in the mental well being of others. This is an excellent placement for a counselor. He has great objectivity in dealing with (or counseling) troubled children. Mercury in Aries conjunct the ninth house cusp shows John has a lot of mental energy and a very quick mind. His communication skills are also strong and he is able to get his ideas across to the children with ease and clarity. His confidence shows, so the children feel they can rely on him.

Mercury sextiles Jupiter in John's sixth house, reinforcing his intellectual skills. Mercury trines Neptune in the fourth house of foundation and family, indicating his family ideals come into play. Again, the divorce of John's parents when he was very young was probably a great influence on his choice of career, making it easy for him to relate to troubled children. Mercury is square the North Node in the fifth house of creativity suggesting his intellect may block creative efforts or over-analyze, rather than letting his artistic side flow.

The ninth house of higher education, philosophy, and foreign travel or foreign matters, contains the Sun and Venus. Aries is on the cusp of this house and is ruled by Mars in the seventh house of partnerships; this indicates help from a partner, fire energy, enthusiasm for education and other ninth house matters. Since the Sun is here, most of John's personal vitality and self-esteem seems to emanate from this house. Anything connected with ninth house matters is where he will shine and would definitely be a source of fulfillment.

The Aries energy and drive are a strong motif in this house as well.

The Sun here indicates that John's energy, ambition and life force (or what makes him proud and raises his self-esteem) are coupled with his philosophy of life, his ideals, and higher education. He will be fulfilled when recognized for his ethics. In his choice of career, it will be his ethics in counseling and his expansion of his field that will be a source of enjoyment and increased self-esteem. The Sun in Taurus suggests he is very dependable and takes pride in this fact. He will work steadily toward goals no matter how long it takes. Superiors will recognize his reliability. Venus is also in Taurus, and Taurus is ruled by Venus, so Venus is at home here. The Sun and Venus in the ninth house also suggest that John will go on for a Ph.D. in counseling or teach at college level. Education enhances his feeling of self-worth. As a counselor, this is a good fact to point out. He may want to take a break from classes for a while, but will be very happy if he eventually continues with his education.

The Sun in the ninth may also indicate time spent abroad. He may work as a counselor in other countries, such as in an American military school, and he has discussed this potential with his wife. Venus here also suggests higher education and travel abroad, both of which could bring him enjoyment. John has already lived abroad once, when he was on a a Kibbutz for six months, and his education paid off there, since he was the only one who could speak some Hebrew, some Russian (which he learned in a public magnet school) and English. He was given a job helping interpret for Russian immigrants. Again, helping others is very fulfilling for John.

Venus in Taurus may indicate overindulgence which can affect the health (and the ability to work), and John should be cautioned about this. Venus in Taurus also suggests a love of art and music which may be integrated into a career for even more fulfillment. Venus is conjunct the Midheaven giving stronger impetus to working, at least for a time, abroad. Another area that could be fulfilling to John would be some sort of foreign business dealings or diplomacy.

Venus, as the ruler of Libra, shows strong support for face-to-face interactions including counseling, consulting, personnel work and the like. The Sun is where John will shine. Since it is in the ninth house, he would shine in foreign affairs. He has Libra in the third house of communication and Libra denotes balance, charm and diplomacy. The earth signs of Taurus in his ninth house and Virgo in his second house of money indicate business acumen as well. As you can see, although John is leaning toward counseling, he has many options from which to choose and, as a career counselor, it is good to give John ideas for future options.

The tenth house cusp is Taurus and ruled by Venus in the

ninth house; Venus is also in Taurus. These placements indicate that ninth house matters, including education, are significant for John in fulfilling his career potential. Taurus is the plodding steady worker. Saturn in the tenth house suggests a desire for control and authority within John's choice of career, and also very, very hard work. Since the ruler of the tenth house is in the ninth house, the hard work may very well be in terms of writing, teaching or inspiring people (all ninth house activities). Saturn here will ultimately lead to recognition.

Saturn is in Gemini, ruled by Mercury in the eighth house of government funds. The governmental entity could very well be the school system, or the government may fund programs for his career. It is important to note that on June 2 and 3, 2002, John had a Saturn return. This time of Saturn return could be anticipated as the foundation upon which his career would lie and bring personal fulfillment. His years of hard work would begin to pay off as he achieves his goals. In this first year of actual counseling, John is somewhat like an apprentice, laying a new foundation for future recognition. The Saturn return rewards his past efforts and lays the foundation for his work. Saturn in the tenth house suggests John has a very strong sense of responsibility and again, a need to control any situation.

Saturn in Gemini can be challenging, since Gemini suggests a scattering of energy and Saturn suggests control. However, Gemini helps lighten the Saturn tendencies. Saturn (like Taurus on the cusp of the tenth house) suggests a plodding, hard worker, striving to reach the top. Gemini adds some flexibility so that Saturn's positive traits can shine in the tenth house. Saturn is conjunct the Gemini cusp on the eleventh house connecting dreams, hopes and wishes (eleventh house matters) with career planning (tenth house), as well as large groups (eleventh house). Such groups can be either the school system, large counseling groups, or perhaps big business dealings with foreign countries. However, the nitty gritty is that John's dreams are tied to his career plans. Saturn trines Uranus in the third house of elementary education, and John is counseling at the elementary level. The trine to Uranus suggests he will bring unconventional ideas to his career and that he will be a definite reformer. He should be able to articulate his progressive innovations and fulfill his Saturn contributions to society. If he can do this, he will be very happy and receive honors.

It is interesting to note that John has a grand trine between Saturn in his tenth house, Mars in his seventh house, and Uranus in his third house. This grand trine gives a positive energy flow from the third house (which in John's case is the elementary and school system and communication) to his tenth house (career) to his seventh house (which is the house of contracts and partnerships). He should be able to increase funding for counseling programs, as well as obtain private and public grants to further his innovative, reforming ideas.

John is quite pleased and optimistic at this beginning of a new career, though he would prefer junior high or high school. He is beginning his career and is optimistic. The only counseling I can see that he may need from his natal chart at this time is encouragement to continue with his education. It looks like teaching some college courses woud be potentially beneficial, and he can still counsel children. Also, he may wish to go abroad to work for a time, and his chart shows potential for this as well. The only really strong caveat is the emotional drain from children with problems. The Moon in the sixth house is empathic and nurturing, but too many problems can be overwhelming. John should make sure that he has outlets for himself such as sports or artistic endeavors. This is very important, that he reserve some time for himself, so he can continue to work effectively with others.

The cusp of the eleventh house is Gemini, ruled by Mercury in the eighth house. The eleventh house represents dreams, wishes and groups. The eighth house is government funds, taxes, insurance, other people's money and end-of-life matters. With regard to career, the school system involves government money. John's communication skills (Mercury) are tied to government funding or grants from other people for counseling and his ability to obtain funding and grants for further counseling. We can take this analysis one step further by considering Mercury in Aries, ruled by Mars, which is in the seventh house of partnerships. This suggests an ability to implement partnership programs with either government or community sponsoring, which can lead to a sense of fulfillment as John's programs are advanced. John's business acumen may also come into play here.

The twelfth house is a key to motivation, and the cusp is Cancer which is ruled by the Moon in the sixth house of work. The Moon is in Capricorn and again you can take this one step further. Capricorn, ruled by Saturn in the tenth house, is John's sixth house of work. With Moon here, his ultimate career is motivated by his sympathetic and nurturing Cancerian values. This placement is quite a good one for John's chosen career. Since Cancer is a cardinal sign, a lot of action on John's part is also indicated.

Case Study No. 3—Carole
Background

Carole has worked since she was quite young. She worked the entire time she attended college, and has always had a good job in accounting. She was interested in working in the music or movie industry and had some experience in both fields. She married and had her first child in her late thirties, and shortly thereafter, had two other children. Since Carole had worked all her adult life, the adjustment to staying home with the children, even though she wanted to do so, was more difficult than she had imagined. Then a friend offered her a two-month job working as a production accountant for an independent movie. This was a perfect opportunity for Carole to keep her hand in the business and get out of the house without making a long-term commitment to work. At the time Carole began her job, her children were ages 5, almost 2 and almost 1. Her husband had his office above their garage and was on site for emergencies. She also had live-in help. All in all, this was the perfect situation for her to work a little without having to worry about her children.

As with all things, the situation proved not to be as perfect as she had hoped. Of course, Carole felt guilty working even for just two months and leaving the children, despite the fact that her husband was one flight of stairs away and she also had the live-in caregiver. Her husband was supportive of Carole's decision to take this temporary job. The job itself was exciting and excellent experience. Based on her astrological charts, I felt this job was just a stepping stone to larger opportunties, should she so choose.

After a short time, Carole's husband may have not been so enthusiastic, but he never stated that he did not want her working, and he has a very supportive nature. But some of Carole's family members were negative. The morning she was to begin her job, one family member called to say, "I hope you know someone else will be raising your children." Carole's perception of family members' actions or statements may have been difficult for her to handle, but logically, Carole knew that this was just not the case that she would in any way neglect her children. The job was a great opportunity both for the experience, and also for her to have some of her career identity back, rather than feeling only like someone's wife or mother with no life of her own. Unfortunately, logic does not always take precedence in emotional family situations, so Carole experienced some difficulty at a time that should have been exciting for her. However, the difficulty was not severe and going to work for a few months became a very nice change of pace for Carole.

Carole's Natal Chart
See figure 6.

Carole has Cancer on the Ascendant. She will be happy in a nurturing or helping role. She would also be fulfilled in a business situation. Although you usually do not equate Cancer with business, because of the retentive nature of this sign, Cancerians are often found working in business situations. In fact, the Cancerian protectiveness and shrewdness, combined with nurturing tendencies, suggest Carol will be fulfilled while looking after and protecting a client's business interests. These traits came in very handy when Carole worked in production in the movie industry. Also, since Cancer suggests family orientation and nurturing, Carole will be fulfilled and achieve self-esteem and pride through her family. Cancer is ruled by the Moon which is in Carole's fifth house of creativity, speculation and children, thus reinforcing a desire to work in a creative field such as the movie industry or music and, of course, also a desire for children. Cancer on the Ascendant suggests changes in jobs throughout Carole's lifetime. Anyone with Uranus and Mars conjunct the Ascendant is inclined to be be restless and may often feel bored.

The first house is personal and shows how one is viewed by others. With Uranus in that first house, unusual or unsuspected changes occur to Carole personally. Uranus here also suggests Carole may have an unusual or unorthodox approach that would extend to her career as well define her personally. With Uranus in Cancer, and Cancer ruled by the Moon, a tendency to fluctuate may also be emphasized. Uranus is square Jupiter in the tenth house, suggesting unexpected career happenings or unusual turns. Carole may have some difficulty staying on course with her career. This placement suggests restlessness, independence and mental work. With this Cancerian Ascendant and Uranus, we also see ties to creativity, children, unusual circumstances, and career.

Carole's Sun (where she will shine) is also in the first house. Her self-esteem is tied to her own personal efforts. She will be happy when she is personally shining, when recognized for her strengths and positive actions. Since the Sun is also in Cancer, and again ruled by the Moon, this suggests personal ups and downs. The Sun in the first house suggests personal charisma. Carole is very conscious of how she presents herself to the world. The Sun is trine the Moon in the fifth house, again suggesting that a creative profession and children are sources of fulfillment for Carole. Already you begin to see why going back to work in production is so exciting for her, being around so much creativity. We also see how Carole's children can play on her feelings about not being home enough to nurture them. Although she actually is there enough, the children know how to push her buttons. With three planets and the Ascendant in Cancer, family has quite a strong impact on Carole.

Carole has a grand trine between her Sun, Moon and Midheaven.

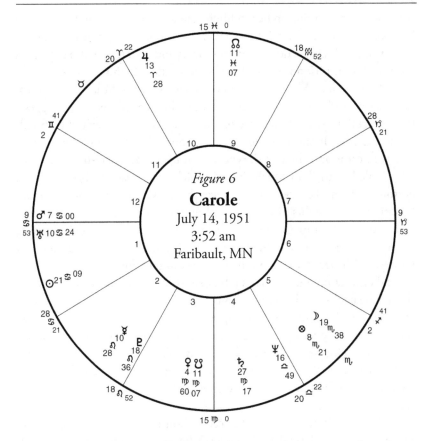

Figure 6
Carole
July 14, 1951
3:52 am
Faribault, MN

This suggests a career involving creativity or speculation, and it just as strongly suggests the Cancerian values of nurturing and family. With the grand trine in water there will be a lot of intuition and emotion involved. This grand trine identifies two very strong and equal themes running through Carole's life—one theme of family and one of a possible career in the arts, entertainment or business. Often, these themes are vying for dominance within her. With this grand trine and Jupiter in the tenth house of career, Carole's opportunities should be extensive. With Jupiter in the tenth house, she will be recognized for her abilities and receive honors. Carole has a very strong chart for creativity in her career.

The **second house** cusp is also Cancer, incorporating values of home, family and nurturing into Carole's personal value system and influencing Carole's decisions about how to make money. Again, Cancer is ruled by the Moon in the fifth house of creativity and children, suggesting that Carole places a very high value on her children, and also that she would be fulfilled if making money in a creative endeavor. The Moon in Scorpio also suggests accounting (which she does), joint resources and research. It also suggests a great deal of intuition upon which Carole would rely in her work.

Carole has Mercury in Leo in the second house of money, possessions and personal values. Mercury in Leo immediately suggests that entertainment or some type of communication field would be fulfilling for Carole. It suggests she will be a very influential and enthusiastic communicator, and also that she will be optimistic and broad-minded. Since Leo is ruled by the Sun which sits in Carole's first house, she brings a lot of personal drive and energy into whatever she does to make money. Mercury here suggests thoughts of comfort and possessions, and with her Sun also involved by rulership, Carole will be ambitious to attain financial security and nice things. She should also be objective and logical at handling her money. With her job as a production accountant for a movie, Carole is around entertainment and has a job of short duration, so she does not feel she will be neglecting her family. Thus, this job seems to be quite fortuitous for Carole at this time. She is strong-minded with the Leo focus. Although the children may have given her a hard time, this job was something she needed to do for herself and she did it. My role as a counselor was to reinforce her positive action, helping Carole to realize self-esteem from a very good position, without feeling excessive guilt about being away from her children part time.

Carole's Pluto is Leo in the second house, and with this placement suggests a grasp of large-scale business or financial affairs (such as accounting). It also suggests generational values. Since Pluto is in Leo, this could be a bond with creativity, the arts and children. We can now begin to see how a job in production accounting is almost perfect for Carole. It combines both the arts and business, a position very true to her second house placements and very fulfilling for her. However, Pluto is square the Moon in the fifth house, again suggesting her children could give her a hard time about going back to work. This square also suggests the natural conflict of time and energy, between time with the children (fifth house) and earning her own money (second house), or we could say Carole's pleasure versus her children's demands. We can see a dual pattern emerging for Carole from her first two houses. The first is work in an entertainment field, the arts, business, or a speculative job, and the second pattern is being with and nurturing her children. The two-month job fulfills both personal quests. Work in either production or accounting is gratifying for Carole, and she is combining both with this job. Plus, she will not be away from her children for too long. Again, Pluto in Leo is ruled by the Sun, and suggests a lot of drive and ambition. Since Pluto is also generational, it suggests that working toward values of Carole's generation, i.e., civil rights, is an option that she could consider.

The third house cusp is Leo, ruled by the Sun in the first house. Carole will bring a lot of personal enthusiasm and energy to third house matters, such as conscious mind efforts and communication. Venus here in Virgo suggests an excellent business sense. Her mind will be precise and practical, efficient and analytical. Carole also exhibits a lot of charm when communicating. She should be able to sway people. Venus here also suggests her thoughts lean toward literature, the arts and entertainment.

Virgo is on the cusp of the fourth house and, since Mercury rules Virgo, it brings Carole's second house themes to the fourth house. This would suggest that home and family are a large part of Carole's personal value system and that she may receive money from family (or spend money on family). Taken one step further, since Mercury is in Leo, she will bring Leo traits to the home. She will want a very lovely or "showy" home for her family. This is part of who Carole is, and so is very important in any career decisions she would make. Saturn is in Virgo here, suggesting both a core drive to care for family and guilt feelings of being away from them, or of doing even the slightest bit less than usual for them. There is a very strong paternal influence working here, and in Virgo this suggests that conscientiousness and attention to detail were very important to Carole's father, and would likely also influence part of who Carole is. Saturn in the fourth house may be tough since it is a karmic placement. Home life could be difficult as a child, and this would reinforce Carole's need for a lovely and peaceful home in her adult life. However, Saturn here also suggests hardworking parents, a family business, a pragmatic home and the like.

There are many motifs upon which Carole draws from her foundation. She will seek a job that does not interfere with home, and at the same time she would want a solid career. With this dual pattern emerging again, a counselor might well suggest that Carole needs to learn not to "beat herself up" when she cannot be all things to all people all of the time. With her first house Sun, she is quite strong, with a strong mind, and is able to handle both family and career, if and when she chooses to do so. She should try to quell any feelings of guilt. In fact, with so much emotional Cancer in her chart, some of the guilt she may be feeling may not be brought on by her childrens' actions or comments, but rather from her own feelings that she should always be there for her children.

Neptune also sits in the fourth house and is in Libra. Neptune here suggests confusion over family matters, perhaps also over the extent of nurturing required to keep the family happy. She may feel she must be the "perfect mother." Neptune also suggests intuition regarding family matters. This is the insight Carole needs to rely on, while trying not to be confused about her role in the family. This placement also suggests that, at a younger age, her parents could push her buttons of insecurity, as well as security, and now her children can push her buttons of nurturing versus neglect. Neptune actually relates strongly to career in respect to whether Carole feels she can balance home and career. Again, this is a typical problem for many women with children, but the planet placements suggest a heavier emphasis on this for Carole.

Neptune in Libra is generational; these are the flower children. The strong familial values Carole learned as a child should correspond to her generation's values (for example, standing up against discrimination). Neptune square the Sun suggests home life as a child may have been personally difficult for Carole. Neptune opposes Jupiter in the tenth house of career, again showing potential confusion as an adult between what to do regarding balance between home and work. In light of this, you can see how the statement, "Someone else will be raising your children," would play upon Carole's guilt and confusion. As a counselor, it woudl be helpful to point out that she is capable of balancing both, if she chooses. She needs to lessen her sensitivity in regard to family duties.

Libra on the cusp of the fifth house is ruled by Venus in the third house. Libra suggests a joy in the arts and creative efforts that should be easily communicated. There is also joy with children. Scorpio is intercepted in this house so there may also be some strong Scorpio tendencies. For example, a viable alternative (which Carole has not yet pursued) could be child psychology, or research work, such as stock analysis or something speculative.

With Moon in Scorpio in the fifth house, Carole is very intuitive, especially when combined with a Sun in Cancer. She can almost run on instinct. The Moon here suggests that work with children, arts and sports are fulfilling for her. Scorpio also rules other people's money so accounting is a good choice for Carole. The Moon in Scorpio suggests a high level of emotional intensity and loyalty, intense maternal instincts and also a strong maternal influence on Carole herself. This influence can be positive or negative, or both, depending on the circumstances. I know that Carole's own mother had problems, and because of that, Carole is very conscious of not neglecting her children in any way. Obviously, the Sun in the first house represents a strong personal drive, and the Moon in the fifth house is a strong maternal drive. Again, you can see this dual pattern of personal conflict emerging. The Moon is square Pluto in the second house of values, so the difficulty in leaving the children to work (even for a short time) is reinforced. The Moon trines the Midheaven so creativity and working with children as a career are also reinforced.

With freedom loving Sagittarius on the cusp of the **sixth house**, Carole should not be restricted by work. She needs not only freedom to "do her own thing" but a position that does not conflict with her high personal ideals. With Sagittarius is ruled by Jupiter in her tenth house, her work will definitely be noticed by superiors and may result in her being pushed to the forefront of her job. She may also travel for work. Higher education is very important for her work and her self-esteem.

Capricorn is on the cusp of the seventh house of contracts, marriage and partnerships. This suggests a reliable, supportive spouse who will be protective and want children.

The eighth house also has Capricorn on the cusp, representing government, insurance, taxes, karma, legacies and other people's money. Capricorn, ruled by Saturn in the fourth house, suggests that family money, as well as Carolo's work, may be a sources of income. It also implies that Carole might choose to work from home in creative or speculative areas at some point in time, so this is another viable option to suggest to Carol. With a Sun in Cancer in the first house, she will probably have many jobs, so an option like working from home may be helpful suggestion.

The ninth house has an Aquarius cusp and is ruled by Uranus in the first house, indicating possible personal travel and self-direction and independence.

Carole has Pisces on the cusp of the **tenth house** of career and honors. It is ruled by Neptune in the fourth house. Already you can see that family is in the forefront of Carole's mind, despite any career opportunity she seeks. Her family is tantamount and often paramount to her career. Her foundation is influential over her choice of career. The Pisces cusp suggests that Carole is very intuitive in career matters. Jupiter is in the tenth house, which is great for people who are willing to work, although it also may suggest the search for the "greatest job on earth," which does not exist. Still, there will usually be career opportunities for Carole. Doors will open even in difficult economic times. Benefic Jupiter here suggests a very successful career, and in Aries, a positive attitude and a pioneering spirit. Jupiter represents a quest for success, and Carole expects to succeed. On the other hand, if we consider Jupiter with the North Node in the ninth house , we might think of travel abroad or a foreign influence on her career. Another possibility is that she could bring people together on a project, or in work as part of a larger project. Jupiter in Aries suggests self-reliance in profession, energy and enthusiasm.

With Jupiter square Uranus, Carole is restless and independent, and work must meet her high ideals. Jupiter is opposite Neptune in the fourth house, and discord between job and home, or the balancing act between home and profession was already discussed. Carole has a pretty good balance between home and career, and both can be fulfilling at the same time.

Jupiter is trine Pluto in the second house suggesting that her career must be based on values and that it should be lucrative. This trine also suggests that her career may involve a large business or group of some kind. With this Jupiter placement, Carole is likely to be noticed by her superiors and receive recognition and honors.

Aries is on the cusp of the eleventh house of dreams, hopes, wishes and groups. With ruler Mars in the twelfth house, Carole's subconscious motivations are a powerful influence on her dreams, hopes and wishes, which would include her career aspirations. Mars in Cancer suggests that Carol could have a nurturing role with regard to groups or be maternal toward her friends.

The twelfth house cusp is Gemini, ruled by Mercury in the second house. The twelfth house is the subconscious mind and hidden matters. The second house has to do with, among other things, personal values. Thus, subconscious motivations strongly affect Carole's personal values. Any childhood repressed feelings, such as possibly not having enough attention or being let down somehow, will influence her values—the way she chooses a career *vis a vis* how she raises her children.

Mars in the twelfth house is in Cancer and conjunct Uranus, trine the North Node and conjunct the Ascendant. Mars shows a lot of inner strength that may not be apparent to others. Because it is in Cancer, high emotions may bubble just below the surface, and unconscious motivations may burst forward from time to time. Also, because Mars is in Cancer, Carole may be a tense mother, which would add to the difficulty she is experiencing in going to work. Since Mars is action, Carole's subconscious may significantly influence her personal action, especially when conjunct the Ascendant and Uranus in her first house. Mars/Uranus indicates restlessness. Carole needs a lot of freedom, variety and stimulation. Her desire for excitement needs to be balanced with her strong maternal instincts (with all the Cancer placements). At times Carole may even surprise herself with her bold actions. Her horoscope suggests a sense of self-confidence with regard to career. Again,

Mars is action and energy. In the twelfth house in Cancer, Mars reinforces Carole's ties to family and nurturing. This placement implies a great deal of her subconscious motivation, and her energy is geared toward her family and in her nurturing roles. Since her subconscious motivations of family are so strong, she is likely to experience strong guilt if her children complain.

Chapter 3

Transit Charts

Once you have delineated a natal chart with a view toward career, you can then look at the faster moving transiting planets to answer current questions. By looking at planets that move slowly, you can plan for the future. Any transiting planet may offer information about your career. However, the outer planets tend to cover global or generational matters, rather than your own personal situation. On the other hand, if you do have a transit of an outer planet prominent in regard to your career, you have a lot of time to work positively and use the motifs indicated by your transits in ways that benefit your career goals. I use about a 3° orb for outer-planet transits (Jupiter through Pluto) and a 5° orb for the faster-moving planets; I will occasionally "stretch" that orb. if it seems to work.

I believe that any time you are reading for someone, you must know about that person's circumstances. The planets, houses and signs suggest many facets of life for each individual. In order to interpret a chart effectively, you must know what your client is seeking at the time of the reading. The use of transits demonstrates this point most of all. A Mars transit, for example, might indicate a new man involved in the situation, or it could point to extreme tension in matters of the house it is transiting (or, for that matter, maybe a new man is causing extreme tension). In the case of Sarah, since we know she has trouble at home, we can pretty well figure that the transiting Mars to the fourth house is pointing to the source of the tension. If she were single and in a relationship that was going places, we might feel the transiting Mars would be her boyfriend moving into her home and taking the relationship to a new level. While we look at the natal chart overall, with all its different facets and complexities, the transits refer to the present time, so we should read them more directly.

The houses the planets transit, and the aspects the transiting planets make to natal (birth) planets, Ascendant and Midheaven are all very important. For example, Jupiter may not be transiting your sixth or tenth houses of work and career, but may instead be making a trine to a planet in your sixth or tenth houses. You could then benefit from the opportunities Jupiter can signify by way of this trine. Therefore, if you are desirous of a new career or some changes in your work, a transisting aspect such as this would be a good time to look for career opportunity.

There are some planets I look at more closely than others with a view toward career. **Jupiter** and **Saturn** are very important in career counseling. Jupiter suggests open doors and Saturn can indicate obstacles in your path. However, Saturn is also a planet I use for karmic interpretation. Where Saturn is transiting in one's chart indicates an area one needs to work on at the current time (and often for a long time). The work needs shown by the Saturn transit are crucial for growth. Although Saturn can be difficult, Saturn should be looked on favorably, even in career situations. With Saturn we build for the long-term. The Saturn theme can be a key to major, measurable accomplishments. Jupiter may show an open door and expanded career opportunities, but Saturn indicates the potential of manifestation—real, lasting results. It can also be helpful to look at **Moon** transits, since Moon moves quickly around the chart (in one month) and is a symbolic trigger for action. You can usually find a time the Moon will trigger something positive for career in your chart within any thirty-day period of time, and then use that time to take action.

Different transits may give you conflicting messages. As with all chart interpretation, you are constantly weighing one factor against another. You can determine which transits are more accurate through the context of the remainder of the natal chart and the other planetary transits. If a transit reinforces tendencies of a natal planet, it will be a strong transit. If the Sun were to transit Mars, both suggest a great deal of energy. Whereas, the Moon transiting Mars would perhaps reflect less energy and might add some emotional tension to the situation.

A planet is said to be retrograde when it appears to be in backward motion; this happens when the Earth passes a slower moving outer planet or Earth is passed by a faster moving inner planet. If a planet goes retrograde and then direct (forward) while aspecting one of your natal planets, the length of time of the transit will be increased. So if you are looking for career opportunity and new offers, and Mercury is direct, retrograde, and then direct again over a planet in your sixth or tenth houses, you have a longer period of time to look for a new job offer. This is a time to be actively looking. Although Mercury retrograde may indicate some confusion, the longer Mercury is at a crucial point in your chart, the more time you have. I do not view the retrograde as a problem. Conjunctions and oppositions of transiting planets seem to be a little stronger than square or trine aspects, which in turn are a little stronger than sextile or quincunx aspects.

Even if no planets are in your sixth or tenth houses, a transiting planet will activate that house. In fact, transits indicate the time to act and are like yellow highlighters to houses with no planets. You are more likely to take action then.

Following are some potentials for each planet in transit:

Transiting Sun

Obviously, the **Sun** is important. The Sun suggests energy, and your desire to shine. The Sun transit is a time for action which will be beneficial. It is a time of recognition and promotion if transiting or in aspect to the sixth or tenth houses, and its transit is even stronger if you have planets in these houses. We are ego-invested (self-esteem on the line) where the Sun is. The downside is a "spoiled brat" or prima donna syndrome. The upside is positive attention and applause.

Transiting Moon

In addition to timing and opportunity, the Moon can also indicate brief periods of recognition.If you have been working on a project that you are particularly proud of, the transiting Moon either directly or by aspect is a good time to present it.

Transiting Mercury

Mercury is also very important in suggesting new ideas, offers and communications. Mercury transits are positive for business decisions, and can also be times for effective mental concentration, or to take classes to further your career. It is a time of paperwork, writing and information. You get new information and inspiration with a Mercury transit.

Transiting Venus

A **Venus** transit to the sixth or tenth houses, or aspecting a planet in the sixth or tenth houses, facilitates things. For example, you may seek to create a nicer working environment during a Venus transit. If you have a particularly difficult task and you can schedule it during a Venus transit, it should run more smoothly—or you might feel lazy and self-indulgent. Teamwork is enhanced with positive Venus transits. Business partnerships can be initiated, or perhaps sacrificed.

Transiting Mars

Take care with a **Mars** transit not to be argumentative, combative or too aggressive. You can achieve a lot during transits of Mars when you use effectively the extreme energy that Mars represents. Mars transits to the sixth or tenth houses can sometimes indicate a new male entering your workplace, or an opportunity for more independence or self-reliance in your work. A Mars transit that relates to the sixth or tenth house by aspect is sometimes easier to deal with that a Mars transits in these houses. You can then focus on accomplishment more easily, when the combative potentials are somewhat toned down. Mars suggests a pioneering spirit and a chance to be first at something.

Transiting Jupiter

A Jupiter transit can be a time to achieve recognition; when your career will move forward. This is a great time to actively seek what you want. You may also want to take educational courses to further your career, or travel for your career. It is a time to reach toward big dreams and schemes. It is also a time of idealism. If overdone, Jupiter themes can lead to **too** much, **too** fast, to excessive idealism or to the "grass is greener" syndrome and grandiose schemes.

Transiting Saturn

Saturn suggests a lot of hard work. but laying a basis for future success. When transiting the tenth house, it can show a peak time of your career success, since previous hard work has laid the foundation for recognition and honors now. Saturn can also mark a time when you begin laying a new foundation for the future. On the other hand, if you have not done your work, Saturn may show your time of downfall—Saturn reflects honor or dishonor. When a Saturn transit is aspecting the sixth or tenth houses, it usually means hard work. If we work sensibly and well within the system, Saturn periods are very productive. Potential downsides are literal barriers, blocks, problems with authority figures, having to face facts, and times when you may feel frustration, inadequacy, fear and anxiety.

Transiting Uranus

Uranus is an outer planet that is often viewed for generational trends. In transit to your chart, personally, it can indicate sudden changes in your life, your work environment or change in the job itself. Changes can be positive or negative. Uranus might be described as throwing everything up in the air and the chips fall where they may. It is unpredictable. A Uranus transit is a time of upheaval. You are being asked to break the rules constructively, to be inventive and innovative. Independence and individuality are advised.

Transiting Neptune

Neptune is also an outer planet that is also viewed as generational. Personally, a Neptune transit can suggest times of confusion or perhaps some sort of misunderstanding. It can also point to periods of great insight and intuition. It can be a tough transit if your career is in business or other mundane fields. Think everything through very carefully before acting. For people in the arts,Neptune transits can indicate great inspiration. For people in helping and healing professions, Neptune symbolizes increased sensitivity and compassion.

Transiting Pluto

Pluto is also an outer planet, generational and beyond. If it is significant in your career arena, you probably have tremendous drive and intensity. Your years with Pluto transits are when you can strongly succeed, but you must take care not to be ruthless. Alternatively, Pluto may mark the time when you change careers, or your when career has some sort of transformation. For example, your company may downsize or you may reinvent yourself professionally. Pluto transits may lead you into a career that is totally new to the world. Pluto transits may also be be active when we borrow money, make investments, get government funding, do research, work undercover, deal with secrets or scandals, confront intense emotions, engage in power struggles, or have to contend with office or other types of politics.

Transits — Three Case Studies

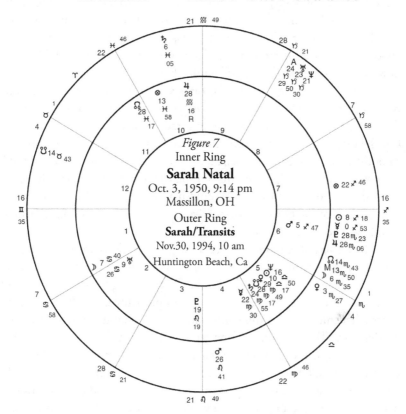

Figure 7
Inner Ring
Sarah Natal
Oct. 3, 1950, 9:14 pm
Massillon, OH
Outer Ring
Sarah/Transits
Nov.30, 1994, 10 am
Huntington Beach, Ca

Sarah's Transits to her Natal Chart
on the Day she Began her New Job
See figure 7, the transiting planets around Sarah's natal chart on this day.

On November 30, 1994, Mars was transiting Sarah's fourth house, which can signify a lot of tension and combativeness at home. As you know, the fourth house sits opposite the tenth house on a natal chart so there is a natural conflict between home and work, at least to some extent, for everyone. However, with the Mars transit the conflict was great. Remember, Sarah's major concentration of planets is in her fifth house of children, so the conflict in her home would more than likely be the difficulty of going back to work, leaving the children, and arguing with her husband about it. This is further suggested by natal Saturn in the fifth house conjunct natal Mercury in the fourth house suggesting a lot of thought and heavy emphasis on home and children. There is a natural difficulty in going back to work in her chart, and the Mars transit underlines the difficulty at this time. Transiting Mars also opposes natal Jupiter in Sarah's tenth house, adding to the conflict between the tenth and fourth house matters. This is one of the last places on Sarah's chart I would choose for a Mars transit on the day Sarah began her new job. It did indicate how going back to work was difficult for her.

Venus transiting the fifth house is a time for creativity and a time to spend with her children, and not necessarily a time for the serious discussions between Sarah and her children when she went back to work. On the other hand, Venus' tact, charm and affection helps situations run smoothly, so this was a very beneficial transit on November 30th. Sarah's Venusian skills did help lessen the tension of separation so that going back to work was not as difficult as it could have been. The Venus transit was the opposite of the powerful combative energy of the Mars transit. Things could have been a lot harder.

Sarah has phenomenal transits for going back to work in her sixth house, but the transits also suggest some difficulties. The transiting Moon indicates change, and obviously the change was going back to work. Since the Moon also symbolizes emotions, it was probably difficult for Sarah to control her emotions and this contributed to her resentment of her husband on that day. The transiting Moon trines Sarah's natal Moon emphasizing a lot of feelings, and it also trines natal Uranus in Sarah's second house of personal values, one of which is taking care of her children and not working while they are young. So, just the transits of Mars and the Moon alone begin to create a picture of how difficult it was for Sarah to be going back to work was at this time.

But, other planets transiting Sarah's sixth house indicate a wonderful time to go back to work. She has Midheaven, Jupiter, Mercury and Sun transits. Mercury and the Sun are conjunct her natal Mars, showing she has a lot of energy and drive. The Pluto transit to her sixth house suggests transformation, but also tension. When Pluto reaches the end of this house and goes into her seventh house (well after the year 2000), Sarah will probably have found a role in which she will be truly happy. This job she begins now is probably a stepping stone to a future career. The concentration of transiting planets is in her sixth house of work. She is laying a foundation for a future career. With her Jupiter transit, Sarah's new job will be rewarding and she will gain self-esteem and the respect of her superiors. Transiting Jupiter sextiles Saturn and Venus in her fifth house, bringing good fortune even though this is a difficult time.

When counseling someone in Sarah's position, it is very important to emphasize the career opportunity and benefits opening up to her as a way of helping her balance the difficulty she is having at home. It is the "silver lining to a very dense and dark cloud." Jupiter here indicates career advancement. Jupiter in the sixth house is an excellent transit to begin a new job. The Sun suggests energy to work and recognition for her work. Mercury represents a lot of thought and communication. The Mercury transit is also an asset to learning a new accounting position.

When planets transit a house they indicate a lot of activity in that area of life, and Sarah's sixth house has four planets and the Moon transiting in it, and her natal Mars is in this house. This is an incredibly dynamic time for Sarah, and even if her husband had not pushed her to go back to work, other events would probably have done so at this time. By stressing this point as a counselor, you can help Sarah deal with her husband more rationally and with less anger, and enable her to decide the fate of her marriage without long-term guilt should she decide to terminate the marriage.

Transiting Mercury conjunct natal Mars suggests a great deal of mental energy and attention to detail. As stated, this is perfect for accounting. It also suggests nervous energy which will help Sarah tackle the demands of both working and taking care of small children. The transiting Sun conjunct natal Mars is a great time to start a new job as there is lots of energy, and this transit could help Sarah discover whether or not she will be satisfied with this job. The transiting Sun squares transiting Saturn in Sarah's tenth house and although this square is challenging to work through, it also uggests significant accomplishments.

Sarah's Natal Pluto in the third house (which among other things is the house of lower education) rules the Scorpio planets transiting in her sixth house of work, and she is working as an accountant in the school system. Natal Jupiter in Sarah's tenth house rules the Sagittarius transits in her sixth house of work, so Sarah's career and the school system seem interrelated at this time.

Overall, Sarah's career potential is actually quite good, but home is where the conflicts in her life lie. If Sarah were single and did not have small children, she would be thrilled at this turn of events regarding career. On the other hand, even though her career is part of the problem at home, without this positive input into her life and the self-esteem arising from it, her home life may have been even more difficult to handle, because she would have no outlet for her energy and her desire for independence.

With Neptune transiting the eighth house, the old order of Sarah's life is passing away even if she does not yet feel the changes, because they are not yet apparent. All of the chaos at home and the return to work is leading up to a major change.

A possibility of Neptune transiting the eighth house, is that someone close may pass out of one's life. This happened to Sarah when, in frustrations that her marriage had become too much to handle, she called a man with whom she had been romantically involved in the past. She was shocked to find out he had died, and this changed her outlook considerably. It was the first time someone who had been close to her had passed on, and this caused her to reevaluate what had been going on in her subconsious. She decided to stay in her marriage and make the best of it for her children, as this is the area of her life where she is most dedicated. Things are smoother in her marriage, now that she has come to this decision. She attributed going back to work as a major factor in making things run smoothly in the marriage but, in fact, it goes far deeper. Her newfound confidence in her ability to support herself and her children gave her more security in the marriage. The real key to improvement was her acceptance of the union as it is. This Neptune transit trined Mercury and quincunxed the fourth house cusp, indicating Sarah was over-idealizing someone and that her domestic life was unclear. In a difficult home situation, someone romantic from the past can easily be over-idealized, thus creating confusion and even chaos.

Neptune transiting the eighth house can also indicate a problem with joint finances, as well as deceit or fraud. As previously discussed at the beginning of Chapter Two, Sarah has always suspected her spouse of hiding assets.

Uranus transiting the eighth house suggests the death of a matter and brings about subconscious changes which in turn will change one's life. Sarah is beginning to feel a sense of freedom and the marriage no longer seems to be a trap from which she cannot escape. Now it is her choice to stay. The feelings of restriction due to the marriage are replaced by the feeling that, "It is my choice to stay." Uranus trining Mercury, Saturn and the fourth house cusp can indicate sudden changes in the home and that Sarah will handle these changes with a new perspective. She is freeing herself from old characteristics that are no longer needed. Sarah's need for independence is an issue, and she feels she has much more freedom with her new career.

I have discussed Sarah's personal life a great deal, as well as her career. In this case, career counseling is predicated upon the happenings in her personal life, and the two cannot be separated. This is why I stated that you must know a person's circumstances to effectively counsel them with regard to career. Sarah's natal chart and the transit chart look great with regard to her career, but her personal turmoil overshadows a very exciting career time.

Over the past few years, Sarah, even though she was unhappy, did not feel she could end her marriage and take care of her children. Now that she is back at work, combined with the mental changes occurring, she feels independent enough to do so. Still, she has now decided against ending the marriage. She is more secure and is becoming happier with her life because of the changes, including her return to work.

As a counselor, the astrologer should stress positive ways in which work changed her life, and by doing so, help Sarah to overcome, rather than dwell upon, her problems at home. When referring to Sarah's chart, the astrologer can choose to emphasize the negative or point out the positive. A well-prepared counselor will emphasize strengths found in the chart, while acknowledging the negative, then use what is best to deal with difficulties. Research in psychology indicates that therapists who regularly emphasize client's strengths are more successful in counseling.

Transiting Uranus opposing natal Uranus is a major aspect in anyone's life that usually occurs around age 41 In Sarah's case, the orb of aspect is a litle wider than I usually use. It really hits hardest for her at age 44, but had been going on for a few years when the orb was tighter. This generational transit markes the mid-life crisis when one is weighing accomplishments such as career and a happy marriage. In Sarah's case her career, marriage and home life seemed to be in constant upheaval, so this transit was particularly difficult for her. She must find internal happiness in order to have her external accomplishments be meaningful to her.

As previously discussed, the changes Sarah experienced within, such as gaining more self-esteem, are leading to happiness within her life. The knowledge that she is choosing her path, and is not trapped, became very important for Sarah's peace of mind. The transiting Saturn opposition to the fourth house suggests that her job will take precedence over her home for the time being, and this suggests a lot of hard work. At the same time, the Saturn transit is laying a foundation for her future success in her career. The transiting Saturn trine to her natal Moon and Uranus suggeset increased stability and this, again, is manifested in her return to work, thus adding to the family income.

I delineated Sarah's charts some time ago. When I reviewed them, I found that, at the turn of the century, she went back to school to become a speech therapist. She will finish school over the next several years, and she plans to work from her home and run her own business. Therefore, as I found earlier, when Pluto leaves her sixth house, she will have the career she seeks. Her years in accounting enable her to run her own business and her accounting for the school system was just a stepping stone. Also, I stated previously that Neptune and Uranus transiting the eighth house were leading up to a major change. Before Neptune and Uranus left that house, her husband had passed away.

When reading for someone in Sarah's position at the time she began her job, if you are not a licensed counselor, you should refer her to someone who is. I am not licensed, and Sarah was going through a very difficult time. I suggested that she she might wish to speak with someone who could help her with her need for release of tension, and that she might benefit from professional guidance.

John's Transits to his Natal Chart
On the Day he Began his New Job
See figure 8.

John began his new job on September 4, 2001. The first transit to John's chart is wonderful. The Sun is transiting his first house, indicating John can achieve personal recognition. He will have a great deal of personal energy and drive. He will get up and be ready to go on the first day of his new career. Sun is square his fourth house Neptune and he will probably have jitters, i.e., "Am I really prepared for this?" On the other hand, the transiting Sun is also trine his natal Sun and Venus in his ninth house. He has an incredible flow of energy and the transiting Sun trine Venus suggests that he can smoothly handle whatever comes up. Again, the Sun is ambition and drive, and John will personally shine today. His superiors will recognize his abilities at the onset.

Transiting Mercury in John's second house suggests a great deal of communication today, based on his own personal values. The conjunction to Pluto in Libra suggests mediation. Pluto also suggests transformation and intraction with a large group. John is beginning to communicate his values to a larger group or organization, and he will draw attention to what is important to him. Mercury conjunct Pluto is a time for intense thought. John will influence others, although he may meet opposition and different points of view. (I will demonstrate these points more thoroughly when I discuss John's Uranus transit.) Mercury is opposing natal Mercury in Aries, which suggests stimulating ideas. John will get a lot of feedback, possibly causing him to adjust his own ideas. Again, this will be discussed further with the Uranus transit that will bring the Sun and Mercury transits into play within a concrete situation.

Transiting Pluto is in the fourth house conjunct natal Neptune,

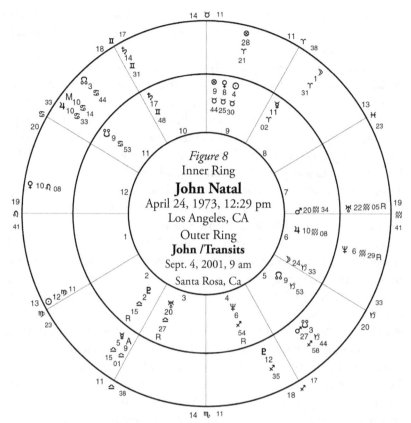

Figure 8
Inner Ring
John Natal
April 24, 1973, 12:29 pm
Los Angeles, CA
Outer Ring
John / Transits
Sept. 4, 2001, 9 am
Santa Rosa, Ca

and Pluto is also opposing natal Saturn in the tenth house. When viewing a Pluto transit in terms of career, we also see significance on a personal level. Pluto traveling through the fourth house of foundation may transform relationships to home and family, especially the parents. For example, if you have been dependent on your family, you may be now breaking that dependence. Obviously, beginning work means less financial dependence or financial help from family. On a personal level, this Pluto transit might also be when John's childhood problems are recognized and conquered. This suggests that the formation of John, the counselor, may be based on family history that led to his desire to help children.

Pluto conjunct Neptune can be a period of personal transformation that indicates an interest in psychology. Pluto opposite Saturn in the tenth house will obviously signify an intense drive in John's career. It is a time of changing circumstances and very hard work. He may feel frustrated at not getting where he wants to go fast enough. John may also be changing some of his attitudes formed by the family unit, and developing his own identity.

Mars is transiting John's fifth house of creativity, and is very widely opposed to his Saturn, and also transiting Saturn in the tenth house. (This aspect from Mars is separating, but it seems to have done its work already). Mars indicates a lot of drive and energy. An opposition to Saturn can symbolize frustration or putting much energy into productive work. Things are not moving fast enough for John. He started counseling in elementary school, but he wanted to work in either a junior high school or a high school, so he is waiting to move up. Mars transiting the fifth house also cries out for creative self-expression or maybe blowing off steam through exercise and sports, and is not necessarily career minded. Since the fifth House rules children, much action with children makes sense. Since Mars is opposite Saturn in the tenth house, there may be a great deal of patience required with regard to career, and John might just keep getting slowly frustrated by circumstances. Working effectively within the rules and establishment may be challenging. Again, when I get to the Uranus transit this will be more clear.

Neptune is transiting John's sixth house of work and service. Neptune may have a very personal significance when transiting this house. John must take care and watch his health so stress does not affect his work, and he also may be misunderstood. More than all of this, the Neptune transit in the sixth house is very conducive to social work and psychology. Therefore, for John, Neptune is a beneficial transit to begin his job, even if there is some confusion around the job itself. Neptune is conjunct natal Jupiter in the sixth house, denoting a time of high personal ideals and a desire to help others. Again, this is perfect. The only caveat with this transit for John is not to take foolish risks, but instead to try to think problems through. However, Neptune also squares John's natal Sun in the ninth house. This can imply depleted vitality, or that ego or idealism gets out of hand and John needs to take care. Also, there may be some uncertainty around work, perhaps because it is not exactly what John wants at this time, since he prefers to work in a junior high school or a high school. Neptune square Venus also suggests a bit of disappointment. Since John's Sun and Venus are in the ninth house, he may already be feeling a need for more education to achieve what he wants. However, any disappointment his is experiencing is far less than the positive self-esteem and recognition indicated by the Sun transit in his first house. All in all, it is a very good day for John. This is what I meant when I stated you must choose what is most prominent when transits conflict. John knows this is a step toward the career he wants.

Uranus transiting John's seventh house, is conjunct natal Mars and trine natal Saturn in the tenth house (albeit by a somewhat wider orb than I usually use, but in this case, it works). Uranus is the planet that symbolizes unpredictable shake-ups. The school had moved small children from their classrooms to various other classes, splitting up friends, and the children were very, very upset. This was done without preparing the children or telling their parents. The school did not value or take into consideration how the children would feel.

When John got to school on his first day of counseling, he had to cross a picket line of angry parents and was immediately asked to defuse the situation. The parents' picketing fir the theme of a John's Uranus transit—something completely unexpected and chaotic. But, we can see how previous placements of transits, such as the Sun and Mercury, helped John deal with this situation. The Uranus trine natal Saturn in the tenth house suggested he could find a good compromise between the Establishment (Saturn) and the upset "revolutionary" parents (Uranus). All his hard work paid off as he was able to handle the situation easily. The parents were satisfied. True to his first house Sun transit, John was able to shine and gain the recognition of his superiors. Uranus trine Saturn allowed him to work within the limits and boundaries of the school system in a positive way, but also a creative way, to defuse the tense situation. In fact, this trine is conducive to professional advancement. Saturn's principles of discipline, balance and hard work were obvious to John's superiors. This unusual and unexpected event (Uranus) was even more fortuitous than John realized at the time.

The Moon is transiting the eighth house of intense emotions and potential power struggles. The Moon in a fire sign indicates a lot of emotional tension and energy with the situation. It was conjunct natal Mercury during that day, indicating a lot of talking and communicating, and emotional versus rational thinking. The Moon in Aries suggests the emotional tension of the parents of the distraught children. There was a great deal of communication in order to defuse the situation.

The next transit we'll consider in John's chart is his Saturn return (transiting Saturn conjunct natal Saturn) in the tenth house of profession. Saturn returns are milestones, and this was mentioned briefly in the discussion of John's natal chart. A major cycle in John's life is closing, and a change will take place. John will reap the rewards of his past years of work. If his energies have been directed positively, he will achieve honor and recognition. John is consciously eliminating negative habits now, so as to go forward in a positive direction and establish his new career path. This is a time of new beginnings. Since John appears to have created a solid foundation over the past years, it is a very positive time. Had he not created a solid foundation, it could have been a time of crises. Saturn's return is the transit that points to maturity. John's years over age thirty will be very productive. The next twenty-nine years will see him working in his field and securing his future so that he can look forward to his older years with the next Saturn return.

Jupiter is transiting the eleventh house of dreams, hopes, wishes and large groups. It is sextile the Sun and Venus in Taurus in the ninth house. Again, this suggests opening up opportunities for John to work, and probably a desire to continue his education. His personal philosophies are expanding and tied to his hopes for the future. Friends and groups should be of assistance now. John will be working and dealing with many people. Jupiter is square Mercury in the Eighth House which is government money, so he will have to work hard for funding for his programs.

Venus is transiting the twelfth house and opposing natal Jupiter, squaring natal Sun and Venus, sextile transiting Mercury, and trining natal Mercury and Neptune. Venus here suggests a time of helping others and charity, but John might give too much and needs to take care of himself. It is also a time to resolve any unresolved psychological matters. Venus is an especially interesting transit because although suggestive of subconscious and hidden matters in this house, it also aspects many areas of John's natal chart. First of all it is opposite natal Jupiter, and John feels as though he can take on the world. Natal Jupiter is in the sixth house of work and John has plenty of confidence to start out in his new career. The Venus transit adds to that promise, although with sixth house health issues, these are aslo aspects for overeating, suggesting that John will probably put on weight this year unless he is very, very careful. Venus square the Sun can imply laziness, but with all the other things going on in his chart, I feel this is a good thing and it may help him slow down a little. He should take time for some recreation for the benefit of his own psyche. Venus square the Sun may suggest conflict, but also successful resolution of the conflict (such as John's successful resolution of the parents' picketing the school).

Venus square Venus may indicate personal challenges, but John can probably work them out smoothly. Remember, Venus symbolizes facilitation, so even in square, it can denote agreement and teamwork.

Venus sextile Mercury suggests commercial transactions. In John's case, it can point to diplomatic speech and smooth communication with distraught parents. His career does require a lot of communication, and he is starting off on the right foot.

Venus trine natal Mercury also suggests a smooth outcome of any situation of difficulty in eighth or ninth house matters. Also, John is probably desperately wanting to fix up his office, to add some color and charm.

Venus trine natal Neptune is great for artistic creativity and imaginative solutions to problems. It also shows that John has a great deal of compassion and understanding at this time. His creative solution to the picket problem was also somewhat visual. He circled the parents around him and let each express their feelings, talk things out, compassionately listening and advising until the situation was defused. The circle virtually gave the parents a sense of connection to each other and a sense of communal power so they felt John would respond to their strength. This Venus transit with all of its aspects turned out to be very beneficial for John. It is in the twelfth house and, although he worked behind the scenes, the affability and interpersonal skills that Venus represents helped John to shine through his first house Sun transit.

As discussed in this chapter, some transits weigh more heavily than others for career, and some transits, like John's Venus transit, are much more helpful than they appear to be at first glance. Venus smoothed many areas of his chart.

In John's position, he really does not need a great deal of counseling. He is starting an exciting career. With John's chart, positive reinforcement as to his choices and direction as well as discussing potential, future opportunity is really just another boost at this exciting time. This is a strong transit chart with which to begin a new career.

Carole's Transits to her Natal Chart on the Day she Began her New Job
See figure 9.

Carol began her job on August 25, 1995. The Moon is transiting the third house and square her natal Moon in the fifth house. The Moon transiting the third house suggests emotional or subjective communication. Since it squares the fifth house natal Moon, there is a suggestion of emotional communication around children. The Sun is also transiting the third house suggesting a lot of mental activity and communication. The transiting Sun is in Virgo implying business activity. All of this describes Carole's life on the first day of her new job, trying to placate her children and working in accounting. The Venus transit in the third house helps the mental transition to work run smoothly. The Venus Return implies personal pleasure and/or financial focus.

As you can see, both luminaries and Venus are suggesting tremendous mental stimulation, and already we see tension with the children as the transiting Moon squares natal Moon in the fifth house. Moon/Moon aspects suggests high emotions but also move rather quickly so adjustment should be fairly rapid. Once again, with the Venus transit, adjustment should be smooth. This is something to emphasize as a counselor. The emotions of the day will pass rather quickly and the transition into the working world should run smoothly.

Mercury is transiting the fourth house, conjunct Saturn in Virgo and opposite transiting Saturn in the tenth house. Mercury in the fourth suggests a reevaluation of domestic life and perhaps a need to do something different. In Carole's case, this need is fulfilled by going to work for a short period of time. Also, Mercury suggests Carole will express her feelings to the family and probably there will be some conflict coming from this new situation.

Mercury conjunct Saturn suggests Carole will proceed cautiously. It is a good transit for accurate mental precision and critical thinking which are requirements for her new position. Natal Saturn opposite transiting Saturn in the tenth house suggests Carole's seriousness regarding this job and her place in the world, as well as her seriousness as a homemaker.

This Mercury transit conjunct Saturn also suggests very hard work. Carole needs to make sure she takes time for pleasure, or work will drain her.

Transiting Mars in the fifth house is conjunct Neptune in the fourth house. The Neptune and Mars conjunction may suggest feelings of discouragement and Carole may be frustrated. She may feel she is doing too much while accomplishing nothing. It is a difficult transit to start something new. Neptune also suggests diminished Mars energy. Since this involves both the fourth house of home and family, and the fifth house of children, it suggests Carole may feel drained at home due to caring for the children after working all day. It is a period of adjustment. Too much idealism or perfectionism could contribute to frustration. On the positive side, active pursuit (Mars) of dreams and visions (Neptune) is possible.

Mars transiting the fifth house suggests conflicts with children. They will rebel and be more difficult to handle in light of Carole's going back to work, among whatever else they will choose to be rebels about at this time. Mars in the fifth house is a good time for physical release such as sports, or

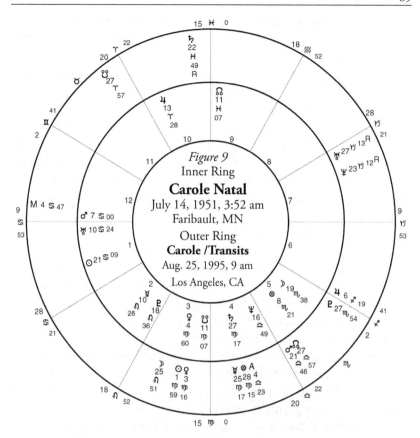

Figure 9
Inner Ring
Carole Natal
July 14, 1951, 3:52 am
Faribault, MN
Outer Ring
Carole /Transits
Aug. 25, 1995, 9 am
Los Angeles, CA

at least some type of physical activity to relieve tension for both Carole and her children. A game of touch football or roller skating after work and school would be beneficial to all of them. As a counselor, this is a very helpful suggestion to emphasize. Physical activity to relieve stress is important at times of change in family dynamics. This will also give the children a little additional attention. Rather than succumb to an energy drain as suggested by the Neptune/Mars conjunction, the physical activity with the children actually is a solution to two situations. It will help increase energy and give the children additional time.

Pluto in Scorpio transits the fifth house. Generally, if you have children, Pluto here suggests a period of time during which you will have an extreme effect on them. Since Carole's children are young, this Pluto transit suggests that she intuitively feels her effect upon them and she takes extreme care to give them positive nurturing during these years. In fact, this is why periodic employment like the two-month job is so perfect for her. Carole will be able to care for her children and have a short, needed break for herself. On the other hand, Pluto can also suggest a kind of power struggle, with the children vying to get their way.

Jupiter has just entered the sixth house of work, suggesting new opportunity. This job was a surprise offer when a previous co-worker called Carole to come back to work. Transiting Jupiter trines natal Mercury in the second house and is almost within orb of trining natal Jupiter in the tenth house. Jupiter's transit in the sixth house is generally a time of good health, which is important for Carol with the additional responsibilities, and it counters the energy drain indicated by the Mars/Neptune transit. Jupiter suggests a period of satisfaction with work.

Jupiter trine Mercury suggests excellent communication, possibly that co-workers will listen to Carole and respect her opinion. It symbolizes an air of confidence and intellectual planning.

Jupiter trine Jupiter is an excellent time to examine and pursue goals, and Carole can actualize goals at this time. Jupiter trine Jupiter suggests a great deal of opportunity. Again, this is why I feel the job is a stepping stone, and should Carole decide she would like more of this type of work and communicate those feelings, she will be able to get it. This is an ideal transit. On a personal level, Jupiter trine Jupiter suggests balance, ease and optimism, so even with any negative family attitude at home, Carole should be very comfortable with her job. This is a good time to start looking at future opportunity and begin to work toward it.

Uranus and Neptune are transiting Carole's seventh house, and Neptune opposes natal Sun in her first house. Both trine Saturn in her fourth house. First of all, Neptune and Uranus suggest confusion and chaos around marriage, perhaps Carole's spouse realizing how difficult it can be without a full-time partner at home. Uranus transiting the seventh house suggests a time to make needed changes in a relationship or at least escape the daily routine. Carole escaped the daily routine with the job. Neptune transiting the seventh house suggests problems in communication, misunderstanding with a partner, or keeping feelings to self, although I feel with her other chart placements, that Carole is avoiding this by expressing herself and her desire to work. Positive options for the Neptune transit (since Neptune transits a house/sign on the average of thirteen to fourteen years) are sharing dreams, aesthetics and spirituality with a spouse, practicing healthy forgiveness in relationships, and building a more beautiful partnership. Neptune opposite the natal Sun can denote somewhat depleted energy but, again, the Jupiter transit in the sixth house helps balance this out. Neptune is excellent for imaginative, aesthetic, or creative pursuits. Neptune transits also imply misunderstanding or miscommunication if ideals get out of hand or if a person gets distracted. Since this is a first-house and a seventh-house problem, it may be miscommunication with the spouse, which is perfectly understandable with Carole's new, hectic schedule. Neptune trine Saturn suggests a balance between what Carole dreams of and reality. Carole senses what she needs and this probably aids in her decision to take the job. She is able to work very hard now.

Uranus trine Saturn in the fourth house suggests a time for self-discipline and Carole will seek constructive changes in her life; thus, adding the job. This is also a good time to start advancing in her profession. Unusual opportunity and hard work are suggested.

The final transiting planet is Saturn in the tenth house. It trines natal Sun in the first house. This appears to be as strong or even stronger than the Jupiter transit in the sixth house for career opportunity. Anytime Saturn transits the tenth house, you can reap rewards of past education and experience and lay a foundation for the future. It seems to me that Carole is reaping the reward of her business education, as well as her experience in both accounting and working in the entertainment industry, while accepting a position which lays a foundation for future, independent work on specific projects which will fit her schedule. Saturn here is honor and with the trine to natal Sun, Carole will be recognized for her ability by superiors. Saturn trine Sun is a time to act.

The Jupiter and Saturn transits to Carole's natal chart clearly suggest a positive time to work and achieve recognition and set the groundwork for future employment should she so choose. Carole's chart is a very good example of the importance of Saturn and Jupiter transits to career.

Looking at Carole's overall situation and planetary placements, it appears as though she may need encouragement and reinforcement that she made a right choice, but I do not feel she is so stressed as to need professional counseling. Unlike Sarah's chart, she does have a strong work theme running side by side with her desire to take care of her family, and she has the ability to handle both. The point to stress as a counselor is that this opportune time should be enjoyed.

Chapter Four

Derivative Houses

I find the use of derivative houses especially helpful in career counseling, and I use transits to the derivative houses when looking for career opportunity in the Natal Chart. I often delineate derivative houses in the Solar and Lunar Return charts, as well as the transits to these houses when looking for further career opportunity. Therefore, I will discuss the derivative houses briefly in this chapter so, as you read on through the chapters on return charts, my use of derivatives will make sense to you.

Definition of Derivative Houses

There are twelve houses in a chart. Each house reflects parts of your life (as defined in chapter 1). However, each house is also the first house of the part of your life it reflects. For example, the tenth house is your career house, and it is also the derivative first house of your career. Thus, the eleventh house (of dreams, hopes, wishes and groups) is also the second house of money to your derivative first house of career. Then, the twelfth house (of subconscious and hidden matters) becomes the third house of communication to the derivative first house of your career. Likewise the sixth house is your house of work, service and health so it becomes is the derivative first house of your work, service and health. Then the seventh house of partnerships and contracts would become the second house of money to your derivative first house of work, service and health.

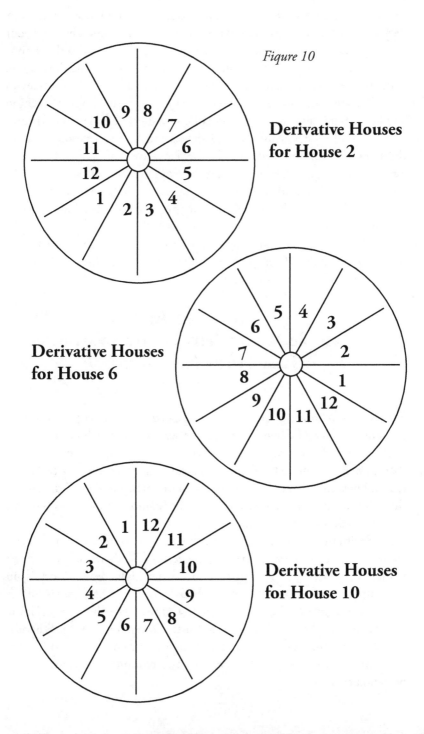

Figure 10

**Derivative Houses
for House 2**

**Derivative Houses
for House 6**

**Derivative Houses
for House 10**

The eighth house would be the third house of communication to your derivative first house of work, service and health. The second house is your house of money, possessions and personal values, and it is also the derivative first house of money, possessions and personal values. The third house is the house of communication but is also the second house of money to your derivative first house of money. The fourth house is your foundation and home but is also the third house of communication to your derivative first house of money. I usually find the second house of money and the third house of communication to be the derivative houses most helpful in career counseling. This gives you a lot more options to work with when trying to help a client find career opportunities. Not only do you have more options to look at with each house, but you have the aspects and transits to consider as well.

When looking for career opportunity, try to use the derivative houses for houses 2, 6 and 10 for further input. See figure 10 for the derivative house outline for career counseling.

Three Case Studies
Sample Natal Chart Derivative Houses
Case Study No. 1— Sarah
See figure 4.

Sarah's chart shown in Chapter 2, is repeated on the next page for your convenience. Her third house, which is her derivative second house of money, possessions and personal values, has Cancer on the cusp; Pluto in Leo sits there as well, suggesting her family is of great value to her and a career which falls in line with generational values is also important to her. With Cancer, she will probably be retentive and guard her company's assets, so business would also be a good career choice.

Sagittarius is on the cusp of her sixth house of work and service to her house of money and values, suggesting Sarah wants freedom to work as she pleases and a job that meets her high ideals. Pisces is on the cusp of the tenth house of her house of money and values and is ruled by Neptune in the Fourth house, again showing home and family importance in light of any career. The North Node in Pisces opposes Saturn and Venus in Virgo suggesting the push/pull pattern of career and family.

As you can see, the derivative houses reinforce the motifs of the natal houses.

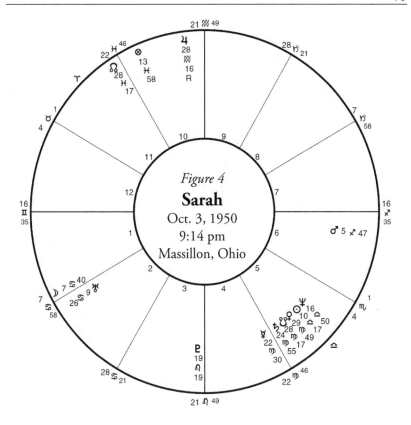

Figure 4
Sarah
Oct. 3, 1950
9:14 pm
Massillon, Ohio

Case Study No. 2 — John
See figure 5.

John's second house is his derivative first house of money, possessions and personal values. The derivative second house (of the second) is the third house. It has Libra on the cusp and Uranus in Libra. This suggests John will exhibit both charm and an unusual approach to earning potential.

His derivative sixth house to his first house of money and values has Aquarius on the cusp and Mars in Aquarius. This suggests visionary ideals associated with work and tremendous energy geared toward work. Uranus in the (derivative) second house rules Aquarius, further pointing to an unusual approach and far-reaching ideas. Mars suggests there may be tension at work as well.

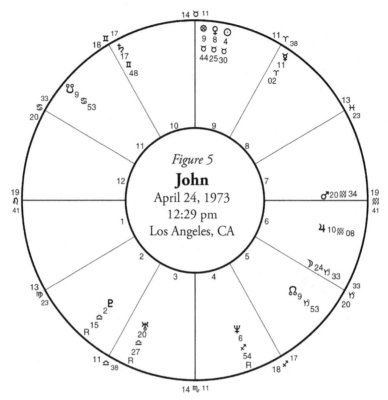

Figure 5
John
April 24, 1973
12:29 pm
Los Angeles, CA

Gemini is on the cusp of the derivative tenth house (of the second) suggesting John may have more than one job/career at a time, or he may do many projects for his job at one time. Gemini is ruled by Mercury in the derivative seventh house (of the second) suggesting career help from his spouse. This reinforces the natal delineation in that he is working for two schools, and his wife is a teacher who would be supportive of his career as a school counselor.

Looking a little deeper into John's derivative houses, his natal ninth house is the derivative twelfth house to his natal tenth house of career. His ninth house Sun squares Jupiter, and since the ninth house is the derivative twelfth house to his natal career house, it suggests work behind the scenes of his career. A counselor does work in the background. Since this is where his Sun is, he will shine.

Case Study No. 3 Carole

Carole has Leo on the cusp of her (derivative) second house of money and personal values, suggesting that something in entertainment

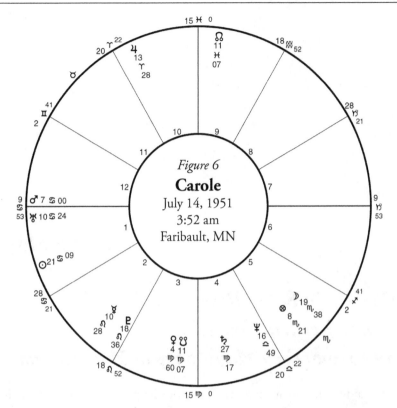

Figure 6
Carole
July 14, 1951
3:52 am
Faribault, MN

would be a fulfilling career. Since Leo is ruled by the Sun in what is the derivative twelfth house to her first house of money and personal values, it suggests an inner drive and ambition and perhaps work behind the scenes. Thus, her work as a production accountant which is behind the scenes in the entertainment field reinforces the derivative house delineation. Venus here (in Virgo) suggests charm, and Virgo suggests work requiring detail such as accounting or business.

Carole has Capricorn in the cusp of her (derivative) sixth house of work, service and health which is the derivative of her second house of money and possessions. The Capricorn cusp suggests work in the area of business. Capricorn is ruled by Saturn in the (derivative) third house of communication and mental processes, suggesting mental activity around work.

As you can see, the derivative house delineations also reinforce the delineation of her natal chart.

Chapter Five

Planets in Solar Return and Lunar Return Houses... and How They May Apply to Your Career

Solar and lunar return charts are based on the placement of the Sun and Moon, respectively, in your natal chart. This will be explained in the following two chapters.

Planets in a solar return chart deal with the focus of your life for a particular year. Any changes suggested by your solar return chart, including career, are focused over the year's period of time and may occur anytime during the year or take the entire year to materialize. All changes are potential and, of course, it is up to you if you want to take advantage of the solar return planetary placements. Different areas of your life may be more prominent in a given year than in previous years. There is the potential to work on these prominent areas during the solar return year. Potential changes may be internal or have to do with external factors. In any given year, there are indicators of where possible job and career opportunities are, as well as suggestions of potential difficulties to be avoided in your job or career.

Planets deal more with potential change and emotions in a lunar return chart than they do in natal or solar return charts. Even if certain planets are not necessarily associated with change or emotional issues, they will manifest what they symbolize in the areas of change, emotions and values. This is true in the area of career just as it is true throughout the entire chart.

The following are some suggestions of planetary significance in both the solar and lunar return charts.

The Sun in Solar and Lunar Return Houses

The Sun in the first house suggests a lot of personal activity, drive and ambition. You should shine personally. This month or year is a good time to present yourself to a new employer, seek a promotion, or go to school for further training. The difficult side of this placement is concerned with you being too aggressive or overbearing. These are traits you should watch out for. Use your leadership drives constructively.

The Sun in the second house suggests drive toward subjects or work that complement your personal values. Energy is directed toward finances and acquiring possessions. The difficult side of this placement is trying too hard, or being too demanding in the acquisition of possessions. Extravagance can occur. Enjoy the material and sensual world, but avoid extremes of hedonism.

The Sun in the third house suggests you will have a great deal of thought and communication this month or year. This is a good time for any work that is mental and a time when you may receive a call about a job offer or promotion. The difficulty with this placement is an emphasis on thoughts way beyond feelings, so you need to seek a balance.

The Sun in the fourth house suggests that your drive and your interests center around home and family. This would be a good time to begin a business out of your home, or at least work at home for a short period of time. You may neglect your work for home now. The downside is the issue of dependency, either your family on you or you on them, and you need to find a compromise. Family dependency on you can be a drain and affect your work. Perhaps you can work with a loved one or motivate family members to support your vocational efforts.

The Sun in the fifth house suggests a great deal of creativity and you will risk other areas of your life in order to be creative, or you may just take risks. If you teach or work with children, this will be a good month or year. Promotional or sales work may go well. Be wary of being too dramatic about what you want.

The Sun in the sixth house suggests a time when you will have a great deal of activity around work and is a good time to ask for a promotion. You may have a job decision. The difficulty of this placement is that more may be demanded of you at this time. Also, the Sun in the sixth house is work- rather than career-oriented. Although you may have job advancement, it may not be the career that you want at this time. You can, however, be very productive now.

The Sun in the seventh house suggests your strength this month (or year) is around partners. It may be a good time to sign an employment contract. Teamwork and aesthetic efforts are favored. Your partner may be more important to you this month (or year) than your career.

The Sun in the eighth house suggests your strength may be working with other people's money, with taxes or insurance. You may also choose to end a matter at this time, which could include your job or career. Look to other areas of the chart to reinforce this. You may help your partner or spouse with money issues this month or year. This is a time for self- evaluation.

The Sun in the ninth house suggests a spiritual nature and thoughts of higher values. You may also decide to continue or complete your education to further your career. You might travel abroad for either pleasure or career. One difficulty with this placement is that this is a time when you question your belief systems. You could abandon some beliefs that really do not live up to your standards. It is often uncomfortable to abandon what you are used to. You are seeking inspiration and can provide it to others as well.

The Sun in the tenth house is a time to receive recognition or advance in your career. You will probably feel pride in what you do. If you are not happy with your career, you may wish to change your career path altogether. This is a time to shine in your career. The difficulty with this placement may lie in authority issues. Either you must supervise well or, if working for others, work hard and you are more likely to achieve recognition for your abilities.

The Sun in the eleventh house suggests your ambition will be based on your dreams and wishes for the future. You may work with groups on a project you feel is worthwhile. However, your individuality and what you want for yourself is of utmost importance. You will seek the freedom to be who you want to be. One difficulty with this placement is that your desire for freedom may conflict with others around you. Some friendships may begin, and others may drift away. Originality is on the rise.

The Sun in the twelfth house suggests your drive is coming from deep within, on a subconscious level. This is a time to listen to your inner self with regard to what you want for your career, and to begin to make necessary changes to achieve your deep-down desires. One difficulty with this placement with regard to career is that this is not a time for recognition. Another difficulty is a lack of sociability at this time. You may wish to work by yourself.

The Moon in Solar and Lunar Return Houses

Remember, the Moon is the most important planet in the lunar return chart, signifying areas where you have potential for change, as well as an area of emotion. What applies to a month in a lunar return has a year to manifest in a solar return.

The Moon in the first house suggests a personal desire for change and emotional needs or emotional support from others this month. These desires and needs may affect your job or career, or you could at least start the wheels in motion for change in your job. Since the Moon symbolizes emotions, you may experience moodiness.

The Moon in the second house suggests a need for financial security and may spur you on to make job changes in order to gain this security. You may have sudden financial fluctuations this month. For example, your car may break down totally and you have to work overtime to earn enough to fix it. Or, you might have your hours cut at work this month and be short of money. You may also be asked to work overtime and have your finances increase.

The Moon in the third house suggests emotional thinking or thoughts of a change. You may consciously seek a job or career where you feel comfortable and secure, where you feel you will almost be part of the "family." This placement may be challenging in light of the fact that your emotional planet is sitting in the house of thought and mental processes, so you may be torn between your heart and your head. You need to integrate both emotional and mental processes. Neighbors or siblings may also become a focus this month.

The Moon in the fourth house suggests that matters of family, security and emotions may be more important than career this month, or you may wish to change your job or career to further your family's security. You may move or change things in your home. Change in your emotional circumstances may be uncomfortable or you may be overly sensitive to things at home.

The Moon in the fifth house suggests you may wish to work with children this month or you may seek a creative outlet for your emotions as a break from your job or career. You may also take risks this month based on emotional reactions. You may start a new romantic relationship. You must be careful lest a strong need for emotional outlets leads you to go to extremes.

The Moon in the sixth house suggests a desire for emotional security through work. Work may also affect your health this month. The Moon suggests change, and you may have opportunities for changes in your job this month, or at least a change in what you do on your job. One difficulty may be that you experience ill feelings due to your emotions. Also, feelings about colleagues could affect your own work. Supportive, nurturing work is favored.

The Moon in the seventh house suggests emotions around partners or a spouse, and perhaps a change in circumstance around partners this month. You may tend to act based on emotions rather than logic around your partners or spouse and should watch out for this. You may receive a partnership offer or contract this month. Joint endeavors go well when your feelings are in sync.

The Moon in the eighth house suggests emotions around joint finances or fluctuation around joint finances, be it a spouse or a business partnership. It may also suggest the beginning of the end of a matter. You must watch tax matters as well. Monitor yourself in how you react to family and act with tact. Your intuition could increase at this time.

The Moon in the ninth house suggests a change of heart toward higher education or a decision to receive some sort of higher education for your financial well-being and/or for your emotional feelings about yourself. It also suggests you may be changing your higher philosophies which could affect what you wish to do careerwise. Also, there may be a trip overseas. The challenge with this placement is discarding beliefs that do not work anymore.

The Moon in the tenth house suggests it is a good time to initiate a change in your career, or to initiate a complete change of career if this is what you are looking for. The change may not manifest itself in a month's period of time in a lunar return chart, but it is a time for beginning anew. If in the tenth house in the solar return chart, you may or may not take the year to change. Be aware of being too emotional around your career. Do not make business issues emotional ones.

The Moon in the eleventh house suggests emotional issues around what you want for the future and dealing with the feelings of friends. You may also wish to work with a group that shares your ideals. There might be fluctuation around the finances of the company for which you work. You may find it difficult to work toward something you desire because of opposition from family or friends. An independent attitude could lead you to feel that others are not very helpful. You probably want to go your own way.

The Moon in the twelfth house suggests deep emotions and a time within which your subconscious motivates you. ou may not act as rationally as you usually do. Thus, you should watch your emotions around work since you may feel unappreciated or overreact to matters. This is also a time of intuition which could be a tremendous asset to your career.

Mercury in Solar and Lunar Return Houses

Mercury in the first house suggests a great deal of thought and communication on a personal level. It is a time to communicate your ideas to those around you, and this would include those with whom you work. Your thoughts will be fast and furious this month, and you can contribute new and exciting ideas to your job. One potential difficulty with this placement might be nervousness and anxiety due to too much thought about any problems that arise.

Mercury in the second house suggests thoughts of money and possessions this month, along with thoughts of what is of value to you and what is of value with regard to your career. It may be a good time to analyze your investments. The difficulty with this placement is that you may question your own worth or question whether others see value in you. Using your intellectual skills to increase your material comforts is a good idea.

Mercury in your third house suggests a great deal of mental activity, mental work, or work involving meticulous details. It also may suggest a call with a job offer. It is a good time to interview for a new job. You may be given additional tasks to perform. This placement can also suggest possible mental anxiety. Don't sweat the small stuff.

Mercury in your fourth house suggests thoughts of family are important, and may take precedence over a job or career. You may wish to work at home, or something may happen to a family member that causes you to do a great deal of thinking. Thoughts of your foundational values are important to what you do.

Mercury in the fifth house suggests thoughts of creativity or that creative endeavors will be fulfilling to you. It could also represent thoughts of children. You may receive an offer which involves some type of risk or gamble. You need an artistic or dramatic outlet this month for mental sanity. You may also be thinking of romance. A potential difficulty is overanalyzing your relationships.

Mercury in the sixth house suggests a lot of mental activity at work and perhaps quick decisions around work. You may also receive an offer of a new position in your company, more responsibility or a new job offer. You must watch your health and not let mental fatigue take over. Practicality and efficiency serve you well on the job and with your body.

Mercury in the seventh house suggests thoughts of partners or spousal matters. If you have good relationships, this is a time of positive thinking to advance your situation. If you have a negative relationship, this is a time of reevaluation. There will be a lot of communication with partners. There may be an offer of a contract such as an employment contract.

Mercury in the eighth house suggests intuition in your life and this may include intuition into your job or career. It may also suggest mental activity over taxes or insurance, or around joint finances. You should watch being too objective about matters, or ending matters without thinking about your emotional needs. This would also include career matters.

Mercury in the ninth house suggests possible higher education and learning. It also suggests issues dealing with philosophies. Your career must meet your higher ideals or you may, at least on a subconscious level, begin thinking of ways to obtain a career which mentally satisfies your aspirations. The ethics of your job will be important. You may also travel overseas and this could be for your job. Something might be going on behind the scenes of your job and you may have a mental hint but not know what it is.

Mercury in the tenth house suggests thoughts of career and a serious attitude toward your career. You may have a decision that will change your career, or begin some sort of training for a change in your career. This is a good time to communicate with others on a professional level. The challenge of this placement is a tendency to overanalyze everything related to your career or to overthink situations.

Mercury in the eleventh house suggests thoughts of the future, dreams, hopes and wishes. It also suggests a lot of communication with friends or involvement with groups. Your thoughts may tend to be rebellious or at least be thoughts of personal freedom which could conflict with group settings. These thoughts may overflow into an individualistic approach to your career rather than a "good for the company" attitude and should be monitored and kept at a constructive level.

Mercury in the twelfth house suggests you may not express yourself to others, or that there may be misunderstanding. This is a time to reflect on what you really desire on an inner, core level rather than what you consciously think you should want. It is a time for review. You tend to be more intuitive with this placement. The challenge of this placement lies in your ability to express yourself clearly to others at this time. You also may find a dichotomy between what you have always desired and what your subconscious is telling you that you really want. This can go for any area of your life, including career.

Venus in Solar and Lunar Return Houses

Venus in the first house suggests a gentleness to your personal approach, and is a good placement if you are working with people. You would have a lot of tact when requesting promotions, raises and the like. You could do so without seeming overly assertive, but could still be firm about your desires. One potential difficulty could be trying to help others too much at the expense of your own needs. You may also be at odds with your spouse or partner at this time. Venus suggests a quest for personal balance and security, and this could manifest itself in the quest for a job that would afford you security.

Venus in the second house suggests an increased desire for material goods or financial increase. You want to be surrounded by what is beautiful. It is also a good time to seek monetary advancement at work, or to change jobs for an increase in salary. The difficulty of this placement is that you may feel some type of ethical conflict. You might reexamine what you are doing, especially what you are doing for money, or to make a living. This is the house of personal values and with Venus here, you will desire to achieve your highest personal potential without compromising your values.

Venus in the third house suggests a subtle confidence to your communications with others, and that others will listen to what you have to say. You will be charming and persuasive. You may wish to study at this time. There will be social contacts, and you can use these contacts to further your career. The difficulty of this placement is your ability to handle things and keep a balance when it comes to gratification; you may overdo. An example would be to use your charm to get what you want at work even if you know it is not really the best situation for the company (not that it would necessarily hurt, but it might not be the best thing).

Venus in the fourth house suggests that you may want to retreat to your home or that matters of the home are most important to you. Your desire for a secure home may help direct you to a job or career that would ensure domestic safety and tranquility. Because of your desire to retreat to a nest, it may be a good time to work from home or start a home-based business. The difficulty with this placement is that the natural opposition between the home (fourth house) and your career (tenth house) is intensified and this may be a time of career versus family competition in terms of time and energy.

Venus in the fifth house suggests a time of creativity. Any job that would require creative efforts would be very fulfilling. This is also a good placement to work with children. Venus in the fifth house, especially in the lunar return chart, can suggest a very romantic time—a time where your attention may be directed toward romance rather than work. This is also a good placement for speculative ventures.

Venus in the sixth house suggests good health and an ability to work with grace and charm. You may desire to improve your health and in turn improve your mental attitude toward work. This is a time to establish good relations with fellow employees and/or employers. You should try to dwell on the positive aspects of your job rather than worry about any negative ones. You are probably working with financial and tangible benefits in mind. Another challenge with this placement is a tendency to be lazy, or to get complacent on the job.

Venus in the seventh house suggests relationship potentials and relationship importance. This would be a beneficial time to form a business partnership. However, a danger is allowing a relationship to over-shadow your own identity. You must try to achieve a balance that benefits both or all parties.

Venus in the eighth house suggests issues of financial security with partners and also sexual issues with partners. You may be seeking a balance between yourself and your partners (business or spousal). Since the money of other people is an issue with this house, both your job and your partner's job security may manifest in this house.

Venus in the ninth house suggests a blending of your higher conscious values with the world around you. You may also travel for pleasure or for your job. Your beliefs about your partnership might come up for review. The downside of this placement can be relationship difficulties stemming from your review of a relationship, business or spousal, in light of your higher philosophies.

Venus in the tenth house suggests you may seek security through a career that affords you the better things in life. You may have issues with authority, whether you are the person in charge or whether there is someone over you. This placement suggests a decision about career. Your decision could be very good for your career or, in the alternative, it could create difficulty with your career. You must look for what is mutually beneficial for you, those you work with, or your company, for a decision that will benefit you in the long run.

Venus in the eleventh house suggests involvement with friends and groups but with less personal involvement or more detached relationships. It suggests you are weighing your desires in light of group goals. Involvement in the arts or drama, in a group setting, would be a very good outlet for you. On the other hand, you may actually want to work in the arts. The downside is to not want to work at all, but spend your time in social activities. This is a good placement for work with humanitarian pursuits.

Venus in the twelfth house suggests spiritual or psychic ability. You may desire to work with chemicals or around water. You may also feel like abusing chemicals, which is not a good idea. You will probably value spiritual ideals more than material ones with this placement. A strong career may not be as important to you as it would be at other times in your life. It may be difficult to get motivated into a strong career right now. If you have a strong career, you will need to take time for meditation or some sort of release.

Mars in Solar and Lunar Return Houses

Mars in the first house suggests a time when you will have a great deal of energy and drive. A downside to this is that you may be too aggressive and may have to curtail your enthusiasm a bit. This is a time of self-confidence. It is a good time to look for a career change or advancement since your confidence will come across to others and influence their decisions. You must guard against too much selfish involvement and try to develop positive personal traits. You should also avoid trying to do too much and actually draining yourself of energy or becoming short tempered. Entrepreneurial efforts usually go well.

Mars in the second house suggests a push toward material possessions or pleasure. You will definitely hustle for advancement in finances. On the other hand, Mars here can suggest tension because of a decrease in salary or perhaps a job change, so you have more freedom but less money at the present time. You will want personal control over your finances, and the downside to this would be arguments with your partner or spouse over finances. You will also look at how others value you with Mars in this placement and make necessary adjustments to win their respect if need be.

Mars in the third house suggests a quick mind, communication and motivational skills. You can act quickly, but possibly without really following through with a whole project. You should be wary of letting anger get out of control. You should also watch using words as a weapon against others. If you emphasize the positive qualities of quickness and communication skills without falling into Martian pitfalls, you can do a lot with this Mars placement. It is excellent for mental work that requires rapid responses.

Mars in the fourth house suggests your energy is geared toward your home and family. However, it may also suggest issues of freedom and a desire to be free of family responsibility at the current time. There is a dichotomy in your attitude toward relationships, and family members may be confused as to whether you want them close and enjoying your high level of energy, or if you want them to back off and leave you to expend your energy as you please. Take care that resentment from the past does not erupt. Since this is in opposition to your tenth house, you may resent your career at this time or at least you may feel a great deal of competition between your home and career.

Mars in the fifth house suggests a strong attraction to drama and the arts. It is a good time to take up an artistic hobby as a release from work tension. You also may need to be more independent of romantic relationships at this time. A new relationship may be very exciting but short-lived. Romance could also be a diversion from work. Be careful that tension or frustration with children does not carry over into to your work environment. High energy for sales, promotional or motivational/coaching work is possible.

Mars in the sixth house suggests you will probably desire to work independently. If you cannot work alone, at least no one should be watching over your shoulder, or you will be quite frustrated. You will tend to work very hard and have a lot of drive right now. You tend to be efficient and take your job very seriously. If you notice problems in the workplace, try not to criticize and make everyone unhappy. Rather, give positive suggestions without pointing a finger or being negative. This positive use of Martian energy can be very beneficial. If you are not tactful and anger easily, problems will ensue. Health problems might affect your work at this time so take care with health and try to alleviate bad habits. A sensible exercise program and assertive efficiency are likely to keep your spirits up and your health good.

Mars in the seventh house suggests your partner or spouse can help you begin projects you may not necessarily take up without their encouragement. It is a time to pursue mutual goals. On the other hand, this is a time to watch your temper and anger at a partner. You may be too quick to anger and should let matters lie and not allow this frustration to spill over into your career. Doing lots of new or exciting activities with a partner provides a positive outlet for this feisty energy.

Mars in the eighth house suggests a strong-minded person with regard to issues of joint finances or sexual matters. Either you or your partner will probably want to control the finances and tension can occur. Also, Mars here suggests long-buried resentment about something. All in all, this can be a rather difficult Mars placement with both you and a partner or spouse being strong-willed and in need of compromise. All of this tension also may spill over into your work, so take care. This placement can be well directed into tenacity, research, or assertive pursuit of government funds, investments, and joint financial accomplishments.

Mars in the ninth house suggests active involvement with your life philosophy or ethical and spiritual issues. They are very important motivating factors for you and you are courageous in your beliefs. Mars here also suggests quick trips and they may or may not have to do with career. There is probably tension behind the scenes of your work that you feel, which has not surfaced yet. Perhaps, there will be a turnover of management that employees do not know about yet, but there are whispers and rumors that something is in the works. Everyone could be on edge. You may also choose to go back to school at this time. You probably have lots of energy to pursue long-range goals.

Mars in the tenth house suggests aggressiveness in business or in the pursuit of your career. It is a good time to focus positively on your career goals and begin constructive action toward them. On the downside, you may have problems with authority figures and need to work on getting along with them or at least not clashing with them. You may also wish to work alone on projects. Your high energy and work ethic should be noticed with this placement. Since the tenth house deals with career choices, Mars here may suggest a time when you may choose a new career path. Entrepreneurial options may appeal.

Mars in the eleventh house suggests a desire for personal freedom, to do as you choose. You may set new goals for yourself this month/ year. Since you will have a lot of ambition and energy and may choose something new for yourself, others might feel that you are being too independent and want the old you back. You may work with groups, for social causes or political causes, or with new technology.

Mars in the twelfth house suggests you may wish to work on projects behind the scenes. You will want to be alone to work your own way. You will not appear aggressive and will tend to keep quiet when things bother you. On the downside, you may not be able to express anger or defend yourself in situations, including business situations. On the other hand, power can come from deep within. Mars here suggests a very quiet, but strong, individual whose power is so strong they do not need to verbalize it. It is just there when needed.

Jupiter in Solar and Lunar Return Houses

Jupiter in the first house suggests an expansion of your personal quest for what will fulfill you and this would include career. You desire to express yourself in all that you do. You are expanding your horizons. The challenge here is to act and not let opportunities slip away.

Jupiter in the second house suggests an opportunity to expand your financial situation. You may examine and expand your own belief system or personal values as well. If your work is not fulfilling or you find parts of it unethical, this is a time you will look for a change. The downside of this placement is that you may be comfortable with your circumstances and miss an opportunity that comes your way by resting too much on your laurels.

Jupiter in the third house suggests a great deal of mental activity and communication. Your daily life will be very busy. The challenge with this placement is concentration. Distractibility is common. You must focus on each task at the time you are doing it, rather than being too scattered.

Jupiter in the fourth house suggests that you feel the ideal situation (at this time) is a nurturing home life and security. You may wish to make changes or improvements to your home, or you might enlarge your home, or people/pets could be added to household or family. The changes would tend to be aesthetic. One challenge is that the fourth house opposes the tenth house of career, and you may wish to focus more on home or domestic expansion rather than career expansion. You may feel there are limitations on your career at this time.

Jupiter in the fifth house suggests a time of creativity and also, perhaps, a time of risk taking or speculation. You are looking for the dramatic. You also may have a new romantic relationship. If you are in a good relationship, this is a time for romance with your partner. It is also a good time to try to have children, or a time where focus will be on your children. One caveat is not to demand too much from your children at this time. Anything pertaining to career would be very fulfilling if you could be creative in your work.

Jupiter in the sixth house suggests your job will be valuable and enjoyable at this time. You may also have an expansion of duties, a promotion, or a raise in pay. This is a time to put in for a new position at work. One caveat here is not to over indulge and to exercise to relieve nervous energy. Weight gain is easier than usual, so take care.

Jupiter in the seventh house suggests you put a lot of faith and trust into relationships, either a business partner or spouse. You may begin a new endeavor with your partner. Be aware of going too far too fast. Monitor what you are doing, since you can overdo at this time. Partners can offer insight, and relationships can grow and improve. On the other hand, your partner may be needy, and you may acquiesce to your partner at your own expense.

Jupiter in the eighth house suggests an expansion of joint finances and also expansion of how you value the intimate relationship with your mate. Your outlook may be too expansive, and you may desire more than your mate is able to give. You may face some moral situations which cause you to really determine just what your ethics are.

Jupiter in the ninth house suggests you may desire more education in order to fulfill yourself as an individual or perhaps for a better career. You seek understanding. You might also travel overseas. Your mind will constantly be moving, and you may write at this time. One thing to watch for is expansion or change going on behind the scenes of your career. If you feel a hint of this, it is a good time to get in on the changes coming rather than being left out.

Jupiter in the tenth house suggests an expansion of your career and that you set very high goals for yourself. You place a great importance on your career and it may "define you" at this time. This is a good time for advancement in your career, or to expand your business if you are self-employed, or to begin a career. You should be wary of over-expansion or having ideas that are really not practical.

Jupiter in the eleventh house suggests a great desire for independence and freedom. You will want to pursue your desires to the fullest. Your employer should be well funded, or if you are in business for yourself, your business should be financially sound. You may even expand at this time. Beware of being overly rebellious or trying to do too much.

Jupiter in the twelfth house suggests a search for the spiritual, or expansion of your spiritual side. You may be overwhelmed by circumstances affecting your psyche. Although you can feel overwhelmed, Jupiter here suggests some security and a sense that you can handle what is thrown at you. Keep control of a tendency to be over- zealous.

Saturn in Solar and Lunar Return Houses

Saturn in the first house suggests personal responsibility or limitations. You will do what is necessary but not necessarily what you would like. You will identify with hard work but may not take advantage of opportunity because of past fears. It is a time to start long-range plans or a time when you will personally receive reward from past action.

Saturn in the second house suggests a quest for financial control or learning to live within strict guidelines financially. You will work hard for gain at this time. It is a time to work toward the future. You may feel that your employer does not value you. If you have not paid attention to your finances in the past, it may come back to haunt you. If you have paid attention, you will probably have a stable financial situation at this time.

Saturn in the third house suggests a time of study and you may feel you are limited by a lack of education. Your siblings might be difficult. This is a time of major decisions which may include your career, but the decisions will probably involve your family, not just yourself. Recognizing life's realities is a factor with this placement. Issues of control are also a possibility with this placement.

Saturn in the fourth house suggests family responsibility. You may be overwhelmed with family issues. You may care for an elderly family member or start a family. You may be a caretaker in your career at this time. Something in your life during the solar or lunar return will probably involve nurturing. It is up to you whether you take the responsibility and learn and grow from it, or become despondent over it.

Saturn in the fifth house suggests you will be more structured in your creativity and less experimental. This may spill over into any creative effort you put forth in your job. You might have a romantic relationship with a younger person. You may either look for criticism as a way to grow, or be overly critical of others. Should you choose to have a child at this time, the first few years could seem very restrictive for you and you may find the responsibilities of coping with both a child and career to be quite demanding.

Saturn in the sixth house suggests a structured work environment where you may feel limited. You might meet obstacles when trying to get ahead in work. This is a time to buckle down and work toward long- range goals. If you have been working toward a long-range goal, this could be a time when you receive the rewards of past hard work. You must be practical about your body and sidestep chronic health problems which could interfere with your work.

Saturn in the seventh house suggests limits or obstacles in relationships with either your spouse or partners. You may have a deep, strong commitment, but what you are working toward could be delayed. There might be power or control issues with your spouse or partners. Differences may be more apparent at this time. If there is not a strong commitment, it is a time when a partnership may begin to break apart. On the high side, tangible achievements through teamwork are possible.

Saturn in the eighth house suggests joint financial concerns, restrictions, limitations, or structure and practicality. You will share financial responsibility with your partner. You may also have issues over intimacy or sexual matters and should beware lest anxiety over these issues spill into other areas of your life such as your work. You may be less financially secure at this time, or you may begin working with a partner toward financial security in the future.

Saturn in the ninth house suggests learning which will help you in the years to come. You will look for structure and order in your belief system. During the time Saturn is in the ninth house, you will probably discard beliefs which no longer apply to you. This is a time when the company for which you work is reorganizing or may have some sort of limitation on business, but it is not yet known. These matters will be in the background.

Saturn in the tenth house suggests a time to begin to work toward career goals, or a time when the hard work of the past will be rewarded. Career opportunity may be slow at this time, or you may make a move to something different. This might be a time for retirement, the ultimate reward of past work. Or, it could be a time of forced retirement that you feel limits you and which you do not want. This is a time of career responsibility or career limitation. You will focus on what is tangible and practical.

Saturn in the eleventh house suggests you are thinking over your goals and wishes for the future and possibly making any adjustments needed for the person you have become. You will work hard toward these new goals. You may also work with groups for a common goal. You will rethink any friendships that no longer work for you, or make new friends who share common goals with you. You might work toward humanitarian goals. The company for which you work could be tightening the budget at this time or restructuring finances.

Saturn in the twelfth house suggests that unconscious motivations may block what you want to do. Saturn here also implies that these unconscious motivations can give you a core stability or realistic attitude which helps you take control over your life. You may seek a higher power or deny it altogether. The key to this placement is to learn to take appropriate responsibility, disregard irrational parts of your being and come into your own. You may choose to work on a mundane level as opposed to a spiritual level.

Uranus in Solar and Lunar Return Houses

Uranus in the first house suggests personal, dramatic change and a great need for freedom. The changes usually involve major areas of your life such as career, marriage, moving, and the like. It is difficult to predict what area the change will be in since Uranus is likened to throwing poker chips into the air not knowing where they may land. You may take risks and do so with great energy and enthusiasm no matter what the consequences.

Uranus in the second house suggests great fluctuation in your financial situation, either up or down. It is fluctuation in your earning potential. It may also be a total change or dramatically different approach to your personal value system. You may seek employment that will afford you the greatest freedom from financial worry.

Uranus in the third house suggests changing mental attitudes and lightning speed thought processes. You will need to be in a position where you can work and think quickly, and speed from one thing to another or risk boredom. You may also receive some sort of training at this time. You will tend to be the rebel and the reformer. Above all, you must be free to think and do things on your own terms. Keep constructive outlets (i.e., exercise, meditation) for nervous tension or anxiety which could arise.

Uranus in the fourth house suggests a disrupted home life. It could be a move, family members leaving, or new ones arriving. The changes may be physical, emotional, or both. Whatever was wrong or held back will come out at this time. There may also be considerable tension between home and career at this time. You will probably desire freedom now.

Uranus in the fifth house suggests a time of great creativity, inventions and imagination. If you have children, they will pick this time to rebel and become independent, so make sure that frustration with children does not affect you at work. You may also be attracted to persons you would never have thought you would, or meet unusual people. Above all, your desire for freedom and creativity will be strong and may conflict with a formerly calm lifestyle. These unusual desires can spill into your work since they would be in the background of your mind while you are working. There may also be tremendous upheaval behind the scenes of your job.

Uranus in the sixth house suggests you will want freedom to work in your own way, without restriction or supervision. There may be dramatic changes at work. For example, your company may merge with another, or obtain a new account which creates a lot of new work or new jobs. No matter what the change, it will be dramatic and probably unexpected. In fact, "expect the unexpected" is a good way to look at Uranus in your sixth house. Job changes are likely whether within the same company, or actually a new job. You may have sporadic health concerns and you are probably open to alternative ideas both in terms of taking care of your body and accomplishment on the job at this time.

Uranus in the seventh house suggests a new relationship, dramatic changes in existing relationships or sudden and unexpected breaks in relationships. They can be with a spouse or business partners. If you have existing relationships that are sound, they may change, but do not break up. You may rebel or want freedom to do as you please at this time. Although it can be a difficult time because of transition, the relationships that are good will survive, and probably become better.

Uranus in the eighth house suggests changes in joint resources, either with spouse or partners. They may be positive or negative. You may desire to work in an area that will give you financial freedom from worry. There may be a change in sexual attitudes as well. Your psyche is heightened and you will be aware of the motivations of others at this time.

Uranus in the ninth house suggests that unusual and unexpected shake-ups with regard to your career are in the works, but not necessarily apparent to you yet. You may desire more education in order to pursue a different career or a different position in your career. On the other hand, you may experience a disruption in your education due to unusual circumstances at this time. You may travel and unexpected things will happen during travel. Philosophical and cultural matters will be important at this time. Above all, you will probably desire personal freedom.

Uranus in the tenth house suggests dramatic changes around career and also a desire of freedom in the career you choose. You may switch careers, change jobs within your company, begin a new business, or make any type of independent career choice that appeals to you. If you do not make changes, you will feel frustrated. You may make decisions too quickly and should make sure you think things through rather than taking sudden action without much thought. You will look for a career that is unique by your terms and in which you will feel a sense of freedom.

Uranus in the eleventh house suggests dramatic change and reassessment of your goals. You will toss aside friendships that do not work for you anymore and make new friends who share your humanitarian ideals. You may join groups that share your ideas for progress and the future. The financial condition of the company for which you work may have dramatic changes, either positive, negative, or both, this year. The philosophy and the way your company values its employees may also change (positively or negatively) at this time.

Uranus in the twelfth house suggests dramatic subconscious changes and a core "rebel" nature at this time. You may act erratically without really realizing why. You have an innate desire for freedom. You will look for constant change in your existence at this time. The trick is to find an outlet for this need for change, while still keeping your life in balance.

Neptune in Solar and Lunar Return Houses

Neptune in the first house suggests a time of personal intuition and a time of spirituality. It is a time of higher consciousness or a state of the self as a small part of a higher order. You must beware of taking on the problems of others and making them your own. You will tend to be scattered in action, and might not finish mundane tasks that you start. Also, it can be a time of over-indulgence that you must monitor and control. It is a time for contemplation of higher values and direction, rather than personal action and direction. You can regroup on a spiritual level, so in the future you will be better equipped to work on a mundane level.

Neptune in the second house suggests an uncertain financial time. Rumor may affect your company's finances causing concern and, in turn, perhaps you will not get a raise at this time. You might have personal financial anxiety. On the other hand, you will realize that personal values are often more important than financial success. Your focus will probably be on your values rather than finances. Your intuition should be right on with regard to investment. You can make money through spiritual endeavors.

Neptune in the third house suggests an openness to new ideas of inspiration and imagination. Thoughts of higher values tend to creep into your mundane daily activities. On the other hand, you may be too dreamy or distracted and get little done at this time. You may be indecisive at this time. This is a time to explore something new, possibly an art class, rather than making decisions regarding your future and future employment.

Neptune in the fourth house suggests uncertainty with regard to your home. You may desire a beautiful home and lovely family life but may be unsure at this time regarding financial or emotional family situations. This is a good time to cosmetically improve your home. You could aid or assist members of your family. Since the fourth house is your foundation, the spiritual side of your foundational values is very important now. You may have a push/pull relationship between home and career with regard to what is most important to you.

Neptune in the fifth house suggests sensitivity to children. Working in the arts or in a creative field may help you increase your sensitivity or spirituality at this time. You may romanticize a lover and see him/her through "rose-colored glasses" only to be disappointed at a later time. You might have insight into situations of risk, or could be completely confused about risk. Creative, aesthetic, "selling a dream" pursuits are likely to go well.

Neptune in the sixth house suggests working in a job that does not appeal to you, or that you are seeking the "ideal job." Or, you may not be working, and do not know exactly what you want to do—you just know that you want to do something you really like. If you are working in a job you like, there may be some type of uncertainty about it. Perhaps there is new training that you do not feel you picked up very well, or perhaps you feel unsure about new people or responsibilities. Your senses are heightened and you feel the problems of others around the workplace as if they were your own. It is a time to communicate realistically with those in your workplace rather than to try to figure things out on your own. Also, you may have minor nagging health problems, especially if you are "spaced out" instead of taking care of yourself. Listen to your body and be sensible.

Neptune in the seventh house suggests uncertainty around relationships or partnerships, and this may be a source of anxiety. On the other hand this can be a time when you intuitively help your partners and are very supportive, especially if they are having personal uncertainty themselves. It is a time for compassion. You may tend to take on your spouse's or partner's problems as your own, and you should guard against overdoing this. Another possibility is that there could be uncertainty around finances at your work, causing you confusion or concern.

Neptune in the eighth house suggests uncertainty around joint finances, either spousal or partnership. It is a time when signing an employment contract could be uncertain, or the conditions of the contract may be confusing and unclear to you. You may have issues over money and power. On the positive side, you will tend to be quite intuitive at this time.

Neptune in the ninth house suggests you may be seeking a higher understanding or spiritual understanding. You may also feel a need for higher education even if you do not know just what you wish to study. You can always begin with general courses. You may be confused over your belief system, or question it, and may take some time to resolve these questions.

With regard to your career, you may feel something is going on in the background that is disconcerting, but you cannot put your finger on it yet.

Neptune in the tenth house suggests uncertainty with your career or your goals with respect to your career. There may be fluctuations in the company for which you work. Or, you may desire the "ideal job" and be dissatisfied with your present situation without knowing how to extricate yourself. If you make a career change with this placement, it will tend to move you toward what you are more spiritually cut out for. You can begin to make far-reaching decisions or daydream about changes and never get anywhere. Aesthetic, imaginative, healing and compassionate pursuits are favored.

Neptune in the eleventh house suggests an almost spiritual need to be with others or to be in a group setting that you can identify with. It is a time when you have a great deal of empathy for others and when you can do good works, either for others or with others in a group setting. Take care that your friends do not take advantage of your compassionate nature at this time. With regard to career, it is a time of financial uncertainty at your place of employment or perhaps you are starting your own business and you are very uncertain about your financial future. Any business started now will be directed toward your long-term goals and based on your ideals and wishes.

Neptune in the twelfth house suggests uncertainty or confusion on a subconscious level. You may act without any recognition as to why you are acting. You feel a need to blend in with the universe and a "higher power." Anything in the arts will help you to feel this higher sense and give you an outlet for the confused feelings. Your intuition is good, but you also tend to dream a lot. Take care with decision making at this time. Think things through.

Pluto in Solar and Lunar Return Houses

Pluto in the first house suggests a time to take personal control over yourself. This means you must recognize what has blocked you from doing what you want to in the past and get beyond it. You will be able to do whatever you desire to do. Pluto suggests personal power and control. It also suggests a probing or investigative nature, so any work that involves investigation, research, and the like would be personally fulfilling at this time. You must take care not to go to extremes. Pluto suggests transformation. In a return chart, Pluto takes on a personal nature, so you are probably going to experience some type of personal transformation (physical, emotional, etc.) with Pluto in the first house.

Pluto in the second house in a return chart is personal and suggests change in finances. The change may come from your own career or job with tenth house or sixth house activities or connections. You may retire from work. Whatever the transformation, control of your own finances will be an issue. There may also be transformation of your personal value system. You may begin throwing out values that do not reflect you, and take more control over how you handle your life. You could increase your feelings of self-worth.

Pluto in the third house suggests a need to understand conscious versus unconscious motivations. You are seeking in-depth communication that goes beneath the surface of superficial discussions. Your power lies in understanding the deeper meaning of what others say, and of the issues at hand. You may have intense interactions with siblings. You may have issues of mental control. You will be intuitive and interested in subconscious manipulations. This is a very good placement for research and learning.

Pluto in the fourth house suggests moving from your home to another home. If you do not move, there will be a transformation of the home within which you live. With Pluto here, the emotions around the house may be tense. Pluto suggests that there will be resistance to change in the home, even if the transformation is needed. This may come from the tenth house of career opposition. Perhaps you move for your job, but do not desire to do so. There might be power struggles within the home as well. Emotional persistence and loyalty are highlighted.

Pluto in the fifth house suggests power struggles with children. There also may be power issues with someone with whom you are romantically involved. In each instance, there is a transformation of your relationship with another person. You may struggle to let the creative side of yourself grow. Issues of power and love may be seen in a creative context or a context of personal expression coming from deep within yourself. There may also be transformation in the background of your workplace which is not apparent yet, but which you feel is coming. There may be feelings of unrest at work. Also, there may be behind-the-scenes power struggles at work.

Pluto in the sixth house suggests that issues of health and control over your body are important at this time. Transformation of work is more likely and your office may totally reorganize, move, begin completely new tasks, change bosses and the like. This is a good time to transform your own workload by eliminating unnecessary tasks and becoming more efficient. This way, you can handle a larger workload if it is placed upon you. There will be power issues between you and those in control or, if you are in control, between you and subordinates, or issues between your superiors themselves. It is a time of manipulation and change.

Pluto in the seventh house suggests issues with relationships and/or power struggles in relationships. There may be a tendency to manipulate or be manipulated by your spouse or business partner. You may also seek to find a deep, below-the-surface meaning in your relationships at this time. Since Pluto suggests transformation, it is a time to compromise rather than manipulate, and to take your relationships to a new level of understanding through conciliation and compromise. There may be transformation of finances around your work as well, i.e., power struggles over finances, such as heads of departments vying for money for their pet projects or for more control.

Pluto in the eighth house suggests power issues in joint finances and dependency versus independence. Your financial situation with your spouse or business partner is likely to change. You may also have difficulties with insurance or tax matters, so you should watch your finances very closely and not rely on your partner for financial security at this time. You may also be seeking more self-awareness at this time and discover you have become much more intuitive.

Pluto in the ninth house suggests you are seeking transformation through education, religion or spiritual matters, or travel to foreign places, and that your higher conscious philosophies are changing. You will seek new ideas and disregard what no longer works for you. Your belief system will gain strength and this may mean you are less tolerant than you should be. Guard against a lack of tolerance at this time. There may be a complete transformation going on behind the scenes of your career now. Again, issues of power will arise between heads of departments, mid-management and top executives, etc. Observe carefully lest, before you know what is happening, you inadvertently get caught up in power struggles not your own. Although transformation may seem difficult, it does not mean the results will be negative. Change is often perceived as difficult.

Pluto in the tenth house suggests issues of control and authority, how you relate to those in charge, or how you relate to those you are in charge of. You need to feel in control of your career. You may push persistently for success. Although this is not bad in and of itself, you must take care not to push too hard or beyond reason, thus hurting your chances of success. Ambition is fine, but an obsessive desire to achieve can be detrimental. Your career itself may be changing due to changes within the company for which you work, or you may actually change jobs with this placement. You may have a major decision to make regarding your career and the direction you wish to take at this time.

Pluto in the eleventh house suggests transformation of your goals and desires for the future. You may work within a group that is trying to transform society in some way, perhaps a political activist organization, a charitable organization, or something like Amnesty International that deals with human rights issues. You will tend to bond with friends who share your desires for the future. You could discover power plays in a group setting, and should watch for manipulative situations. There might be a transformation of the financial condition of the company for which you work, perhaps a merger, stock split, major acquisition or the like.

Pluto in the twelfth house suggests a time for behind-the-scenes activity or actions in order for you to advance later on. It is not necessarily manipulation, but a time for subtle work toward what you wish for yourself. On the other hand, Pluto also suggests activities that are not so altruistic, and that you should be on guard against (such things as deception, excessive fantasy). Pluto suggests transformation on a subconscious level of what you really desire, and you may not realize this transformation for a time. Pluto here suggests a transformation of how the company you work for presents itself to the public, or a conscious change in strategy.

Chapter Six

Solar Return Charts

The second chart I use in career counseling is the *solar return chart.* This is a chart calculated for the moment the Sun returns to the exact degree, minute and second that the Sun occupied at your birth. It is a chart to be considered for the next year of your life. It should be calculated for the place that you are, at the exact moment the Sun returns to your birth Sun placement; if you are in a city different from the city within which you live, use the city where you are to calculate the chart. The solar return chart is always within a couple of days of your birthday, if not on your birthday.

You should delineate a solar return chart much like a natal chart, so you can follow the outline in Chapter One. However, this delineation method does need a little tweaking for career counseling. There are three specific distinctions to consider.

Remember the solar return is for the current year only and not patterns extending over your lifetime. This is one reason why it is so useful in gauging current career opportunities.

First, look at the Ascendant to determine your personal outlook and personal approach to your life this year. It will also be your approach to your career this year. It is often useful to compare the solar return Ascendant with the natal Ascendant to see how the solar return Ascendant can complement and add strength to your approach. If your solar return and natal Ascendants are at odds with each other, this is a time to use your solar return Ascendant to gain advantages you do not often get with your natal Ascendant.

Planet placement is the most important consideration for career counseling in a solar return chart. I usually only consider (or consider with heavier emphasis) the houses that contain planets, unless seeking to find opportunity with transiting planets. Chapter Five contains interpretations for each planet in each of the solar return houses.

As a general rule I have found that if a majority of planets are contained in houses 1 through 6, you will be more private in terms of career and tend to work in the background. If a majority of planets are in houses 7 through 12, you will be more public or tend to be recognized for your work. If a majority of planets are in houses 10 through 3, you will have more personal control over your career than if a majority of planets are in houses 4 through 9, where others would influence your career. This is quite obvious when considering that the tenth house represents your career and honors, the first house represents your personal effort, the second house represents your finances, and the third house represents your ability to communicate. By contrast, the fourth house represents your family's influence, the seventh house represents your partner or spouse's influence, and the eighth house represents other people's money. If planets are evenly distributed, you should move along steadily toward your career goals.

Planet qualities of cardinal, fixed, and mutable, discussed in Chapter One, are important considerations for your career growth during the year. I feel that planet placement by house, quality and element should be weighed more heavily than the astrological sign. I usually weigh planet placement with quality and element at about 80% or more, and the astrological sign at about 20% or less. Since the Sun in your solar return chart is always in the same sign as it is in your natal chart, its house placement becomes far more significant than the sign. **This is one of the important distinctions in the solar return versus a natal delineation when doing career counseling.**

Obviously, since this is a solar return chart, the Sun, the very basis of the chart, its house placement and aspects are very important to career opportunity (or the lack thereof) in a particular year.

The Moon house placement and aspects indicate areas of change or fluctuation, so the Moon is a place to look for career change.

Jupiter and Saturn are also very important, just as their transits are to natal chart delineation. Jupiter represents opportunity and Saturn shows lessons for the year. Lessons may initially appear to be obstacles, but they are also opportunities for growth.

In a solar return chart, the outer planets' house placements take on a more personal nature while still retaining their generational qualities. For example, Pluto in the tenth house may suggest a transformation of your career personally as opposed to work in an area with generational values that might normally be associated with Pluto—or possibly both would occur. **The outer planets' personal nature is the second important distinction in career counseling with the solar return chart.**

Just as in a natal chart, I look at the ruler of a house cusp in the solar return to see where planetary themes may help. This is especially true for the sixth and tenth houses, if they do not contain planets. You will be able to ferret out opportunity for your clients' careers by looking to the ruler for significance in any house with no planets. I also look at aspects the planets are making to each other for insight into career opportunity. The use of transits of the faster-moving planets and the aspects they make are also helpful in determining career opportunity. The outer planets will not move fast enough for you to consider their transits in a solar return chart, unless they are at a cusp and move from one house to another. Then their transits should be considered where applicable.

The third important distinction with regard to career counseling is determining whether a natal house cusp lies well within your sixth, tenth or second houses on your solar return chart, or if a solar return cusp lies well within your natal second, sixth or tenth houses. This is an indication of where difficulty or obstacles may lie this year (if any) with regard to your career. This is very useful in determining where you must put extra effort, tread lightly, or handle people with tact in order to advance your career.

Again, the solar return delineation is much like the natal chart delineation. As you constantly weigh one planetary symbolism against another, a clear pattern will emerge. Thus, you can use the definitions and methods supplied in Chapter 1 and 5 with the distinctions noted in this chapter, when you are considering the solar return chart in career counseling.

Now, let's look at the solar returns for the three people whose natal charts were delineated in Chapter 2—Sarah, John and Carole. The natal and solar return charts should reinforce each other in terms of career opportunity. If something is prominent in both charts, it suggests a very strong opportunity. Also, you may find some new opportunities this year that were not apparent in the natal chart alone.

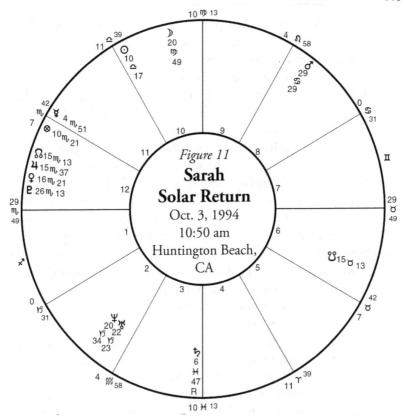

Case Study No. 1 Sarah
Solar Return Chart

The first thing I would look at in Sarah's solar return is her Scorpio Ascendant. This suggests that Sarah will be intense, emotional and determined in her approach. She will be able to ferret out facts, look beneath the surface for hidden meanings and solve problems. However, the Ascendant is 29 degrees Scorpio and Sagittarius is intercepted in her first house. An interception is a sign that is contained within a house but not on any cusp, and may indicate where tension, obstacles or problems lie. Thus, the Sagittarius traits of idealism and desire for freedom will be displayed this year by Sarah, who will want to be free to do what she pleases. Also, what she does must meet her own personal high ideals. This is our first indication in the solar return chart that Sarah may have personal tension if being pushed back to work is not her desire. Remember, Sarah's natal Ascendant is Gemini, suggesting versatility, a quick mind, and adaptability. The solar return Scorpio Ascendant, with its likelihood of intense emotions, is coupled with a Sagittarius interception, indicating a desire to be free to do what is important to Sarah herself. This suggests a breeding ground for animosity toward her husband for pushing her back to work. The natal Gemini adaptability and "roll with the punches" attitude that her husband is accustomed to in Sarah is now traded in (by her solar return) for emotional intensity and a quest for personal freedom that her husband is unlikely to suspect in his attempt to get his own way with her.

Sarah has nine planets in houses ten through three, suggesting her individual effort, along with her recent courses in computers and accounting, will pay off. This also indicates that she will control her own destiny. This heavy emphasis of planets also suggests she will be more self-reliant and develop an inner strength which will help her through this very difficult year. Six planets are contained within houses ten through twelve: honors, groups and subconscious. Both luminaries and Mercury are in the tenth and eleventh houses suggesting she will have to integrate her activities to include working with others or in a group setting (the school system is definitely a large group). With only two planets in mutable signs, Sarah will have to find a way to adapt to her new work routine. She is balanced in fixed and cardinal signs, which implies she should adjust well.

Sarah has no planets in fire signs, so she is probably concentrating on her immediate problem, rather than looking toward the future, and may not yet realize that this job is a stepping stone toward something better. Right now all of her energy is expended on work and taking care of her family. She may feel at a loss or just plain tired. With only one planet in an air sign and six planets in water signs, she could be very emotional about any decisions she makes. The lack of air signs might also lead her to feel she is not quite ready for her new job. She must tone down feeling insecure because she is really quite capable of handling both her new job and her family. The abundance of water signs can lead to anxiety rather than the love of family it also symbolizes. It would be unwise to let her emotions overrule her usual Libran logic. This is particularly true since she faces major changes this year. She should keep reminding herself that she can handle whatever comes her way.

Both Uranus and Neptune are in Capricorn, a cardinal sign suggesting action, in the second house of money and personal values. Capricorn is ruled by Saturn in the third house of lower education (remember she went to work for the school system) and also conscious mind and mental activity. Uranus suggests unusual circumstances around finances. Although Sarah never worked as a financial clerk for the school system (others who were applying for the job had done so), her superiors were very impressed and enthusiastic by her experience, especially that she had worked for Mayor Bradley. They stated they wanted a new approach to the position they were offering, so Sarah got the job.

Neptune in the second house of her solar return suggests money issues, and since her spouse has terminated his partnership, this is certainly true for Sarah. Also, Neptune can indicate deception of some kind and, again, Sarah felt her husband was hiding assets. Sarah feels the financial tension here, but also that money is not as important as her children. Uranus conjunct Neptune in house two of the solar return suggests chaotic change in finances. (Or it could also be read as financial independence and making money through Uranian fields.) Since her husband quit his law partnership, obviously, there has been a change in finances, and as previously described, Sarah's job was not enough for the family to live on. Uranus here can also suggest a change in personal values, but in Sarah's case it feels more like a disturbance of her personal values.

With regard to career, both Neptune and Uranus trine the Moon in the tenth house of career, and this is an indication that her new job should be beneficial and a good way to begin to make money. Uranus trine the Moon in Sarah's solar return tenth house suggests that a financial upset could give her an opportunity for a career move. In Sarah's case, she felt that she must pursue the career because of financial hardship, so her new career choice was not viewed as an opportunity, but instead as something she was obliged to do. However, in the long run the opportunity will be revealed, since this job is the door opening to her future career.

Neptune trining the Moon in this solar return chart might indicate deception by a family member (in her case, her husband). Also sometimes knowing the truth can feel worse than not knowing. In Sarah's case, certain truth would be the knowledge—rather than just the suspicion—that her husband is hiding assets. Self-deception allows the situation to continue, and in turn leads to more emotional estrangement with her husband. Had Sarah confronted her husband about the financial situation, and gotten everything out in the open, the fight that probably would have ensued would soon be over. They could have continued their relationship in a more open fashion. Instead, Sarah let her emotions fester, which caused delays in the healing process of their relationship. This is a very important point which you, as a counselor, should emphasize. Although Neptune and Uranus are in Capricorn, which suggests business, it is the Neptune and Uranus planetary qualities that are strongest here. Again, I place less emphasis on the sign, although it is the Capricorn cusp of Sarah's solar return chart that suggests a business type job (accounting) as a way to make money.

The next solar return planet we come to is Saturn in the third house. Saturn is where obstacles lie and where lessons are learned. Saturn is in Pisces, ruled by Neptune in the second house, again suggesting lower education (the school system) as one possibility for income. Thus, this placement is true to Sarah's new job. Saturn here suggests a lot of mental and organizational work, and conscious responsibilities. For Sarah, this seems to be the case: accounting and conscious conflict between work and children. Saturn here suggests that Sarah experiences a very difficult time mentally but she is consciously trying to cope. However, in noting that Saturn trines Mercury in the eleventh house of wishes, I sense that Sarah feels her wishes can somehow come to fruition, so she will keep going. The cusp of the third house of Sarah's solar return is Aquarius, so Sarah should have unconventional and far-reaching approaches in her mental processes toward her new job.

Sarah has only one planet in houses five through nine, and that planet is Mars. Mars can suggest conflict or tension, as with her husband pushing her to go back to work, but her chart indicates that she is controlling her own destiny, even though she feels her husband is pushing her into action. Mars can symbolize lots of energy to work. Mars is in the eighth house which, in part, is government money or the school system's money. Since Sarah is working for the school system and with finances, Mars here does hint at the nature of her new job. Mars suggests changes in eighth house issues, or a keener awareness of them. Since the eighth house is also her spouse's derivative house of money, changes, tension and cost cutting are suggested due to her partner's activity. (Again, Sarah's husband quit his law partnership causing drastic changes, and this is part of the reason Sarah had to go back to work.) Her spouse's actions caused Sarah to feel resentment toward him. The square of Mars to Mercury in Sarah's solar return eleventh house of wishes suggests that he is thwarting her true desires.

The cusp of the solar return eighth house is Cancer, ruled by the Moon in the tenth house, suggesting that Sarah's career (a tenth house matter) could be tied to government money. Since the Moon also suggests nurturing roles, this is another indication that Sarah would rather be home with her children than working. On the other hand, Mars represents raw energy. Since the ruler of the house Mars is in, Cancer, is the tenth house of the solar return, Sarah might use this energy to push ahead and forge a career path. Her drive is very much in conflict with her spouse's values, but it was his financial action that is causing Sarah to go back to work, thus creating the tension.

Now comes the good part. If Sarah had to go back to work, what a fortuitous placement of both luminaries (Sun and Moon) it is that both are in the tenth house! First of all, the cusp of the tenth house is Virgo, suggesting meticulous, organized and business type work. This describes well her new accounting position. Virgo is ruled by Mercury in the eleventh house which is the derivative financial house to Sarah's career, so the job seems well-funded and it seems Sarah will be working with the funds. This also suggests that, at the onset, Sarah is thinking about a future position more suited to her own eleventh house desires.

The Moon is the biggest indicator of change in the Solar Return chart, and sits in Sarah's tenth house suggesting a change or a new career for her. The Moon here suggests very beneficial changes even though there may be some emotional disturbance or high emotions involved with the change. The Moon generally indicates a major change in work or recognition for work, and it also implies that Sarah will be involved in some way with the public. Obviously, going back to work after years of being at home is a major change, and working in the school system is working with the public, even though it is a local government position. In fact, to backtrack, Mars in the eighth house of government symbolizes a lot of drive and energy around a government job.

As the year progressed, Sarah's superiors recognized her abilities and contributions to her job. The Moon trines Uranus and Neptune in Sarah's second house, suggesting financial benefit. These trines also indicate that the new job will not conflict as much with her personal values as she feared it would. Again, she has a job during the same hours when her children are in school, so she is home with them as much as possible. The Moon/Uranus aspect suggests change and, obviously, going back to work is the change. The Moon/Neptune aspect suggests that Sarah has insight into her work. This is another point to emphasize as a counselor. It suggests that she may want to talk to a professional to help her through this difficult time.

The Sun is drive and ambition—where Sarah is putting her energy this year—and as such, is the most important planet in a solar return chart.

The Sun is in Sarah's tenth house, and in a solar return this indicates a best time to push forward for career change, and career fulfillment. Since the Sun is where strength and drive lie, this is a time when Sarah has control over her career and what she wants to accomplish. Please note that her natal Sun affords Sarah much less control over her career, since it lies in her fifth house, suggesting that children are her main focus, along with creativity. With her solar return Sun placement, she should receive positive recognition this year, and she can use that to forge ahead.

As I illustrated in the delineation of Sarah's natal chart, if her spouse had not pushed her to go back into the work force this year, something else quite likely would have done so. Again, this is a positive point to bring up, so that Sarah can deal with things more rationally. Her solar return chart also shows a need for counseling this year, considering the Neptune and Mars placements noted earlier. Sarah's stress is tremendous, so if you are not also a licensed professional counselor or therepist in a case such as this, you should refer her to someone who is, and can help her cope with the stress.

Sarah's solar return chart even more strongly emphasizes going back to work than her natal chart did. For a further example of this, Mercury sits in the eleventh house of the solar return in Scorpio, suggesting a great deal of thought going into Sarah's hopes and wishes for the future. Since the eleventh house also represents groups, it points toward thought or work within a large group (again the school system). Sarah will probably be weighing her personal goals in balance with what she can contribute to the school system. This placement is a very good example of why I like to use derivative houses in career counseling. The eleventh house is the derivative second house of money to Sarah's career house. Mercury placed there suggests thought and meticulous work around money (the accounting clerk). Mercury is in Scorpio which is ruled by Pluto in the twelfth house—the derivative third house to Sarah's career house. This represents, among other things, lower education. Again, this is a link to her work in finances and the school system. Scorpio is co-ruled by Mars in the eighth house which, among other things, is government, and thus another link to the school system.

Sarah has three planets in her solar return twelfth house: Jupiter, Venus and Pluto. Jupiter and Venus are conjunct. Pluto is conjunct Sarah's Ascendant and trine Mars in the eighth house. With planets in the twelfth house, Sarah has some unresolved issues she must deal with, especially since Pluto in Scorpio suggests issues that must be reexamined. This is obvious in

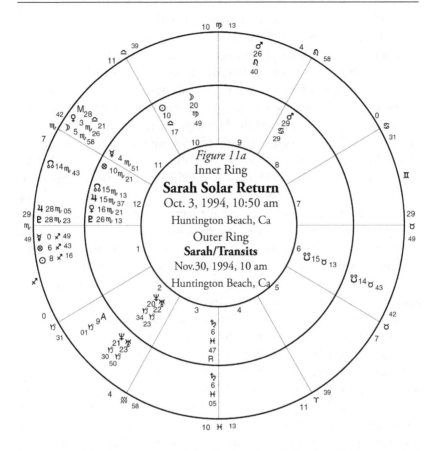

Figure 11a
Inner Ring
Sarah Solar Return
Oct. 3, 1994, 10:50 am
Huntington Beach, Ca
Outer Ring
Sarah/Transits
Nov.30, 1994, 10 am
Huntington Beach, Ca

light of Sarah's relationship with her husband, and she should be counseled not to sweep her issues with him under the rug. Her job was a good excuse to delay dealing with her marriage problems, which then caused them to last longer than they needed to. This presents a precarious situation for a counselor. Should you advise Sarah to deal immediately with her marriage problems, and take a chance that her work will not suffer because of even greater tension at home? Or might her work suffer because she is not dealing directly with her inner feelings regarding her marriage? When I look at Sarah's entire chart, I am inclined to let the marriage matters alone for the immediate future, while Sarah and her children adjust to Sarah working. But this is truly a subjective call and a dilemma for the counselor. The marital issues can wait for a few more months, so long as the problems are resolved sometime during the year. Pluto in Scorpio here suggests skeletons in the closet may be discovered and she needs to feel secure in her job before taking any more chances with her marriage.

Pluto is in the twelfth house and both the twelfth house and Pluto have to do with hidden actions and situations. Therefore, whatever is hidden is very deeply buried. Again this placement indicates that Sarah may have an affair or at least desire one. Pluto near the Ascendant indicates changes of significant magnitude formulating and they will begin to take shape when Pluto enters the first house and does not retrograde back into the twelfth. Although the solar return chart is only for one year, the Pluto placement represents a beginning of transformation that will come to fruition in the years to come. Pluto trines Mars. This can suggest power struggles. With Mars in the eighth house, the struggles may be over joint finances. In Sarah's case, her struggles were related to being forced back into the workplace and the reduction of joint finances when her spouse terminated his law partnership. Even though a trine implies an easy flow of energy, the planets themselves and their placements suggest difficulties with motivation, power struggles, and joint finances.

Venus in the twelfth house suggests that emotional and spiritual qualities are more valued than material success, which makes going back to work even harder since Sarah would much rather live with less money than leave her home and children to go to work. This is also often indicative of a hidden love relationship. Again, had the person from her past been available, she probably would have had an affair. Venus widely trines Saturn in the third house and Saturn indicates possible restriction of a relationship. Thus with this placement, if a relationship is poor there will probably be a breakup. Also, Sarah must conserve fiscally for the next year (the exact amount of time her husband did not work on a steady basis).

Jupiter in Scorpio in the twelfth house implies overwhelming emotions. Since the sixth house in Sarah's natal chart is where Scorpio is located, Sarah's work overshadows all else at this time and sets the tone for the next year, causing overwhelming emotions. The prominence of work is especially hard on her sons. It takes approximately one year for small children to fully adjust to a mother going back to work, and the home life is not easy for anyone during that time. However, Jupiter is like a guardian angel here in that it gives Sarah a sense of protection and cloaks the stress. Sarah feels a kind of faith that she may not have felt very much in the past. Again, this feeling of faith could be enhanced by spiritual endeavors and, as a counselor, you should stress the need for spirituality.

The stability of Saturn's energy in the third house of conscious mind also keeps Sarah from going crazy *vis-à-vis* all the subconscious mind twelfth house planets. Jupiter is a fortuitous planet and suggests all of the changes should be rewarding. Also, Jupiter suggests optimism and a faith that the universe will supply what is needed in order to cope. Jupiter here is very two-sided, but with great benefit. Venus conjunct Jupiter suggests an inner, subconscious strength to carry through. Venus in the twelfth house suggests that strength in spiritual or inner values is more important than financial gain, so the school system provides a job which Sarah can cope with regarding her children.

Pluto is the planet of unconscious motivation and, when in the twelfth house of subconscious mind, it suggests a great deal of hidden meaning and growth not yet recognized. All of the changes occurring will probably come to fruition when Pluto goes into the first house, and Sarah will determine exactly what she wants and how she will get what she wants. This is a very turbulent inner time. Again, Sarah has now gone back to school and determined a solid career path along which this job was just a stepping stone (the same as with her natal chart). Although Pluto here suggests many issues, this delineation is geared toward career counseling. Sarah going back to work and pushing money issues to the forefront comes to fruition when Pluto crosses into the first house. Sarah is transforming herself for the future, which includes her career.

Transits on the Day Sarah's Began Her New Job

The transiting Sun and Mercury are transiting Sarah's solar return first house (*see Figure 11a on page 111*) suggesting a lot of personal and mental energy the day she began her new job. These transits are very helpful when starting a new job.

You will notice that Mars by transit has moved into the ninth house in Leo, suggesting a lot of energy and tension behind the scenes at work. Sarah took over a desk that had apparently been empty for a while. She had a tremendous amount of basic preparation before she could begin to work effectively. It took a lot of Mars energy. Also, her tension from home was in the background at work, since obviously she could not show her stress on the new job. The transiting Ascendant is in the second house of money on the day she began her new job, suggesting that she will personally be earning the money or funding through her own personal efforts. This also implies that she is consciously aware of her own values of home and family versus the value of making money at their detriment.

The transiting Moon in the eleventh house suggests that Sarah's hopes for the future are changing, and this is further reflected in the delineation of the twelfth house.

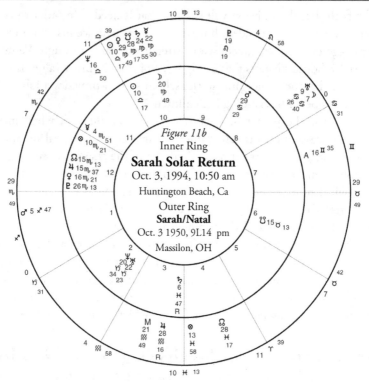

Figure 11b
Inner Ring
Sarah Solar Return
Oct. 3, 1994, 10:50 am
Huntington Beach, Ca
Outer Ring
Sarah/Natal
Oct. 3 1950, 9L14 pm
Massilon, OH

Cusps Affecting Sarah's New Job

Sarah's natal chart is figure 4 in Chapter 2.

If you look at where Sarah's natal chart cusps lie directly in her solar return houses, it is another indication of where obstacles lie this
year. (See Figure 11b.) Sarah's natal 16 Gemini Ascendant sits right
in the middle of her solar return seventh house, another suggestion of
personal conflict with her partner. Sarah's natal 21 Leo cusp of her
fourth house lies directly in the middle of her solar return ninth house
suggesting conflict between home and her personal philosophies. Sarah's
natal fifth house cusp lies about 1/3 way into her tenth house of career
suggesting conflict between her children and career. Her natal seventh
house cusp lies directly in the middle of her solar return first house
suggesting conflict with her spouse. Her natal tenth house cusp at 21
Aquarius lies directly in the middle of her solar return third house,
suggesting conscious conflict with career and conscious mind and lower
education. In other words, she is not mentally ready to go back to work
for the school system. Her natal chart eleventh house cusp is about 1/3 of
the way into the fourth house of her solar return chart suggesting conflict

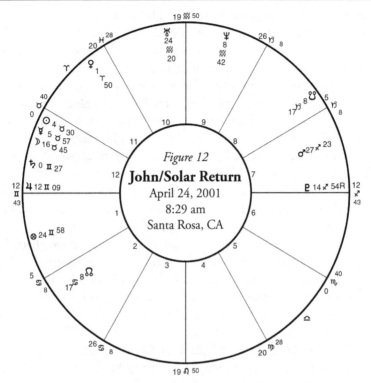

Figure 12
John/Solar Return
April 24, 2001
8:29 am
Santa Rosa, CA

between wishes and home. These cusp to house comparisons further emphasize suggestions made by her planet placements in the solar return chart.

Sarah's solar return chart is a perfect example of enhancement of the natal chart as to what a particular year brings to an individual. This is one reason I use both charts along with the lunar return (explained in Chapter 7) to effectively counsel in career areas.

John's Solar Return Chart
See Figure 12 above.

John has a Gemini Ascendant on his solar return chart. His approach to this year suggests he is quick-witted and adaptable. He will use verbal skills and rely on rational, logical thought. Since Gemini is a dual sign, he may do more than one task or job at a time. His Ascendant in Gemini is also the approach he will bring to his career. He is working in two schools. The solar return Ascendant is a good complement to his natal Leo Ascendant which affords a great deal of energy and quick action to his solar return Gemini with its quick and adaptable mind. This is a tremendous combination to start a career. The ruler of Gemini is Mercury in the twelfth house, suggesting John will bring his subconscious motivations into his choice of career. If you remember from his natal chart, working with children is quite a strong possibility, partially because of childhood trauma around divorce as a motivating factor.

Every one of John's planets in his solar return is above the horizon, suggesting he will be recognized for his work. Since he is starting his career, this is very important. His first year out, he should receive accolades, and his superiors will definitely notice his work.

John has seven planets in houses ten through three, and three planets in houses four through nine, suggesting he is largely in control of his career this year. Even though this is fairly balanced, and he is in control, he may not get all of his choices, i.e., he is working at the elementary school level rather than middle or high school, which he would prefer.

John has a majority of fixed planets in his solar return chart. Usually, five fixed planets indicates little change, which is contrary to John's situation this year. I tend to view this dichotomy as John really staying within his personal goal plan, not changing his goals, and the balance of four mutable planets suggests a change in circumstance or a step upward toward his goals.

There is only one cardinal planet and John would prefer to focus on just one thing in that area (Venus in the eleventh). The cardinal sign is in the eleventh house so he is focusing on what he wants for the future, and his focus may deal with groups. Despite that preference, the emphasis on mutables shows many demands and possible distractions.

John's planets are well balanced between air, earth and fire but there are no planets in water, only the North Node in the second house. This suggests a conscious detachment or a time of intellectual activity. This actually appears to be good since a first-year counselor runs a risk of letting childrens' problems become his/her own and may become overly emotional. This should help John get started with empathy rather than becoming emotionally drained.

The second house of money has Cancer on the cusp and is ruled by the Moon in the twelfth house, suggesting subconsciously motivated work, or work in the background, as a way to make money. Again, a school counselor works in the background. This also suggests John must have a position that is in harmony with his subconscious motivations. There are no planets here, but the North Node is in Cancer and sextile the Sun and Mercury and quincunx Neptune. If we use derivative houses, Neptune is in the derivative twelfth house of his career house, again suggesting work in the background. The Sun and Mercury are in the derivative third house of his career house suggesting work in lower education and a great deal of communication. Both of these things seem to describe John's work this year. Although John is sort of working in the background, with all of the planets above the horizon, again he will definitely be noticed for his work.

The sixth house of work, service and health has Scorpio on the cusp and is co-ruled by Mars and Pluto in the seventh house. Pluto is opposite Jupiter in the twelfth house and opposite the Ascendant. Pluto suggests transformation and understanding through deep psychological influences. When looking at this placement in terms of career, Pluto is in the seventh house of contracts, and Pluto involves a change or transformation, so the contract that John signed with the school system seems to be the change in his life. In fact, John did sign contracts for two schools.

Pluto opposite Ascendant implies personal change and the beginning of John's transformation from a student himself to a counselor. Since Pluto is in Sagittarius and opposite Ascendant, John may not be as personally free to do what he would like with this contract job.

The second planet we come to is Mars in the seventh house, again showing a great deal of drive and energy around a contract job. In Sagittarius, this also suggests John's wishes to be more free in his approach and shows that his work must meet his ideals.

The seventh house is the derivative second house of money to the sixth house of work and service, suggesting John will put a lot of energy into looking for future funding. With Pluto here, John may have some transforming ideas on how to get money. This choice was apparent in John's natal chart as well. There also may be tension around funding. This is not surprising, since he works for the school system and schools are always in need of money. Mars here suggests John will be energized in sharing his experiences with his wife and they may also have some arguments in adjusting their lives to the new scheduling.

The next planet we come to is Neptune in the ninth house. It squares Sun and Mercury in the twelfth house, and trines Jupiter and the Ascendant.

Neptune is at home in the ninth house linked with higher philosophy and enlightenment. These ideals would come into play in the way John approaches his career. Also, it suggests John is already thinking of further education. But more than this, when using derivative houses, the ninth house is the derivative twelfth house to the tenth house career. There is a square to the Sun which is in John's twelfth house of hidden or behind the scenes matters and which (when using derivative houses) is the third house to John's career house. Thus, there are two themes running side-by-side which affect career. The first theme is the solar return as it is delineated on its face, and the second theme is the solar return using derivative houses. Both seem to suggest the same thing. There seems to be a lot of behind-the-scenes activity with regard to lower education, and some obstacles as well, when using the derivative houses. There also may be some confusion or misconceptions in the background of career along with the insight suggested by Neptune. Neptune in Aquarius suggests John's high ideals will come into play with his career and must be the background of any career he chooses.

The potential obstacles appear to be offset somewhat by the trine to Jupiter. This trine suggests expansion of John's work in the background of the educational system. Jupiter is trining Neptune in the ninth house which is the derivative twelfth house of John's career (the background happenings to his career) and sits in the third derivative house of John's career representing lower education. This trine also brings subconscious motivations and intuition from John's solar return twelfth house into the superconscious philosophy of John's solar return ninth house, another suggestion that John is coming into his own as a person, as well as with his career.

The Mercury-Neptune aspect suggests working with empathy and concern, which is excellent for counseling, even if difficulty arises with the square energy. The Sun square Neptune indicates heightened intuition, also excellent for a counselor, even though he may encounter difficulty.

Aquarius on the cusp of the tenth house suggests a profession with high ideals and far reaching consequences, and is ruled by Uranus which is the next planet we come to in the tenth house of career. A sign with its own ruler is very strong and it is in an angular house. Thus, this is a very strong indication of career change (Uranus can mean radical change and Uranus here sextiles solar return Mars, so the changes are likely to be large). In John's case, he changed from an ivory tower student to a responsible counselor. Uranus suggests he wants freedom to work in his own way and will buck the system if need be. Uranus is the planet that symbolizes unusual occurrences. Remember from John's natal chart that the day he began his new career, he was thrust to the forefront to handle picketing and angry parents. His entire time at his new job will probably be filled with unusual situations.

The next planet we come to is Venus in the eleventh house. It squares Mars and sextiles Saturn. John's mediating skills (Venus) brought positive attention from parents and authorities at work (Saturn). Venus in the eleventh house suggests new friendships, dealing with group dynamics and expanding interests. Friends may play a part in helping him toward his goals. This is a nice placement in combination with a heavy career load. It gives John a break. When looking at career, this is the derivative second house. Venus is in the money house of career suggesting reward for work. With a sextile to Saturn, it may mean a promotion or more responsibility. For John, this translates to a new job and earning full-time employment income for the first time. Venus here also suggests that his career is well funded this year.

Finally comes the largest concentration of planets, five planets in two signs in the twelfth house. Again, there are two themes running here, the twelfth house of the subconscious and things hidden, which is also the derivative third house to the career house. With all these planetary placements, this is an excellent place to look for career opportunity.

The first planet is the Sun in Taurus ruled by Venus in the eleventh house, suggesting that John's unconscious motivations about what he desires for the future are coming to the forefront. The Sun here also suggests a lack of personal recognition, but with Uranus in the tenth house and all planets above the horizon, I doubt this is the case. It seems more that, unconsciously, John would want to work in the background, but will be recognized anyway. Also the Sun in the twelfth house can imply a drain of energy that would accompany the physical and mental drain of a new position.

On the other hand, since this is the derivative third house of the career and the third house is lower education and communication, it suggests a great deal of energy and vitality in his new job with the school system and in dealing and communicating with the children. Both luminaries are here in Taurus fully supporting John's new position. The Moon here suggests twelfth house deep emotions on a subconscious level, but implies the change in career to the derivative third house education position. Again, although John does not want to work in an elementary school, it is a good start to his future. The Moon here suggests emotions kept below the surface which help with the detachment needed to counsel. The Moon has a 150 degree aspect to Pluto in the seventh house of contracts, so it also triggered the contract with the school system.

Mercury in the twelfth house suggests control over his thoughts and secrets. It is a good time to reflect on issues and look at himself, a time for review and organization. It is a time for deep thinking and possible repression of thoughts. However, again this is the derivative third house of communication and lower education to the career house, so Mercury shows a great deal of activity and communication with the new job. Mercury and the Sun square Neptune in the ninth house, and John may have trouble censoring what he says at conferences with superiors when he feels strongly regarding issues. Mercury-Neptune aspects suggest working with compassion, a humanistic approach—truly a good placement for a counselor. Because of the square, John will have to work hard to overcome any blocked energy. Sun-Neptune and Sun-Mercury aspects suggest a great deal of intuition at this time and suggest helping those in need. Both the Sun and Mercury aspects with Neptune indicate potential drug and alcohol use. Should John indulge in this, he must watch the tendency to overindulge when unwinding from hectic schoolwork.

Saturn in the 12th house can indicate a need to overcome inhibitions. It suggests a feeling of responsibility even when there is no reason to be responsible. It is a time to look at any personal weaknesses that you let stop you from becoming what you really want to be and move past them. It is a time to grow. This is a tough task for John who is taking on a great deal of responsibility. On the other hand, this is the derivative third house to the career house, and Saturn is hard work but also the foundation from which a career in education will grow over the next fourteen years. If he works hard, he will be where he wants to be. John's sense of responsibility is very important to him this year. There is a lot of mental work and focus which Saturn symbolizes. Also, Saturn in Gemini points to a mental focus that keeps John from being too scattered while he is going from one school to another. It is a necessary stabilizing factor in the solar return chart. Decisions he makes will affect the future of the children, so he needs the Saturn focus.

Saturn also helps stabilize Jupiter expansion, so things do not seem out of control for John. Jupiter is the next planet sitting in the twelfth house. Jupiter in the twelfth house is wonderful, especially with Saturn there. It suggests that on a subconscious level, no matter what, John will feel he can handle whatever comes to him. This is good since Jupiter's expansive nature also suggests feelings of being overwhelmed and the area at issue is found where Jupiter sits in the natal chart. (In John's natal chart Jupiter sits in his sixth house of work, service and health, so work may seem overwhelming this year, especially going between two schools.) Since the solar return twelfth house is the derivative third house to career, Jupiter suggests a lot of activity and a balancing act of all John has to do. Since it is in Gemini, this is intensified. I am not surprised that John is working at two schools; Gemini is a dual sign. Fortunately, Saturn helps with concentration to get everything done efficiently. Jupiter here would also involve ethics and career or situations where ethics would come into play. One example of ethics coming into play happened shortly after school began. John had to report suspected child abuse—a very difficult decision as the word "suspected" is the key.

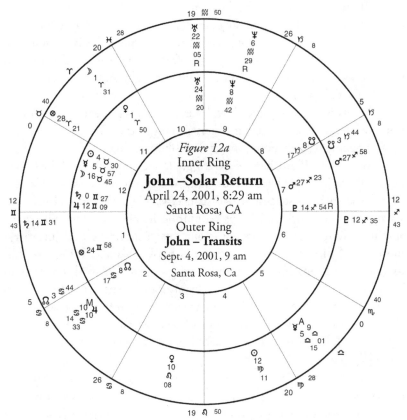

Figure 12a
Inner Ring
John –Solar Return
April 24, 2001, 8:29 am
Santa Rosa, CA
Outer Ring
John – Transits
Sept. 4, 2001, 9 am
Santa Rosa, Ca

Transits That Pertain To John's New Job
See figure 12a above.

Saturn transiting the first house of the Solar Return when John started this job suggests heavy responsibilities and great successes. Saturn was transiting the first house on the day John began his new job. This implies a new period of personal hard work and overcoming obstacles, combined with a time when past efforts are rewarded. Obviously, this is a picture of a new career based in past education. This transit of Saturn is now directly opposite Pluto suggesting two things, the success of efforts of the past fourteen years (or from the time when John entered high school and Saturn was conjunct Pluto through college) and now the realization that he probably must put more effort into his education and work to really succeed. This is a time of personal growth. There is a suggestion of disappointment with reaching goals and, again, John is trying to get into a middle or high school rather than elementary.

There is a transiting Midheaven and Jupiter in the second house of finances. The Midheaven suggests career opportunity and Jupiter is expansion. Jupiter here suggests making money. Since this is the house of personal values, John is also bringing to fruition what is of value to him, i.e., helping children. This is a time for John to really look at what he wants out of life, and to go for it.

Venus is transiting the third house, which represents lower education—where John is counseling. Venus also suggests his social life may pick up and he might have more contact with siblings.

By transit, Pluto had been retrograde and now sits in John's sixth house of work and service. Pluto transiting the sixth house on the day John began his job suggests health concerns. John has strained his back since beginning work and keeps re-injuring it. He probably will not be able to fully recover until school is out this year and he can quit carrying carts of files, etc., from school to school. This also brings psychological motivations into work and suggests John will work on ways to transform counseling, as suggested in his natal chart. Transiting Pluto is opposite Saturn and the Ascendant suggesting difficult personal and power issues, and striving for control—either control over others or vice versa. John must watch to avoid being combative when asserting himself.

The transiting Moon was exactly conjunct his solar return Venus on the day he began work. The Moon triggers change, and it showed the exact day John began his new job. Both were at one degree Aries, a very critical degree for a new beginning.

Cusps Affecting John's New Job

If you look at where his natal cusps fall well within his solar return houses, you will see where any difficulty would lie. Likewise, matching cusps show strength of purpose and where things should run more smoothly. John's Ascendant is 19° Leo and the cusp of his solar return fourth house is also 19° Leo, suggesting his personal approach and quest is allied with his foundational values this year.

John's 11° Libra natal cusp of the third house lies within his solar return fifth house, suggesting that this is not a good time for speculation and thoughts of starting a family of his own will be delayed. Also, it is likely he will not have a lot of time for creativity.

His natal seventh house cusp lies directly on his solar return tenth house cusp indicating support from his partner with his career and, of course, signing a contract with the school system for his first job.

The next conflict is suggested by the cusp of the ninth house lying well within the eleventh house. There appears a philosophical conflict of some sort with groups, or (again) maybe butting heads with school administration, or perhaps delay in wishes for the future. It also suggests challenges to the career house regarding money. One major challenge is that elementary education must find funding each year for counselors and, thus, two schools shared John since neither had enough money for a full time counselor. John will have a challenge in getting programs funded.

As you can see, John's solar return reinforces his natal chart with regard to career. Both show so much activity, as a career coun-selor I would suggest

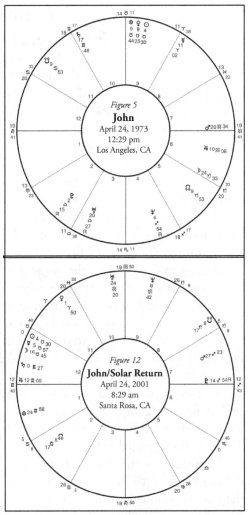

that John set aside time every week to do nothing but play sports to relieve stress and relax with a mindless book or computer game. He needs breaks in order to work effectively. I would also emphasize what a great career start he is having, so when he gets feelings of being overwhelmed, he will remember this is an exciting beginning and being overwhelmed at the onset is part of it. I would also stress that the Saturn placement shows not only a culmination of past work, but also a beginning of something new to work toward. Even though he may not want an elementary position this time, let alone working in two schools, it is the start he is supposed to have to grow.

Carole
Solar Return Chart
See figure 13.

Carole has six planets above the horizon and four planets below the horizon, suggesting her work will be slightly more public than private or she will be recognized for her work. Her planets are almost evenly distributed in houses ten through three and four through nine, so this is very balanced as far as control and prominence.

Carole has five cardinal planets, three in Cancer and two in Capricorn. The Cancer planets are in an angular house, as well as Neptune in Capricorn. She has two fixed planets both in succedent houses. She also has three mutable planets. This is also a very good balance. She can do as she wishes and make her own decisions, and she will think rationally. With five cardinal planets, change is indicated, but it is up to Carole. This also suggests a lot of activity. She could not have more activity with a new, short-term job and three young children to take care of and at the same time, keeping her relationship with her husband in sync. She can feel overloaded at times.

The Ascendant is Sagittarius suggesting that Carole approaches her life and her career this year with a desire for freedom to do what she chooses, as well as a career which aligns itself with her ideals of family life. Already we see from just the Ascendant that a short-term job is perfect for her family situation, and does not create conflict with her ideals. She is doing as she chooses to do without compromising her values. This was also suggested in her natal chart.

Neptune in the first house is in Capricorn, ruled by Saturn in the third house. We see a correlation with conscious thoughts of what she can do personally to be more self-fulfilled. Neptune here suggests a look toward spirituality and also suggests helping others. This is a time when Carole is going back and forth in her mind to determine what she wants. Neptune in this house symbolizes permeable membranes. Carole will take on the influence of her surroundings (either consciously or subconsciously).Therefore, she will feel all the tension of her family with her return to work. Neptune rules her solar return third house and Carole will instinctively know what others around her are thinking and will feel their emotions with them. Neptune trines Mars in the ninth house which is very helpful for work behind the scenes (as in production accounting) and this work will advance Carole's career later on.

Neptune is opposite the Sun in the seventh house, so there may

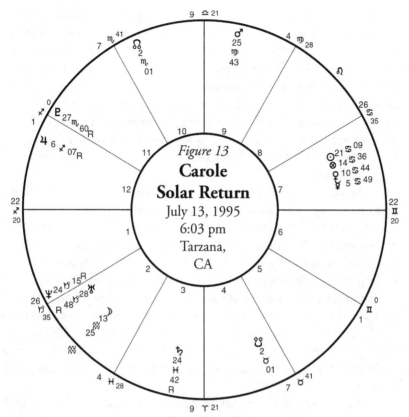

Figure 13
**Carole
Solar Return**
July 13, 1995
6:03 pm
Tarzana,
CA

be some tension with the spouse, but more likely there will be personal conflict about whether Carole should work or be home for and with her spouse. The Sun/Neptune aspects suggest Carole is growing into more awareness of others. Since the Sun is in the seventh house, more awareness of her partner's needs may cause personal conflict in going back to work, and not because of any actions on the part of her spouse. She is personally feeling that work may be taking her away from others. There are a lot of emotions around the marriage at this time.

Mars trine Neptune suggests surprise in what happens, and even the best-laid plans do not always work out. Jobs can be an issue. Neptune is conjunct Uranus giving Carole an unusual bit of money for the time being (Uranus is in the second house of money and possessions). Obviously, a temporary job will give Carole a bit more money for the time being. This is a time to lay a foundation for the future.

There also may be some sort of deception around the job. Since this job is accounting, it may have something to do with taxes or the appropriate categorizing or allocation of money. There also can be drug or alcohol problems indicated around the job (not uncommon in the movie industry). Neptune in Capricorn indicates a very good intuition for business. Neptune in the first house of a solar return chart indicates a higher, spiritual consciousness. Self-centered needs are diminished for the good of the whole. This, combined with the Mars drive in the ninth house, creates a higher consciousness that is very powerful. In actuality, Carole is beginning to experience a spiritual growth she is not consciously aware of yet, and it is even more obscure because of the turmoil created by her career versus her family at this time.

The cusp of the second house is Capricorn, ruled by Saturn in the third house, suggesting a lot of communication and hard work.

Uranus in Capricorn in the second house indicates financial ups and downs, and the Moon in Aquarius indicates fluctuation and unusual situations. The sign of Capricorn stabilizes the fluctuation. Aquarius is ruled by Uranus and this implies very unexpected financial conditions, unique occupations, employment and/or money gained through friends. In Carole's case, the opportunity for the short-term job, which came through a friend, was very unexpected and created definite financial ups. Changes can be positive or negative and may occur at different times while Uranus is in this house. If one is not working, she may find a job (in Carole's case) and, if working, may change jobs.

Also, Carole was required to defend her position of going back to work *vis-á-vis* the standard of others and she was required to define her own priorities. Although this was only a two-month job, her family and in-laws applied pressure on her to keep the status quo. She stood her ground and let those around her know that everyone in a family has a time when his/her needs take priority, and this was her turn. This does not conflict with the "good of the whole" in that allowing herself fulfillment as a person was beneficial for the family unit. As a counselor, this is a very important point to stress and will help Carole overcome some of the guilt.

Uranus opposite the Sun in the seventh house again suggests tension with spouse and work. It also implies Carole is working as much for personal fulfillment as for money. In addition, Uranus here suggests Carole may defend her actions to her family. She must be able to express her need for personal fulfillment, and that may be the real issue.

The Moon is in the second house. Again, the Moon is a great indicator of change in a solar return chart, and it trines the Midheaven, so the change is with career and money. The Moon here also suggests that emotions are manifesting themselves in a need for security or financial stability. As there appears to be a desire for more self-fulfillment, it seems to be tied to a desire for financial independence (if she were ever to need it). This does not mean she is seeking to leave a good marriage, but desires to be more self-secure. The Moon here symbolizes the change of income that her job is creating. The Moon can represent money changes and also personal values that are evolving and lending themselves to a need for independence and security—to be her own person. After several years at home, having worked her entire adult life, being financially dependent on her husband was difficult. This job played a definite role in assuaging the need for financial independence. It also let Carole keep her hand in a business within which she loves to work. Uranus in this house indicates changes in values and morals.

The next planet we come to is Saturn in the third house. Saturn trines the Sun and is opposite Mars. Saturn here suggests a year of mental activity and hard work. Carole may feel mentally stressed and should try to communicate her feelings to relieve the stress. Everyday life can be bothersome and take on more of a complex nature than usual. So while Carol has strong mental focus for work, the little things of life can be annoying. Saturn is the planet of karma, so Saturn here suggests that the decisions Carole makes about work will greatly affect those around her. What was begun this year will require future efforts to complete. In Carole's case, major decisions arise this year around responsibility for herself and responsibility for others. She feels her personal needs directly conflict with the needs of others. Carole must search for options and run the risk of depression if she cannot find positive solutions. The depression could lead to fatigue. Although Carole felt her fatigue was from working and caring for a home and children, she did have live-in help, and the fatigue could partially be emotional fatigue due to the conflict.

Saturn opposite Mars suggests Carole has an opportunity to work toward her goals and the energy to do so. There may be stress due to Carol wanting faster action (suggested by Mars) but meeting obstacles (suggested by Saturn). She is working with deadlines and delays, typical of the motion picture industry. Mars is opposite Saturn across the third and ninth houses indicating the conscious versus the higher conscious mind. Carole must realistically assess the situation and work toward completing long-term goals and appreciate the efforts needed to achieve them. Saturn is practicality, and plans cannot be implemented unless they are realistic. Frustration is common here. In Carole's case, the frustration is between work and family, and knowing it will be a long time, if ever, before she goes back to a career. She must realistically see that, with such young children, her choice may be a career as a mother and homemaker rather than in the business world. When she feels she can work, a part-time job or a job from the home might be best. Part of her frustration is realizing there are limitations on her options.

Saturn trine the Sun in the seventh house of partners suggests that the structure of her marriage is an asset at this time. Saturn is in Pisces (ruled by Neptune in the first house) suggesting a lot of self-evaluation as to what Carole really wants. Saturn is where obstacles lie, and Carole is having a difficult time mentally with her decisions, i.e., to work.

The Sun in the seventh house is opposite Uranus, indicating Carole has a desire to make radical changes, but they will be disruptive. Of course, going back to work is disruptive. However, this also goes deeper and these changes are at issue with boredom and restriction, and emanate from Carole's desire for some freedom and creativity in a working environment. What you, as a counselor, must help Carole overcome are feelings of guilt with regard to working and being her own person.

The Sun is trine Pluto in the eleventh house (which has to do with working with groups of people, enhancement of dreams and wishes). Carole's employment is with a very large group—the movie industry. Carole is having increased awareness of her own power in everyday situations, and she is more able to recognize psychological motivations, as well as her family's attempts to manipulate her. This is probably why her family could not really deter her from taking the short-term employment. Carole is learning to deal with life on a deeper level.

Venus in the seventh house indicates the importance of a partner (a spouse or business partner). Carole must learn to negotiate, as well as compromise, at this time and with this situation. This experience will lead to an easier time of negotiations and compromise with future situations. Carole's wishes may have been superceded by the needs of others, but she was able to negotiate and compromise enough to take the short-term employment which she very much needed for her own growth and peace of mind.

With this placement, there is a tendency for Carole to let the needs of others suppress her identity, a common pitfall of mothers. By taking the job, Carole helped avoid this pitfall. Venus is trine the North Node in the tenth house which indicates luck in career. The North Node in the tenth house is in Scorpio which is ruled by Pluto in the eleventh house (again indicating larger groups, dreams and wishes), so there is again an indication of working with large groups. The movie industry is quite a large group. Carole's Venus is in her seventh house and this rules Libra which is on the cusp of her tenth house. Again agreeable, this placement aids Carole when dealing with her relationship with her spouse and her career.

The planets in the seventh house are in the sign of Cancer, which is ruled by the Moon. The Moon is in the second house of money, possessions and values. Carole is exerting her self-worth and value by taking the job in spite of any conflict or guilt she feels regarding the marriage and partnership. There is also an indication that her employer may wish to work as a partner on future projects after this solar return. Venus is square the Midheaven, suggesting difficulty with relationships or partners, and with what she wants from her career.

Mercury in the seventh house is conjunct Venus, squares the Midheaven (the cusp of the tenth house of career) and forms a trine to the North Node (also in the tenth house of career). These placements indicate fortunate partnerships and associations versus disquiet in the marriage *vis-à-vis* the career. Mercury here indicates a lot of talking and planning with others, but these plans are not easily finalized. (Taking the employment was not an easy decision.) Personally, it is a time for Carole to clarify her role in marriage. Professionally, it is a good time to work with others in her field. The danger here is letting her family dominate her thoughts.

Mars is in Virgo in house nine opposes Saturn in the third house. Mars is also trine to Neptune and Uranus, and square to Carole's Ascendant.

Mars in the ninth house suggests a strong identity with philosophical beliefs. Carole will further develop her own personal philosophy and code of conduct. Mars here suggests that Carole may react to past injustices, and she must be careful not to react to present situations based on past experiences with others. It is a time to negotiate fairly with her family. Virgo is ruled by Mercury which is in the seventh house of partnerships, and Carole must be careful of anger with her husband. Her new job has made Carole feel like she has a tremendous amount of responsibility. Her frustration at an overwhelming amount of work is not created by her husband, and she should not take it out on him.

The trine by Mars to Neptune implies that Carole has ease in her work, and Mars trine Uranus in her second house represents Carole's unexpected income. This is quite true since a two-month, short-term job is easy to accept and the offer (which came out of the blue) created some unexpected income for Carole.

The tenth house of career, profession and honors contains the North Node (benevolent lunar node) in Scorpio which is ruled by Pluto in Carole's eleventh house of dreams, wishes, friends and groups. Her career benefit did come through a large group—the movie industry. The North Node is also trine to all the planets in the seventh house, and a future business partnership may be in formation at this time—there for the asking if Carole wishes to take advantage of it.

Pluto is in Scorpio in the eleventh house of dreams, wishes, friends and groups. Pluto is quite at home here and is in Scorpio, which it rules. Pluto identifies with the group as a whole, not the individual. Accomplishments will be through the group effort at this time. Individual needs will be set aside. As Carole learns more about herself (remember her ninth house), she will learn more in the way of negotiation, as well as the dynamics of the group. Carole will be looking within herself as well as outside. Changes in goals will begin to occur, and Carole must watch out not to block the changes based on past circumstances. Since Pluto is trine Saturn, there should be a great deal of communication with groups, and Carole will begin to develop who she is to be. Again, the entertainment industry is a tremendously large group. Although Carole's job may be a small part, it is part of the whole, and the dynamics of change are occurring (although with Pluto here they will not be realized for some time). Pluto is transformation, and the transformation is not always evident at the time it is occurring.

Jupiter is in Sagittarius in the twelfth house. Jupiter also rules Sagittarius—another planet at home with its ruler. Jupiter represents open doors of opportunity and, in the twelfth house, the door is not yet apparent to Carole, but it is opening. She will be aware of it in the future. Sagittarius has to do with matters foreign; in Carole's case it would not surprise me, if in the future, her career path led to a company with a lot of foreign invest- ment or that dealt with foreign matters. In fact, there was probably foreign investment in the movie she was working on.

Jupiter in the twelfth house indicates overwhelming emotions that Carole will have difficulty in controlling. Jupiter is the planet of growth and the twelfth house rules the unconscious. Carole's unconscious may grow disproportionately to the rest of her psyche at this time of change. Feelings can run amok and the stress can be overwhelming. Extremely strong feelings can drown out reasoning. However, Jupiter here is not bad even though it seems difficult. While going through psychological stress, Carole's own belief system is evolving. This is coupled with Pluto in Carole's eleventh house and her development with the group dynamic.

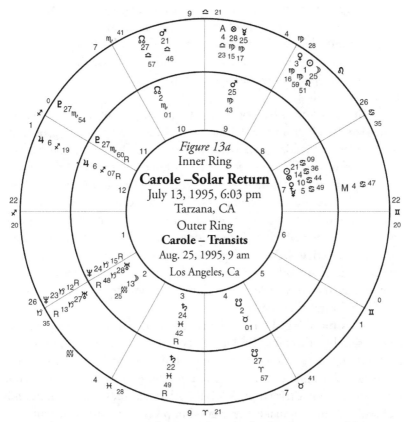

Figure 13a
Inner Ring
Carole –Solar Return
July 13, 1995, 6:03 pm
Tarzana, CA
Outer Ring
Carole – Transits
Aug. 25, 1995, 9 am
Los Angeles, Ca

When Jupiter crosses the Ascendant to the first house, problems may intensify, but it is a rewarding time. Around December 1, 1996 through January, 1997 the changes occurring at this time begin to appear. Carole may also be afforded the career she wants at this time, or choose not to have a career. She should be very secure in her choices whatever they may be.

Transits That Pertain to Carole's New Job
See figure 13a above.

The transiting Midheaven is conjunct Mercury in the seventh house of partnerships suggesting a lot of communication about her career with her spouse and also perhaps signing a contract for the short-term job.

The Moon, Sun and Venus are transiting Carole's eighth house of government, taxes and other people's money. Carole is working with other people's money as an accountant. As suggested in Carole's natal chart, she may also be dealing with taxes or tax problems and creative accounting. The Sun and Venus in Virgo suggest meticulous work and attention to detail. Again, this describes accounting. This is the derivative third house of communication to the sixth house of work and service, suggesting a lot of mental activity and communication. The Moon transiting the eighth house can draw you to powerful people such as those in the movie industry.

The transiting Mercury is at the exact degree of Carole's solar return Mars in Virgo on the day she started her job. This is a good time for study and education to advance in her career. The ninth house is also the derivative twelfth house to the tenth house. Remember, the twelfth house represents behind-the-scenes activities and Carole is working behind the scenes in production accounting. This behind-the-scenes work is for advancement of Carole's career in the future. There are a lot of communications involving abstract ideas with others at this time (also a ninth house activity). Mars is opposite Saturn and this is an appropriate aspect for mental work requiring discipline. However, this also implies a very serious time for Carole. She is thinking about the world and her place in it. It is a time of changing values.

Mars transiting the tenth house can represent positive energy and recognition by others for Carole's efforts. It also can indicate tension with the fourth house (the home) since a great deal of energy is put into the tenth house and this opposes the fourth house. Those in the home feel Carole is not recognizing their needs. With the Mars transit, Carole's ambition is aroused and she will make a very good impression on others for offers in the future. These people will be in a position to help Carole in the future.

Cusps Affecting Carole's New Job

Carole's first house cusp at 9 Cancer sits well within her solar return seventh house suggesting personal tension with the partnership. With five planets in water, Carole is probably intuitively picking up frustration, even when it is not openly expressed. She feels personally at odds wih her family. Also, this frustration is coming through to her via her partner's family members.

The third house cusp at 18 Leo sits well within the eighth house, suggesting mental activity and frustration with other people's money, so her position as an accountant for a movie may be frustrating work at times. There may be problems with taxes.

The fifth house cusp at 20 Libra sits well within the tenth house, suggesting conflict between children and career.

The seventh house cusp at 9 Capricorn sits well within the first house, again implying personal turmoil with partner.

The 18 Aquarius ninth house cusp sits well within the second house of personal values. As Aquarius, I think it refers more to values than money. This suggests Carole is struggling with her needs and her decision to work.

The eleventh house cusp at 20 Aries is well within the fourth house, so it indicates a struggle over personal desire versus home.

There seems to be a lot of personal questioning and conflict, but since Carole is working on a short-term project, job matters should be okay.

In looking at Carole's solar return chart, I feel the abundance of water planets shows her overly emotional focus. Her husband is a very

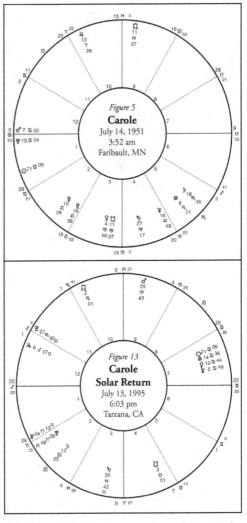

Figure 5
Carole
July 14, 1951
3:52 am
Faribault, MN

Figure 13
Carole
Solar Return
July 13, 1995
6:03 pm
Tarzana, CA

nice and supportive person. Even if he told Carole 50 times a day to "take this short-term job, everything is all right," she would immediately tune into any little daily frustration he may have because she is not home. Her guilt feelings also fit this abundance of water. As a counselor, it is important to stress the real cause of these feelings, and help Carole feel good about her decision to take the short-term job. There is nothing in this chart that suggests Carole needs professional counseling. She really just needs some encouragement and knowledge about the cause of her feelings of guilt. This is the type of situation where you, as an astrological counselor, can do wonders for a client.

Solar Return Birthday Trip

You may choose a solar return birthday trip when you feel very frustrated with a particular area of your life. For example, if you feel like the romance has gone from your life, you have no prospects, have not had any prospects for months or years, you may choose to be in a location that would place planets such as the Sun, Venus or Mercury in your fifth house. The same holds true for the other houses and what they represent as well. For this book, I am dealing with a solar return birthday trip for career opportunity.

Some astrologers swear by solar return birthday trips, and others feel that since you just come back home, where you live is where your solar return should be based. I have found that just as your natal chart is your natal chart no matter where you move, your solar return chart is your solar return chart based on the exact place you are at the exact time the Sun's placement is identical to its placement at your birth, no matter where you live. I find being in a location about one day before and one day after your exact solar return is a sufficient amount of time to be in one place for the solar return birthday trip. Some astrologers feel you should be in the location for a longer period of time. Being in transit at the time of your solar return is really difficult.

A solar return birthday trip can be very helpful if you wish to work on a certain area of your life and, thus, it can be very useful as a tool in career counseling. You must be very careful when planning a solar return trip so that other areas of your chart are not adversely affected. With today's astrological computer programs it is easy and feasible to play with a chart until you find a good solar return birthday trip which would enhance career opportunity and not adversely affect the rest of the chart.

I will discuss my own solar return birthday trip compared to my natal chart since it is a very good example of how opportunity can open up. Although I did not plan the trip for publishing, it just worked out that way. My natal chart is figure 14 and my solar return chart is figure 14A.

Before I delve into my solar return birthday trip, I will jump ahead a little to the advanced methods section (Nodes and Yods) and a discussion of the asteroid Chiron since they pertain heavily to my solar return birthday trip chart. Although they are a little advanced for this section, once you read the brief descriptions and then look at the comparison, they will make sense.

Lunar nodes occur when the Moon intersects the plane of the ecliptic (the Earth's "path" around the Sun). The North Node is the point

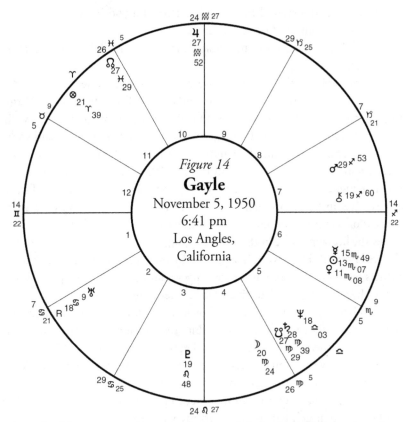

Figure 14
Gayle
November 5, 1950
6:41 pm
Los Angles,
California

where the Moon crosses from south to north latitude, and the point where the Moon crosses from north to south is the South Node. Though they are not planets, the North Node is considered relatively benevolent and the South Node is considered a bit more challenging in nature. Karmically, the South Node suggests past lives, and the North Node is where you are this lifetime, and a point to work out Karma.

A yod is a combination of aspects. It is two planets that sextile each other and both are also quincunx a third planet. Points of a yod can also be Nodes, Midheaven, Ascendant or Descendant, as well as planets. Yods are often called "fingers of fate." Thus, a yod in a natal chart suggests lifelong patterns. A yod in a solar return chart sets up a pattern to be used for a particular year, affording you opportunity you do not necessarily have all the time.

Chiron is a small body located between Saturn and Uranus. By definition it suggests philosophy, healing, life values, looking beyond limitations, desire to control, and an unusual or radical approach to money and possessions. In the second house and as part of a yod it would deal with money, possessions, and personal values.

I will not discuss my entire natal chart, just highlight items pertaining to career.

Uranus is in the second house of money and values ruled by the Moon in the fourth house (the foundation). The Moon is in Virgo suggesting a "critical mother" so one of the first motivations I have is striving to improve based on foundation. The Moon also suggests a hardworking, conscientious or compulsive mother. Although I do not feel my mother was extremely critical, she did push us to be "the best" we could be, always reaching higher. Venus, the Sun and Mercury are all in the sixth house of work and service, in Scorpio, ruled by Pluto in the third house, indicating work in areas of communication, writing and lower education. Eight planets are below the horizon, as are both luminaries, suggesting private work or work in the background. Hard work is suggested by three planets in the sixth house. Planets in the sixth house in Scorpio suggest an interest in metaphysics, the occult, health, religion, detective work and ferreting out facts.

With Jupiter in the tenth house I should be lucky with career opportunities and should receive public recognition or honor. However, this is diminished by so many planets below the horizon.

I also have a T-square between Saturn in my house of creativity, Mars in my house of contracts and the North Node in my house of groups and wishes, so getting a contract for something creative is a challenge. I've worked pretty much true to my chart my whole life.

I work as a certified paralegal which involves a lot of writing and communication, but is behind the scenes since the lawyers are the public figures. Because it is not a large firm, I am noticed by clients and other attorneys or paralegals, since I deal directly with them on a daily basis. If I worked for a large law firm, I would probably not have nearly as much contact with people on a daily basis. I certainly would not get to know all the clients as well as I know each and every one of them. So Jupiter takes hold a little in the type of firm for which I work.

Jupiter is in Aquarius, ruled by Uranus in the second house, so I should have unusual opportunities for money, and work must be aligned with my personal values. There is a tendency toward humanitarian work. Thus, there is my other work, astrology. Over the years, true to my sixth house in Scorpio ruled by Pluto (in my third house of writing and communication), I have published many articles about astrology and helped people with readings, etc., but did not really push for recognition. It was

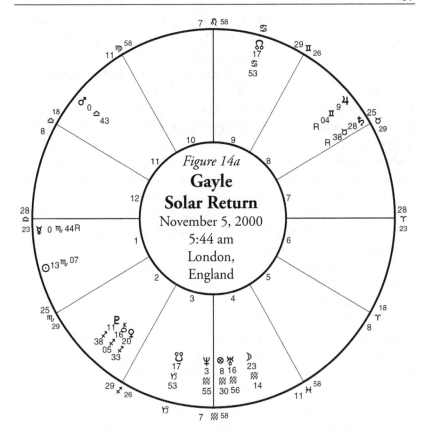

Figure 14a
Gayle
Solar Return
November 5, 2000
5:44 am
London,
England

just fun. I became interested in career counseling; after a lot of work with people changing jobs or looking for new careers, I wrote an article which later turned into a manuscript, which I submitted to ACS.

I took a birthday trip to London, England in 2000. During the year 2000, I was told ACS was interested in publishing this manuscript. If you look at the solar return birthday trip chart (figure 14a), you will see why the opportunity opened up at this time.

The first indication of publishing is the yod. The yod consists of Chiron and Uranus sextile and both are quincunx the North Node.

Chiron is in the second house (of money) and Uranus is in the fourth house (of home) in Aquarius which suggests unusual opportunity in the home, which is where I write. They point to the North Node which is in the ninth house of publishing. This yod is combined with the Sun and Mercury in the first house suggesting a lot of personal drive and communication this year, a year where I will shine personally. 2000 is the year I got curious and called ACS regarding the disposition of my manuscript. In fact, I called several times (Sun energy and drive) and was told that they were interested in publishing it.

There is a grand trine from Neptune in the third house of writing to Saturn in the eighth house and Mars in the eleventh house of wishes. So it seems opportunity for creative writing with Neptune and wishes to publish this particular manuscript are also suggested by these placements. I still have most of my planets below the horizon but the Sun in the first house suggests I will personally shine and Mercury suggests personal communication and writing. I also have six planets in houses ten through four, suggesting I will have more personal influence on what I want this year.

Jupiter and Saturn are in the eighth house, which is the derivative second house of money to the house of contracts, suggesting hard work and a lot of reward for any contract signed.

Though Pluto and Venus in the second house suggest financial good fortune and there are other work factors in this chart, it is the publishing that really stands out and the opportunity for it that is suggested by the chart. On the other hand, Uranus and the Moon are in the fourth house and Uranus here can suggest disruption or change in the home, or health problems of elderly family members. The Moon suggests mother, and my mother has been quite ill. I actually did not sit and calculate a chart for my birthday but picked a place where I wanted to go. Had I calculated it first, I would have been very concerned about the fourth house placement. This is an example of why, when you take a birthday trip to enhance an area of your chart, you should be careful that it does

Chapter Seven

Lunar Returns

The lunar return chart is calculated for the exact degree, minute and second that the Moon occupied at your birth, which occurs once every 28 days. Like the solar return chart, it should be calculated for your location at the exact moment the transiting Moon reaches your birth Moon placement. If you are out of town, use the city you are in to calculate the chart. The lunar return is the third chart I like to use in career counseling. **You will have 13 lunar return charts during a year so using a lunar return chart gives you 13 different charts with which to look for career opportunity throughout the year.** It is a very helpful tool for timing and to find opportunities when they appear limited or do not seem to exist in the natal or solar return charts.

You should delineate a lunar return chart much like the solar return chart described in Chapter 6 with **a few distinctions**. The solar return chart suggests patterns for the current year. The lunar return chart **suggests patterns for the current month**.

The lunar return is very helpful when seeking opportune times to act. The Moon symbolizes change. If you have a month during the year when the Moon is in the second, sixth or tenth house, it is a good time to seek career opportunity, to make changes in career, or to make changes in your job itself. This placement also suggests fluctuations in earning power. If the Moon is making an aspect to a planet in your second, sixth or tenth house, it is also a good time to act.

Since I delineate the lunar return in a similar fashion to the solar return chart, I have highlighted my approach below. It was explained in detail in the solar return chapter. The similarities and distinctions of the solar return and lunar return delineation are as follows:

In a solar return chart, the Sun is the most important planet and it suggests where you will shine this year. In a lunar return chart, the Moon is the most important planet and it suggests opportunity for change in a particular month.

Look at the Ascendant for your personal approach to your career. For example, if the Ascendant is Aries you will probably work with energy and enthusiasm.

If you have a majority of planets in the first through sixth houses, you will be more private in terms of work, or recognition for your work, this particular month. It is not a time to try to achieve recognition, but may be a time to be patient and wait for recognition.

If you have more planets in your seventh through twelfth houses, this is a month where you will be more public with your work, or receive more recognition.

If you have more planets in the tenth through third houses, you will take more personal control over your career this month.

If you have more planets in the fourth through ninth houses, you will take less personal control over your career this month, but move steadily toward your career goals.

If the lunar return has a completely different motif from the solar return chart, this is the month to use the lunar return placements for advantageous motifs not found in the solar return. For example, suppose you want public recognition for your work and your solar return has a majority of planets in the first through sixth houses, so recognition may be challenging. But, you have a lunar return sometime during the year with a majority of planets in the seventh through twelfth houses. This would be the time to try to achieve public recognition. Let's say you have a small on-line business selling crafts to local businesses, and you wish to expand to national or international markets. Perhaps your solar return has a majority of planets in the first through sixth houses, and they are in fixed or mutable signs and/or houses. Suppose your lunar return chart has a majority of planets in your seventh through twelfth houses, and these planets are in cardinal signs and/or houses. That month would be the time to push forward with your expansion ideas. The lunar return can show you opportunities at certain times that you might not have with your natal or solar return charts.

Just as in the solar return chart, I look especially hard at Jupiter for opportunity, and Saturn for a place to work hard toward your goals.

The outer planets take on a more personal nature (just as they did with the solar return chart). Aspects the planets make to each other and to the Midheaven are important.

I look at the astrological signs on the cusps of the second, sixth and tenth houses, and then the rulers of the signs to see what other houses may add to career opportunity.

I find that planet placement in the houses slightly outweighs the astrological sign the planet is in, but not as much as in the Solar Return chart. Rather than looking at the house placement versus sign 80/20%, I look at it about 75/25%.

Look at the transiting Moon as it goes through each house this month. The transiting Moon is particularly helpful in indicating opportunity in a lunar return chart.

I use the lunar return in conjunction with the solar return by placing the solar return planets around the lunar return chart. This gives a comparison of monthly opportunity in light of the entire year's opportunity. Usually, sometime during the year, even when the solar return seems a little bleak regarding career, you can find a good time to act by using the lunar return chart.

Planets In Lunar Return Charts As They Pertain To Career

The **Sun** will suggest where there will be action and activity this month. The house the Sun is in is a good place to focus energy and accomplish a lot. If the Sun is in the second, sixth or tenth house, earning and career potential should be strong. If the Sun rules the sign on the cusp of the second, sixth or tenth house, it is also a month where a focus on your career would be beneficial. Remember, the Sun is where you will shine, so when relating to the second, sixth or tenth house, it is a time to shine in your work and career. Oftentimes, it is a month in which you will receive recognition for a job well done, or you will receive more responsibility, or a new project.

The **Moon** (as stated above) is the most important planet in a lunar return chart. The Moon suggests areas where emotional issues may occur. More importantly, in the lunar return, the Moon shows great potential for change. Thus, if the Moon sits in the second, sixth or tenth house, or if it rules the sign on the cusp of the second, sixth or tenth house, you will have opportunity for advancement, greater earning, or perhaps a complete change in what you are doing in your job or career.

As the Moon transits the lunar return chart, you have an opportunity to change with respect to whichever house it is transiting. Therefore, some time during the month should be a positive time to take action with regard to your career. If you have the Moon in the sixth house, and the transiting Moon sits in your second house, there is opportunity to increase your income, and this would be a good time to request a pay raise. If the transiting Moon is in the tenth house, it would be a good time to go after a promotion or plan a new career path.

The Moon suggests change in your position or earnings. In the sixth and tenth houses the Moon may suggest change within the company for which you work. For example, your company may move, merge with another, expand its interests and so forth.

Mercury in a lunar return chart suggests where you are mentally this month, and where communication will center. Thus, if Mercury sits in the second, sixth or tenth house, or rules the sign on the cusp of the second, sixth or tenth house, thoughts are probably of career, work and finances. You have the potential opportunity of a job offer of some type, or of business dealings. Mercury in either the sixth or tenth house suggests you will be very mentally active this month around work. Since this is a lunar return chart, I look at what opportunity for change is suggested by planets, not necessarily what they would mean sitting in one placement a whole year in your chart. Any offer you get will probably require a quick decision on your part. Since this is a chart for the month, you may have to act quickly. Actions upon your decision may be carried out further down the line, but the actual decision may have to be made this month.

Venus in your lunar return chart can suggest monetary change and where you may look for financial security. If your job is tense or overwhelming, Venus suggests a sense of relief for the month. If Venus is in your second, sixth or tenth house, it is an opportune time to increase your resources or salary. Again, act quickly since this chart is only for the month. ou can use this Venus placement to begin a process that can extend beyond the month to increase finances, but you must begin this month. Venus suggests a sense of wellbeing, and, if Venus occupies an earth house, any difficulties at work will be made easier.

Mars in the lunar return chart suggests areas where you will take the initiative, have a lot of energy, or be aggressive. Mars in the sixth or tenth house is a good time to begin a new project at work that will require extra energy, or a time to take on extra responsibility and impress your superiors. You should watch being overly aggressive. You may have tension around your finances if Mars is in the second house. On the other hand, this may be a time of active pursuit of money, extravagance, impulsive spending, or arguments with others about money. You must look to the sign Mars rules in your chart to see where opportunity may come from. For example, suppose Mars is in your tenth house, and the sign of Aries is on the cusp of your fifth house. That would suggest career opportunity may open up in the areas of speculation or perhaps an artistic or creative endeavor and that, whatever you do, it will be with great enthusiasm and energy.

Jupiter in the lunar return chart suggests where opportunity may open up this month. Jupiter in the second, sixth or tenth house suggests new opportunity or expansion of finances and your job or career. Again, this chart is for the month so you must make rapid decisions and act quickly to take advantage of the opportunity. Since the lunar return is the chart of change, with Jupiter in the second, sixth or tenth house, change in your finances, work or career should be expansive and you should have the potential for growth. Jupiter in the second house suggests improved finances. Unlike the solar return chart where Jupiter's placement suggests you have the entire year to expand, the lunar return Jupiter suggests the time to act is now, or at least start something during this month. Perhaps what you act upon will not be as big as if it were backed up by the solar return and natal chart placements, but you can start something and make gainful strides during a lunar return. It can be finished later but must be started now. On the other hand, if your solar return and natal Jupiter backs up your lunar return Jupiter, this is really an opportune month to expand.

Saturn in the lunar return chart suggests a place where you may incur obstacles this month. It is a place of hard work, possibly for rewards later on down the line. Saturn suggests an area of reality and down-to-earth situations. With regard to work, you must deal logically and reasonably with your options and limitations. If Saturn is in the second house, it may not be a time of financial excess but a time where hard work will earn you a living. Saturn in the sixth house can suggest stress from work conditions that may affect your health; you may need to rearrange your work priorities this month for future benefit, including less stress. Saturn in the tenth house suggests career advancement or career obstacles. A lot of Saturn suggestions seem karmic in that you reap the rewards or must begin something new. If you reap rewards, they are based on your actions and work of years past. Saturn here can suggest ending your career with retirement, or moving to another career. Whatever Saturn suggests, you must be responsible and attend to your career, or you will not receive the rewards you want down the line.

Uranus in a lunar return chart suggests change and surprise, fluctuation, or an event causing radical chaos this month. The change can be positive or negative, but it will be a surprise. If Uranus is in the second house you may have an unexpected problem with finances; for example, your roof collapses and it costs you a lot of money. Perhaps the company you work for announces a merger and the stock you have in the company's retirement plan dramatically increases. With Uranus, even if looking at the aspects, house it rules, etc., you often cannot tell where change will come from or what it might be. Since this chart is for one month, it often may be one big occurrence creating a positive or negative cash flow. Uranus in the sixth house can suggest an unexpected change around work or colleagues. Whatever the changes, this month will be exciting, ground-breaking, or it can be just plain chaotic. You achieve more independence or learn new technology. Uranus in the tenth house suggests the unexpected in your career this month. Uranus is unpredictable, and again the changes can be positive or negative. But these unexpected occurrences in the lunar return are often single events affecting this month only. If Uranus is conjunct the Moon, there may be more permanent change.

Neptune in the lunar return chart suggests areas which may be confused, uncertain, or in which your intuition could be a great asset. Thus, if Neptune sits in the second, sixth or tenth house, you might feel uncertain about your job this month or uncertain about your earnings. You may be very intuitive around work and able to recognize potential problems before they start, or you could invest some earnings on a hunch that pays a quick dividend. If you are experiencing uncertainty, the lunar return is only for a month and things should start to clear up next month, so this is not as bad as having Neptune uncertainty all year in the solar return chart. Perhaps you are getting a new supervisor and are unsure of what he/she expects from you. Obviously, this would be cleared up in the near future. Neptune in the sixth house suggests you just may not feel like working this month, and this would be a good time to have planned a vacation, or planned activities dealing with art, beauty, and spiritual matters. Neptune in the tenth house is a time to use instinct, to help solve career differences, and to avoid feelings of doubt in your career.

Pluto is the planet of transformation in the lunar return chart. Since it is for the month, Pluto suggests a place you can begin transformation, but not necessarily that a transformation will take place within the month's period of time. On the other hand, if you have been working toward change or transformation in your career, and Pluto is in the second, sixth or tenth house, this may be the time where something acts as a catalyst to create the change that you have been working toward. A Moon/Pluto aspect suggests a start of some transformation this month that will be completed later on. Control may also be an issue this month with regard to your finances or to activity at work. There may be a power issue between you and others, or between others, that affects you this month. Since this is a lunar return and for only one month, it is better to let things be than get caught up in short-term battles. Look at the "big picture"—not just this one month.

Sarah's Lunar Return
See figure 15 on page 153.

Sarah has Aquarius on her lunar return Ascendant, suggesting she will have an individualistic approach to her career the month she begins work. Her new job is in accounting, and computer work is a good field for someone with Aquarian motifs. However, she is probably already looking for a new approach to what she may consider a mundane job. She may also be looking for new technology to make her job more exciting.

    Sarah has Saturn in her first house, suggesting hard work and a slow but steady nature. Saturn here indicates her sense of responsibility and doing what she must do, versus doing what she would prefer to do (i.e., continue as a full-time mother). With Saturn here, she will concentrate on her new job, but she may not go for the job she would really want for fear of not getting it, or fear of something too new. Saturn is in Pisces, suggesting Sarah is restructuring her fantasies or dreams, becoming more practical in her approach at this time. With Saturn square her Sun in the tenth house, Sarah is experiencing personal conflict about going back to work and personal difficulty or hard work.

    Sarah has Pisces on the cusp of her second house of money and personal values. Pisces is ruled by Neptune in her twelfth house. This would bring a lot of subconscious motivation, plus artistic, imaginative, compassionate, idealistic, and inspirational motifs into the type of job Sarah would like, as well as possible generational themes. Thus, a job in accounting probably does not appeal to Sarah as much as something else. Since she is working for the school system and has the same hours as her children, the job coincides with her personal motivations. Also, if you look at the twelfth house as the derivative third house to Sarah's career, this placement suggests she can work in lower education or the school system.

The next planet we come to is the Moon in the fifth house of creativity and children. The Moon suggests which area of life is changing. In Sarah's case, her life with her children is drastically changing. She has gone from being a full-time mother to a working mother with much less time to spend with her family. The Moon also suggests that the children need some special attention to adjust to the situation. The Moon here also can indicate romance, but in Sarah's case (and because of the conflict with her husband), I feel it strongly suggests emotions and a changing environment for her children. The Moon and Cancer suggest the nurturer. With this placement, it appears as though Sarah really does prefer, at this time, to remain the nurturer at home.

Sarah has Cancer on the cusp of her sixth house of work and again Cancer is ruled by the Moon in the fifth house. Thus Sarah's house of work reflects the change forced upon her children and also suggests her children are of prime concern over any job Sarah would accept. Again, she took a job which probably did not pay as much as other jobs, but had very good benefits (that her family needed since her spouse was not working), and that had the same hours as her children.

The next planet we come to is Mars in Leo in the seventh house of partnerships and marriage. Mars is square the Sun on the cusp of the tenth house of career and semisquare (45°—half a square) the Moon. Mars here suggests tension with the marriage, and also that Sarah's husband will push her to do things she may not want to do this month, i.e., her new job. Her spouse is a strong motivational part of her life this month. His influence may be positive or negative. In Sarah's case, she feels his influence is negative at this time. In the long run, since other charts indicate her job is the start of a career which will go much farther, the outcome should be positive.

At this time, Mars suggests conflict and tension almost on a daily basis. Sarah must be careful not to let this tension filter into other areas of her life, such as her new job. It truly may be a difficult month. Mars in Leo suggests a lot of energy and the possibility of a fiery explosion with her spouse. Mars is square Sarah's Sun on the cusp of the tenth house suggesting conflict with her partner versus her career. But with regard to her career, even with a square aspect, the Mars/Sun aspect suggests a great deal of personal

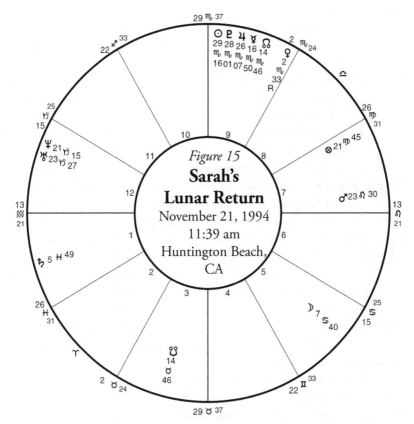

Figure 15
Sarah's
Lunar Return
November 21, 1994
11:39 am
Huntington Beach,
CA

energy and success in her career as long as Sarah does not let tension and anger waste this energy.

This Mars placement seems to be very significant in Sarah's career, and reinforces the delineation of both her natal and solar return charts. Mars is semisquare the Moon in the fifth house, suggesting the emotional tension around Sarah's children and Sarah's very frustrating position at this time. The Moon in the fifth house (representing her very nurturing nature), semisquare Mars (drive and energy) seems to represent a very personal dichotomy in feelings for Sarah. Also Mars/Moon aspects may suggest an affair which was also a possibility at this time, as described with her natal and solar return charts.

Sarah has a grand trine between the Moon, Venus and Saturn, tying in her personal obstacles, hard work with her children, and higher conscious philosophies in the ninth house. Venus, as part of the trine, suggests teamwork and potential pleasure in work. This is a benefit that helps lighten the load a little.

There is a heavy emphasis on water planets. This suggests Sarah is having a terribly emotional month, and her actions are ruled by her emotions. She will probably not be able to react in a logical manner. These emotions mainly deal with herself and hard work (Saturn in the first house in Pisces), her children (the Moon in the fifth house in Cancer), and her higher consciousness and life philosophies (all the planets in the ninth house in Scorpio). Sarah probably feels emotionally overwhelmed and unable to cope. I would strongly recommend counseling to guide Sarah through this very difficult time. The preponderance of water as much as anything else in her natal and solar return charts suggests how truly difficult this time is and how much potential there is for Sarah's emotions to run amok. Saturn in her first house suggests personal rigidity and Saturn has its work cut out for it in helping Sarah remain stable enough to start a new job.

There is also a stellium of planets (Venus, Mercury, Jupiter, Pluto, the Sun, and the North Node) in the cadent ninth house which suggests indecision, scattered energy and difficulty coping with change. Sarah really needs to have time for herself, which she is not getting. As a counselor, I would suggest she take time to meditate, exercise, or talk to someone so she has some release.

Since Venus deals with love and relationships, its placement in the ninth house suggests Sarah is questioning her feelings and beliefs about her relationship, or they are changing in some way. This is coupled with Mars in the seventh house, so her marriage problems at this time appear to be very difficult and suggest a change in her higher conscious outlook on life. This is supported by her solar return and natal charts. Venus could be a desire for more or better, as demonstrated when Sarah called someone from her past. It also suggests reconciling her relationship with her husband in her own mind, as she eventually did.

The North Node in the ninth house suggests Sarah may seek higher education to further her career. Mercury here could mean a time to go back to school for further education, or perhaps a teaching situation. Although Sarah is not a teacher, she is working in a school and has a lot of contact with the students, such as working at the evening football games and collecting money for such things as class photos or yearbooks. But, more importantly, although Sarah did not recognize it during this lunar return, she did realize later that she needed to go back to school .

Jupiter here suggests Sarah may be looking for something spiritual to relieve the tension. A time of daily meditation would be a great help to her. Jupiter here also suggests that her higher consciousness is opening and developing, and it helps Sarah to draw from a higher realm of energy to deal with her problems. It is beneficial for Sarah during this very difficult month. Jupiter here is a good balance for the Saturn in the first house. Sarah has both the ability to work hard toward goals, and the frame of mind and expansion of ideas to succeed. Jupiter here also suggests that Sarah will soon realize the need for more education and plan to go back to school, which she has subsequently done.

Pluto in the ninth house suggests a time of transformation of beliefs and a time of learning. It is conjunct the Midheaven, so career will be an influence. Pluto is conjunct the Sun, so it is very personal for Sarah. Since it is her spouse who is "forcing" change upon her, her transformation is probably most obvious in her interaction with her husband. During this time of change there will probably be a great deal of tension. This is an even stronger suggestion with Mars in the seventh house. The Sun rules the seventh house of partnerships and is conjunct Pluto— suggesting power struggles and joint resources issues. The Sun conjunct Jupiter suggests the importance of long-range goals and values. Pluto here suggests a time of learning, no matter what the source of the lessons, in order for Sarah's higher consciousness to evolve. Because Pluto and the Sun are conjunct the Midheaven and the cusp of the tenth house of career, it is the change in career (or the start of a new career) that is the catalyst for an evolving higher consciousness.

The stellium of planets in the ninth house can also suggest travel or interaction with foreign persons or foreign matters, education, law and religion. That is not the case for Sarah. You must know a person's circumstances in order to be an effective astrological counselor. In Sarah's case, especially with the Sun, Pluto, and Jupiter, the job starts a process wherein she will seek higher education to work in an area which she feels will be helpful to mankind, and which suits her ideals.

The Moon indicated change with her children and their pattern of existence, but the Sun is where Sarah will shine this month, and it is on the cusp of her tenth house of career.

Pluto, the Sun and Jupiter are conjunct at the Midheaven which suggests striving for objectives and an advancement of one's position, or a career crisis. In Sarah's case it was a little of both: a new position or advancement in terms of a new career, and a crisis actually caused by career (going back to work) in terms of her relationship with her husband, and the emotions around leaving her children to work. It is definitely a "double-edged sword."

The Sun is square Mars and Saturn. The Sun conjunct the cusp of the tenth house is a wonderful placement to start a new job. It suggests a very strong, energetic start to a new career this month. It implies Sarah will have positive feelings about her abilities, and she will have control over her career decisions. Although she was pushed into going back to work, she did control the type of job she took—a job with the same hours as her children and one with excellent benefits for her family.

With the Sun conjunct the cusp of the tenth house, if you are working, you will usually advance. If not, you will shine somewhere in your life. If you start a new career as Sarah did, you will shine there. With the Sun here, Sarah will be recognized by her superiors for her hard work and abilities. The Sun placement also suggests strong parental influence over Sarah's choice of career. Sarah came from a very large family and her parents did not fight, so her stress in leaving children and the tension and arguments with her spouse were very difficult in light of this family background. But this background was a major influence in the type of job she chose, one that would least affect her children's lives. The Sun here is very positive for a new career. The Sun is square Mars in the seventh house showing the tension Sarah has with her husband pushing her back to work, and it is square Saturn in the first house, also suggesting personal guilt in going back to work. But Sun/Mars, even in square, show Sarah has the energy needed for her new position, and Saturn symbolizes personal hard work toward her goals.

Neptune and Uranus are conjunct in the twelfth house. Neptune is semisquare Saturn and conjunct Uranus which is quincunx Mars. This is a pretty heavy twelfth house. Neptune here suggests confusion or unclear thinking on a subconscious level and may lead to anxiety. While Sarah's higher consciousness (represented by the ninth house) seems to be expanding and coming into its own, Neptune here suggests that emotionally, she is very troubled and anxious. This is a time of sensitivity and intuition. This month, Sarah will probably have fleeting moments of feeling she knows what to do and which way to go, and then times of confusion and indecision.

Uranus here suggests a time of radical changes on a subconscious or core belief level. This may be caused by an event which shakes your world and sends you in a different direction. For Sarah this very different direction was going back to work well before she felt it was healthy for her children. She is probably reevaluating on a very subconscious level. This also suggests secrets and occurrences behind the scenes: perhaps secret planning for the future and a way out of her current circumstance, or perhaps an affair. You can see that Neptune conjunct Uranus here is quite challenging.

Neptune is semisquare Saturn, so Sarah is experiencing anxiety on a personal level and is confused. With Neptune in the twelfth house and Saturn in the first house, there is considerable conflict with the ideal versus the real. Neptune would like to dream, meditate, and seek beauty and solitude or compassionate pursuits, while Saturn in the first house suggests that Sarah needs to work.

Uranus quincunx Mars suggests she is experiencing radical change because of her spouse and is probably building deep subconscious resentment or gaining deep subconscious strength. Mars/Uranus wants to break free and may feel trapped. Independent action would be a healthy expression of this aspect. Sarah's lunar return is very difficult regarding family, but a very promising chart for her future career. It reinforces her natal and solar return charts.

I feel the stellium of planets, the Sun conjunct the Midheaven, the preponderance of water and the Moon in the fifth house all quite accurately point to Sarah's situation this month.

If you place Sarah's solar return planets around her lunar return chart this month (*see Figure 15a on the next page*), you will see her solar return Mars sits in the sixth house of work and service and trine her lunar return Sun, which is conjunct the cusp of the tenth house. This is very beneficial and suggests a lot of energy, drive and ambition to succeed.

The solar return Midheaven sits in the lunar return seventh house suggesting her spouse is pushing her toward career. Midheaven opposing Saturn in the first house reflects Sarah's personal conflict with career and going back to work. The solar return Moon also sits in the seventh house of partnerships and trines the lunar return Neptune and Uranus suggesting deep emotional changes, on a subconscious level, relating to marriage and partnership.

Solar return Sun sits in the eighth house of government and Sarah works for the school system (the government) so she would personally shine at work. The eighth house also represents joint resources and Sarah went to work because her family needed the money. Since the lunar return Sun is conjunct the cusp of the tenth house of career, this suggestion of personal achievement is very strong.

Sarah's solar return Ascendant is conjunct, to the degree, her lunar

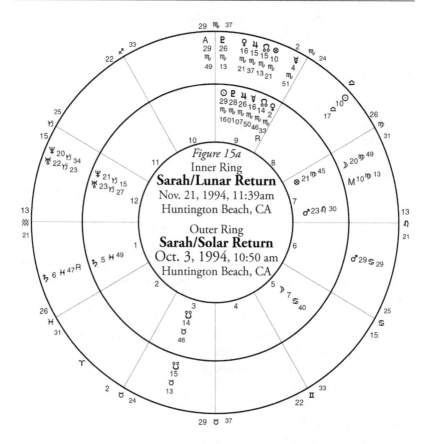

Figure 15a
Inner Ring
Sarah/Lunar Return
Nov. 21, 1994, 11:39am
Huntington Beach, CA

Outer Ring
Sarah/Solar Return
Oct. 3, 1994, 10:50 am
Huntington Beach, CA

return Sun which is conjunct the cusp of the tenth house of career. This
is a very strong suggestion of personal effort and success with her career.
This is a very positive combination to begin a new job. Sarah was able to
personally choose a job that, if she had to go back to work, created the least
personal conflict for her. If she had to go back to work this year, this was
the month to do it.

The transiting Moon on the day Sarah began her new job was conjunct solar return Mercury in the ninth house, (see Figure 15b on the next
page) suggesting Sarah's higher consciousness and philosophical changes
brought about by her new position. The transiting Moon is also three degrees
past lunar return Venus. She began her new job so close to her birthday
that, with regard to transits, the Moon is the only planet of real significance.

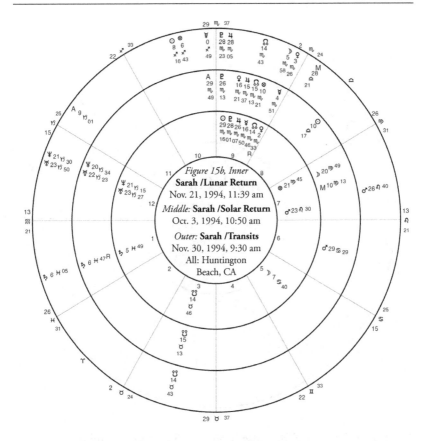

Figure 15b, Inner
Sarah /Lunar Return
Nov. 21, 1994, 11:39 am
Middle: **Sarah /Solar Return**
Oct. 3, 1994, 10:50 am
Outer: **Sarah /Transits**
Nov. 30, 1994, 9:30 am
All: Huntington
Beach, CA

John's Lunar Return

John's Lunar Return chart is figure 16 on page 160.

John has a Capricorn Ascendant in his lunar return chart suggesting a down-to-earth, businesslike approach to his career. Capricorn is ruled by Saturn in the fifth house implying John will be creative in his approach, as well as work hard. It also suggests a personal desire to work with children.

With John's six planets in the seventh through twelfth houses and four planets in the first through sixth houses he should receive recognition for his work this month. His planets are divided evenly between his tenth through third houses and his fourth through ninth houses suggesting he will work steadily on his own, but also listen to others with regard to his career.

Since this is a lunar return chart, I start with the Moon placement. The Moon indicates change and its placement is very important. The Moon

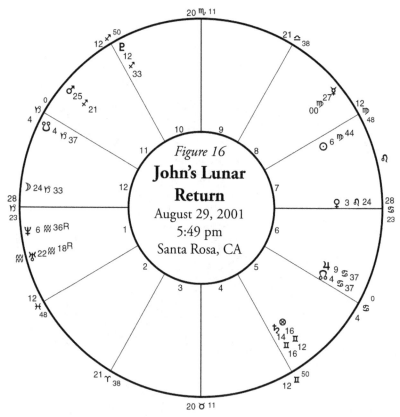

20 ♏ 11

12 ♐ 50

♇ 12 ♐ 33

♂ 25 ♐ 21

0 ♑

4

☊ 4 ♑ 37

21 ♎ 38

♍ 27 ☿
00 ♍   12 ♍ 48

☉ 6 ♍ 44

10   9

11   *Figure 16*
**John's Lunar
Return**
August 29, 2001
5:49 pm
Santa Rosa, CA

8

7

♀ 3 ♌ 24

♌

12

28
♑
23

☽ 24 ♑ 33

♆ 6 ♒ 36R

♅ 22 ♒ 18R

28
♋
23

6

5

♃ 9 ♋ 37
☊ 4 ♋ 37

2

3   4

12 ♓ 48

21 ♈ 38

20 ♉ 11

0
♋

4

♄ 16
14 ♊
♊ 12
16

⊗

12 ♊ 50

is sitting in John's twelfth house conjunct his Ascendant and trine Mercury in the eighth house.

First of all, the Moon is in Capricorn and conjunct John's Capricorn Ascendant suggesting personal insight into what he is doing careerwise. Because the Moon is in Capricorn, the emotions and fluctuation usually indicated by the Moon are somewhat stabilized. With the Moon in Capricorn in the twelfth house, John may not yet be able to express his feelings to others regarding his new position as a counselor, or his feelings about this may change within this position. Since the Moon is conjunct his Ascendant, this suggestion is very strong. John does not yet know how to best communicate in his new situation, so he may suppress some feelings around new superiors and co-workers. With the Moon here, John will likely be very sensitive to those children whom he is counseling.

The Moon is trine Mercury in the eighth house of government and therapy, and again John is working for the government (the school system), as counselor. This trine suggests easy adjustment to his new job. Moon in the derivative third house of lower education to John's tenth house of career also indicates the change to his new job in elementary education. The job includes a lot of communication—symbolized by the third house. You can see already, by just this one example, how important the Moon can be in a lunar return chart with regard to career. John's Moon placement alone suggests change in the area of career and lower education and a lot of communication. Moon trine Mercury (in the house of government) correlates with John's work for a government entity, the school system.

Neptune and Uranus are in John's first house showing insight, intuition, chaos or originality. Neptune here suggests commitment of ideals to what John undertakes but, as with his other charts, he must watch being drained of energy, and of taking on the problems of those he counsels or those around him. Neptune opposite Venus in the seventh house suggests personal concerns regarding finances and financial security with his spouse. Uranus here suggests dramatic changes personally and in John's lifestyle. Since John is beginning his career, the changes are pretty obvious.

Uranus also indicates a desire for freedom and independent work as was also suggested in John's other charts. Uranus is square the Midheaven showing tension between his career right now and his desire to work independently. This also sounds very much like John's solar return and natal charts. Also, this Neptune/Uranus placement suggests unusual or chaotic events happening. As you recall from the delineation of the natal and solar return charts, John arrived on the first day of his new job to face an angry group of parents picketing the school, and the principal placed him in the position of defusing the situation.

There are no planets in the second house of money, but the cusp is Pisces which is ruled by Neptune. Neptune sits in the first house in Aquarius. This suggests it is John's personal effort this month that brings him rewards and affords him a position to earn money. Neptune in Aquarius indicates an unusual personal approach and also suggests that intuition could contribute to earning and to any job he will do. His far-reaching ideas and personal values will help John advance. John will be happy and fulfilled with a job that he feels is beneficial to mankind, but must be left to work on his own.

The next planet we come to is Saturn in the fifth house. Saturn suggests hard work and lessons to learn. Saturn is in Gemini representing mental hard work. It is opposite Pluto in the tenth house of career, implying a lot of mental energy expended with regard to career, and also indicating that John may butt heads with superiors. Saturn is ses-quiquadrate (or sesquisquare) to the Ascendant, indicating personal hard work. Saturn in the fifth house suggests an element of practicality to John's creative solutions.

The cusp of the sixth house of work is Cancer ruled by the Moon. First of all, Cancer suggests John may seek a nurturing role this month, and he did, as a counselor helping children. The Moon in the twelfth house in Capricorn shows that John may feel emotionally responsible toward his work and will be organized and thorough. Counseling would then fulfill his sense of responsibility. This placement implies John may seek a connection to others and be very sensitive; again, a strong suggestion that counseling is a good field to choose this month.

Jupiter is in the sixth house of work and service suggesting new opportunity and this is quite appropriate since John has a new job. Jupiter symbolizes expansion so it represents greater duties than John probably anticipated. He is working in two schools rather than just one, so his duties are expanded. Jupiter here implies joy in working, and is a very beneficial placement with which to begin a career.

Since Jupiter is quincunx Pluto in the tenth house of career, it suggests John may have too much work. Jupiter also suggests John wants freedom to work as he chooses. This may create some conflict with superiors, so he must be tactful. Jupiter here can indicate weight gain which is certainly possible with a desk job, so John should be encouraged to exercise for mental relief and for health.

Venus and the Sun are both in the seventh house of contracts and partnership. The Sun is where John will shine, and he did sign a contract for his job. With Venus here, the contract should be rewarding. Both the Sun and Venus here suggest the new contractual relationship is very important. Also, this is the derivative second house of money to the sixth house of work, so it appears his job is financially stable and John will be rewarded. The Sun is square Pluto in the tenth house, again suggesting personal difficulty with conforming to work. Pluto in Sagittarius suggests that John will want personal freedom in his career.

Mercury sits in John's eighth house in Virgo trine the Moon in the twelfth house, trine the Ascendant, square Mars in the eleventh house. Mercury in the eighth house suggests a lot of insight and an awareness of psychological issues—a good placement for counseling. It is a placement that suggests you will seek counseling or counsel others. A Mercury/Mars aspect can indicate quick thinking and assertiveness, or at its worst, aggressiveness and anger. Since the aspect is a square, John must concentrate on using his quick mind and not becoming frustrated or angry. Mercury/Moon suggests a blend of emotions and intellect, or it could be emotional thinking. Since Mercury and Moon are trine, there is a blend of emotions and intellect that is also an excellent placement to begin counseling. Again, Mercury is in the eighth house of government and John works for the school system. Mercury here also represents thoughts and planning regarding joint finances. Since this is John's first job in his career, there is extra money to plan for the future with his wife.

Scorpio is on the cusp of the tenth house, ruled by Pluto in Sagittarius. Pluto is also in the tenth house suggesting (again) that John, at the onset of his career, will seek reformation in his profession based on his ideals. It indicates that John desires control over his career, even at its outset, and will be very dedicated. Pluto also suggests John's career will deal with groups of people. Scorpio is co-ruled by Mars which sits in John's eleventh house of dreams, wishes, groups and social causes. This implies that John's dreams this month deal with his career and working with groups of people, again a very good placement for a counselor.

The next planet we come to is Pluto in the tenth house in Sagittarius suggesting John will personally try to reform and reorganize his career to his own ideals and standards. Since Pluto is square the Sun it will probably be an uphill battle, but he will probably work very hard to do so.

Pluto in the tenth house suggests a destiny or career move. Since John is beginning his career, this Pluto placement is quite good. While John's career is changing externally, Pluto here also suggests he is probably changing internally as well. A caveat with Pluto in the tenth house is power struggles, and the Sun square Pluto suggests this may be personally difficult for John. He actually did try to stay out of a power struggle between two superiors, and had a difficult time not getting dragged into it. Pluto here suggests both career and personal choices this month.

Mars is in Sagittarius in the eleventh house and square Mercury. Mars here implies a lot of drive and energy geared toward John's hopes and wishes for the future, and, in Sagittarius, suggests an idealism associated with this drive. Mars in Sagittarius symbolizes a strong desire for freedom to pursue goals as he wishes. Although the goals are very personal, with Mars in the eleventh house, they involve others. In John's case, the others are the children he counsels. Also, Mars is square Mercury in the eighth house of government, again suggesting John's ideals and goals may conflict with the established system.

John's lunar return chart seems to reinforce both his solar return and natal charts. When we put the solar return planets around the lunar return chart (see Figure 16a on page 159) we can see the interface of the year's forecast with the current month's forecast. The lunar return can enhance the solar return or it may be at odds with it. The lunar return may suggest opportunity not apparent in the solar return chart.

Of course, the slower moving planets will remain pretty much the same, but the solar return luminaries, the faster moving planets, and the Ascendant and Midheaven are places to look for contacts with the lunar return chart.

John's solar return Midheaven sits in his first house suggesting this is a month of tremendous personal effort toward career that will help John to achieve recognition. It is trine lunar return Saturn, suggesting personal hard work and creativity since Saturn is in the fifth house. Since Saturn is one of the planets I look at in terms of career, it suggests the personal start of a lot of work toward John's ultimate goals. The lunar return Saturn/solar return Midheaven trine suggests a lot of drive and also the ability to push others to success which is good for a counselor. The solar return Midheaven is square the lunar return Midheaven, again implying that John will have a personal struggle *vis-à-vis* career, or have to expend excessive energy to get where he wants to go, or struggle with rules and/or authority figures.

Solar return Venus sits in the lunar return second house of money suggesting a financial benefit or increase. For John, this increase came with his new job.

The solar return Sun, Mercury and the Moon all sit in the third house of lower education and communication. John's new job is in elementary education and the Sun suggests this is where he will shine this month (and this year). Mercury here represents a tremendous amount of talking, thinking and communication, and the Moon brings in an element of sensitivity and also changes of circumstances. This pretty much sums up John's activity as a new counselor. The solar return Moon is square the lunar return Uranus in the first house and opposite lunar return Midheaven, both suggesting personal frustration with some part of the job, as well as with the administration and the fact that John wants to work in a secondary school. The Sun, Moon and Mercury in the third house suggest a level mind in balance between emotions, intellect and subconscious motivations. It indicates a strong mind for counseling. The solar return Sun is square lunar return Venus in the seventh house of contracts, and again, John did not get the contract he really wanted in sec-

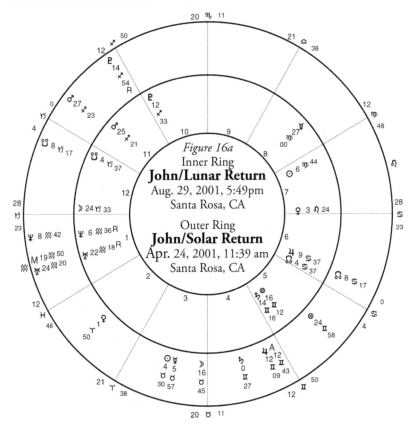

Figure 16a
Inner Ring
John/Lunar Return
Aug. 29, 2001, 5:49pm
Santa Rosa, CA

Outer Ring
John/Solar Return
Apr. 24, 2001, 11:39 am
Santa Rosa, CA

ondary school. Also, the solar return Sun squares Neptune in the first house indicating that John may over-idealize what he wants or be overly sensitive. However, that sensitivity should work well for him as a school counselor.

The solar return Saturn, Jupiter and Ascendant are in the lunar return fourth house. Saturn and Jupiter together suggest realization of goals and combined with the Ascendant suggest a change or new occupation or job. Since these planets sit in the fourth house, it appears the new job may be based on foundational values. As you recall from the natal chart and the solar return chart, I feel John's choice of occupation had a great deal to do with his foundation and family. Again, Jupiter and Saturn are the two planets I really look at in terms of career. Saturn itself suggests John will feel more responsibility for the home which seems true since he is now contributing a full-time income to the home. Jupiter here suggests expansion of security in the home, the security of a full-time career position.

Figure 16b, Inner
John /Lunar Return
Aug. 29, 2001, 5:49 pm
Middle: **John /Solar Return**
April 24, 2001, 8:29 am
Outer: **John /Transits**
Sept. 4, 2001, 9:00 am
All: Santa Rosa, CA

Solar return Pluto is in the eleventh house conjunct lunar return Pluto. Since John's solar return this year, Pluto has moved from the tenth house to the eleventh house suggesting transformation of wishes for the future and also work dealing with groups. It is opposite Saturn again representing hard work and the beginning of work toward a goal.

The placements that really point to John's career and the new job are the solar return Midheaven sitting in the lunar return first house bringing personal effort to career and the solar return Sun, Mercury and Moon in the lunar return third house of lower education where John began his new job. John's lunar return is enhancing his solar return career opportunities.

When we look at the transits the day John began his new job (see Figure 16b above), we again look at the luminaries and faster moving planets. The transiting Moon is in the second house conjunct to the exact degree solar return Venus suggesting change in income. Since it is conjunct

Venus, it suggests an increase in income.

Transiting Saturn is in the fifth house bringing hard work into creativity or with children. The Midheaven is conjunct the North Node and Jupiter in the sixth house of work and service, obviously suggesting the career opportunity opening up with John's new job. The Ascendant and Mercury have moved to the eighth house of government and psychotherapy, and John is working for the government as a counselor. Pluto is again in the tenth house suggesting a career with large groups and for the benefit of generations. The transits also heavily suggest a new career.

Carole's Lunar Return
See figure 17 on page 163.

Carole's lunar return Ascendant is Libra suggesting partnership or a balanced approach to anything she tackles this month, including career. It suggests a personal love of beauty and art and a career choice may be either to work around the arts or to be in a better financial position to acquire that which is beautiful. Libra here suggests a gracious attitude. Libra is ruled by Venus which sits in the lunar return tenth house of career, so a career choice is suggested with this Ascendant.

Mars is in the first house in Libra. Mars in the first house suggests a lot of personal drive and energy, and it is conjunct the Ascendant. Mars is sextile Venus in the tenth house, again bringing personal recognition and career into play. Mars here implies Carole will be more inclined to do what she would like to do this month. The Mars energy helps attain goals and in the first house goals are likely to be involved with self or self-realization. This is a very good placement for the short-term job Carole took, helping her feel a lot like her old self, but not really leaving her children for a full-time career. Mars is in a cardinal house, and very strong action on a personal level is suggested. It is in Libra indicating Carole weighed her decision carefully but was eventually decisive.

The second house cusp is Scorpio. Scorpio is co-ruled by Pluto in the second house and Mars in the first house. Pluto is conjunct the Moon and trine Saturn in the sixth house.

Since this is a lunar return chart, the outer planets, which include Pluto, take on a more personal nature, and in the second house suggest changes associated with self-worth and with personal income. Mars in the first house suggests Carole's personal effort and drive will be involved with finances and self-worth. Again, this short-term job both helped Carole feel good about herself and increased her finances. The Moon indicates change and also sits in Carole's second house. Aside from the obvious fluctuation, and in Carole's case, increase in finances, more important is the change in feelings of self-worth and being able to work in an area that Carole missed for a number of years. The Moon here suggests Carole needs to know that she can create her own financial security, so this job was helpful. The Moon trines Saturn in the sixth house of work, symbolizing hard but rewarding work. Remember, Saturn is where growth starts, so work this month is a good start.

Jupiter is in the third house and suggests expansion of daily activities as would be the case in going back to work. It is the expansion of mental processes, and perhaps overscheduling. It may be hard to concentrate at times. Jupiter here suggests decisions which may include choices regarding how you live your life. In Carole's case, this would be the decision about whether to go back to work, and whether it was okay to leave her children for a short time. Even though she had live-in help and her husband worked from home, it was still a major, soul-searching decision for a mother to make, and not an easy decision for Carole. (I feel this decision was probably best for her.)

Jupiter is in Sagittarius and suggests a mental desire for some freedom. In Carole's case, that was the freedom to work a little. Jupiter is trine Venus in the tenth house of career indicating mental expansion toward career, and it is trine the Sun in the eleventh house of wishes for the future, so this job may be a stepping stone toward future jobs and goals.

Neptune and Uranus are conjunct in the fourth house. Neptune suggests confusion or uncertainty around the home. It may mean some type of relocation but in Carole's case, since it is sextile Saturn in the sixth house of work and service, it seems to suggest the uncertainty of home conditions in light of Carole taking this short-term job. Uranus here suggests chaotic change and disruption at home, and this also seems to be the case with Carole working. It also suggests potential emotional disruption. Family members may be moody and express their unhappiness. Everyone's actions tend to be unpredictable. All of these suggestions seem likely since many children do not like to see their mothers go back to work. However, this chart is only for the month. After the initial chaos, I feel everyone will adjust and grow positively even if this month is difficult. Remember, in the delineation of Carole's natal and solar return charts, it appears to be a positive, growing experience for the children since

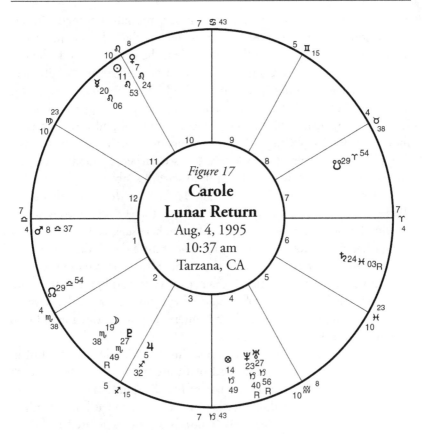

Figure 17
Carole
Lunar Return
Aug, 4, 1995
10:37 am
Tarzana, CA

Carole is only taking a short-term job. They are well cared for, and they can begin to get a sense of independence while Carole is fulfilled as her own person.

The sixth house has Pisces on the cusp and it is ruled by Neptune in the fourth house. Again, work is influenced by home conditions and I would suggest Carole consciously try not to worry too much about the temporary confusion and chaos at home while she is working.

Saturn is in the sixth house of work and health suggesting Carole should watch her health due to overwork and related stress. Saturn here also suggests dealing with the realities of work, which Carole did when she went back to work. Saturn suggests hard work. Saturn is trine the Moon and Pluto in the second house suggesting rewards for her hard work. Saturn here also suggests Carole is laying a foundation for future work.

The tenth house has Cancer on the cusp. Cancer is ruled by the Moon in the second house of money and personal values. It suggests a positive change in finances. Cancer is also the nurturer, and Carole's family still remains the most important job she has, despite any career opportunity she may have at this time. Venus here implies good relationships with your superiors and working with your superiors for advancement. It is a very positive placement to begin or grow careerwise. This is another indication that this short-term job may be a stepping stone for future employment. Venus in Leo suggests work around theater, arts or movies. Again, Carole is a production accountant on an independent movie. This placement also reinforces what we have seen in her natal and solar return charts. This is definitely a good month to start this job.

Carole has both the Sun and Mercury in the eleventh house. This symbolizes clear thought patterns and that Carole is consciously considering her hopes for the future. The Sun here suggests Carole is evaluating what is right for her with regard to her future. With the Sun here, it is a time to act. Freedom to do as she wishes is a major issue and concern for Carole. The eleventh house is the derivative second house to the tenth house of career, so Carole's job should be well funded. Since the eleventh house also has to do with friends, it is interesting that it was a friend who offered Carole the short-term job.

Mercury in the eleventh house implies Carole may be thinking of some personal freedom and of future goals. Since the eleventh house concerns social situations, part of her thoughts may turn to social views of her as the "working mother" versus the "stay-at-home mother" (although in today's society this is not as strong as it used to be). It is helpful to let Carole know this is a good time to experience a little freedom and to allow her children to grow a little also, even if they are young. This is a good time for Carole to reevaluate what she wants for the future, and the short-term job experience can help her make that decision. Does she want to work part-time, work on projects, have a full-time career, or be at home and work full-time in her role as mother? It is really her decision and there is no right or wrong decision, just what she feels is personally right for her and her family.

Now place Carole's solar return planets around her lunar return chart to compare opportunity for the year to opportunity this month. (See Fig. 17a on the next page).

Carole's solar return Midheaven is conjunct the lunar return Mars in the first house suggesting success and advancement in career this month. The solar return Midheaven also sextiles the Lunar Return Sun and Venus, suggesting strong personal career potential.

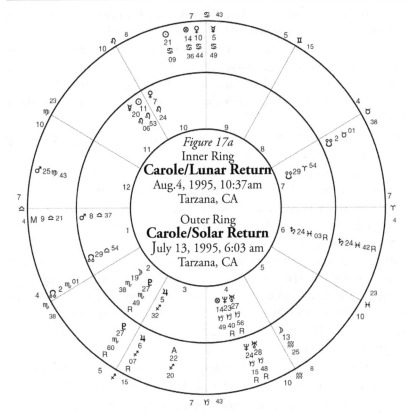

Figure 17a
Inner Ring
Carole/Lunar Return
Aug.4, 1995, 10:37am
Tarzana, CA

Outer Ring
Carole/Solar Return
July 13, 1995, 6:03 am
Tarzana, CA

The solar return Ascendant is in the third house of communication representing a month of logical thinking and communication, and personally dealing with communication, as well as increased daily activity. This is a good placement for any kind of mental work. The solar return Ascendant in the lunar return third house implies Carole has lots of thoughts about what she is personally doing.

The solar return Moon sits in the lunar return fifth house symbolizing emotions around the children and also intuition and nurturing capabilities to handle any problems.

This solar return Moon squares the lunar return Moon in the second house again suggesting the children will be emotional about Carole working. It also indicates an emotional fluctuation in her personal values as she allows herself to go to work.

The solar return Moon in the lunar return fifth house is opposite the lunar return Venus in the tenth house again showing the stress and emotions with the children stemming from career pursuit.

The solar return Moon is trine the lunar return Ascendant and Mars indicating personal creativity and intuition with the job.

Both the solar return Venus and the solar return Sun sit in the lunar return tenth house suggesting this is a good month for a new career and for recognition for her work. With the Sun trine Saturn in the house of work and service it implies that work may be hard, but is beneficial.

The solar return Sun is opposite Uranus and Neptune, again showing the push and pull of home versus the job.

Solar return Mars in the twelfth house suggests inner tension and opposes Saturn in Pisces in the sixth house, suggesting work may be a source of inner tension, and also that Carole should watch for health problems due to stress. Also, there may be drugs around work (this was also suggested in delineation of her natal and solar return charts). Mars/Saturn suggests a need for planning and structure around work or around going to work so Mars energy is not wasted but is used efficiently to get things done. Frustration can be a result of a Mars/Saturn aspect. Mars is trine Uranus and Neptune in the fourth house suggesting Carole does have the inner energy to cope with any problems at home while beginning her new job.

The Mars/Uranus aspect suggests dramatic changes and a desire for freedom. Since Mars is in the twelfth house, these are innate feelings or desires for change. Carole's going back to work was a dramatic change at home. Mars/Neptune suggests Carole's actions are based on no conscious motivation, but come from within, a deep-down need, and even if Carole is uncertain about her actions, she is able to take control and move positively.

Mars in the twelfth house suggests work in the background and Carole is working in the background of the movie industry. Mars here suggests a lot of personal drive, but not open aggressiveness, and a time when Carole will keep anger or resentment to herself. If her family gives her a hard time about work, it may be difficult for her to respond.

The transiting Moon in a lunar return chart is usually important. Carole's transiting Moon is in the eleventh house in Leo. (See Figure 17b.) The solar return Moon in the fifth house suggests a lot of emotions around the children. In Aquarius, it is probably because of Carole's desire for some personal freedom, which the children are not used to. The transiting Moon in the eleventh house implies Carole is re-evaluating her wishes for the future, and part of this reevaluation would

Figure 17b, Inner
Carole /Lunar Return
Aug. 4, 1995, 10:37 am
Middle: **Carole /Solar Return**
July 13, 1995, 6:03 pm
Both above: Tarzana, CA

Outer: **Carole /Transits**
Aug. 25, 1995, 9:00 am
Los Angeles, CA

be her short-term job. Leo represents the movie industry. Also, the Moon rules Carole's Midheaven, or career house. The transiting Moon is conjunct Mercury (by a slightly wide orb) in the eleventh house implying mixed emotions and thoughts about what Carole desires for the future. **Just by this one transit of the Moon and its aspect to the lunar return Moon and rulership, we have identified Carole's position on the day she began her short-term job.** This is a perfect example of how important the transiting Moon is to a lunar return chart.

Again, Carole's lunar return seems to support the delineation of both her natal and solar return charts. This appears to be a good time to take the short-term job and for Carole to reevaluate if she really wants project work, part-time work, or a full-time career in the future.

Chapter Eight

Advanced Methods

"What should I do?" "What am I good at?" "Should I apply for a new job?" "I hate my job! Should I just quit?" These are very difficult questions for an astrologer to answer. A career decision is a major life decision. An astrologer takes on tremendous responsibility when giving clients advice on career opportunities.

In order to advise a client on an opportune time to change careers, begin a new career, advance in a career, go on for further education, in what type of career he/she may do well, etc., I look at midpoints, sensitive points, Arabic Parts, and combinations of planets. I will again emphasize some points from earlier in the book that are crucial, such as transits, aspects, the South Node and planets conjunct the South Node.

As discussed previously, the two transiting planets I emphasize when looking are a client's career are Jupiter and Saturn. Jupiter often shows open doors. It is the planet of opportunity. Saturn is equated with restriction or obstacles. Obviously, Jupiter transiting the second, sixth or tenth house will symbolize open doors for work, career and monetary advancement. Saturn may indicate limited opportunities or restricted advancement for a time, but also suggests a very practical approach, laying a secure foundation for manifestation of material results. At the very least, with a Saturn transit you will have to work hard to accomplish your goals. I do not necessarily find Saturn restrictions a bad thing, since Saturn is the teacher and what you learn with a Saturn transit benefits you throughout your lifetime. A Saturn transit may be a very good time to work toward long-term goals. Jupiter and Saturn transits should not only be looked at when transiting the second, sixth and tenth houses. Look at Jupiter and Saturn as timing mechanisms when transiting midpoints or any points in the horoscope that activate the second, sixth and tenth houses.

Look again at Sarah's natal chart (Fig. 4, pg. 29). Jupiter transited her sixth house of work when she started a good job which met her specifications, i.e., she worked for the school system during the hours when her children were in school so she would need very little day care; she also received tremendous medical benefits for her family. On the other hand, Saturn was transiting her tenth house of career; thus, she had to work hard for recognition and advancement. This job was not her career, but a stepping stone toward what she will ultimately choose as her career. Transiting Saturn sets the stage for what must be done at the current time. Although Sarah wanted to stay home with her children, Saturn was transiting her tenth house, and she had to begin work toward her career (which may include further education), as well as her new job. Saturn opposed her fourth house, signifying conflict between family and work. I also look at transiting Sun, Venus, Mercury and Mars, but I feel a heavy emphasis should be placed on Jupiter and Saturn for work and career.

In addition to the major aspects discussed in previous chapters (squares, oppositions, conjunctions, trines and sextiles), I also look to see if a chart has **unaspected planets** (a planet that has no aspects to any other planet), **stellia** of planets (three or more bunched together), **grand crosses** (four planets at four points in a square), **T-squares** (involving three planets at three points in a square with the fourth missing), **grand trines** (involving three planets at three points forming the trine), yods (two quincunxes that are connected by a sextile), significant **midpoints** (the point half-way between two planets or between two points such as the Midheaven, Ascendant, Descendant, Node) and **sensitive points** (the point on a horoscope that creates an aspect to any planet, Midheaven, Ascendant, Descendant, or Node). If you use any of the major computer software programs, they will list these points and aspects for you, so you do not have to worry about calculation.

Although some of what I will next discuss was briefly touched upon in earlier chapters, I feel it is worth exploring in great depth in this chapter.

Unaspected Planets

An **unaspected planet** is quite significant since it is not strongly connected to the other planets. When an unaspected planet is triggered by a transit, a tremendous opportunity is available to use this usually unharnassed energy constructively. For example, if Jupiter is transiting an unaspected planet, this transit would activate the unaspected planet's motifs, and this would be a very important time to act on the opportunities suggested by Jupiter.

Stellium, Stellia

A stellium of planets is an obvious indication of where a client's strengths lie. You must look at a stellium (or stellia, the plural form) with a view toward how a concentration of planets in a particular part of a chart can help your client choose a career, and this might matter in terms of also opportune times to act regarding the career. For example, Al Gore (figure 18) has a stellium of planets in his first house: Pluto, Saturn and Mars. All are in Leo along with his Ascendant. First of all, this concentration in his first house suggests he will personally shine, and also Leo can indicate a public figure.

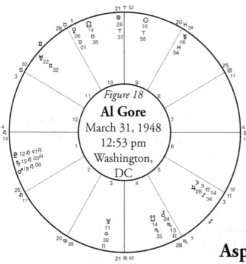

Figure 18
Al Gore
March 31, 1948
12:53 pm
Washington, DC

Pluto suggests working for the "good of the whole." Saturn indicates very hard work (which is karmic and personal). Coupled with Pluto, this can be karmic work for the good of mankind. Mars suggests a lot of drive and energy. This is a pretty good description of a very prominent politician.

Aspect Configurations

Any time a transiting planet activates a point on any of the aspect configurations mentioned previously (midpoint, sensitive point, yod, grand trine, T-square, as defined below, or stellium of planets, etc.], the other points of the aspect are activated as well. **If any one point of these configurations is in the second, sixth or tenth house, you may use the transit to further your finances, job or career.** You may often see where opportunity lies by using one point of an aspect to activate another point of the aspect which is in the house within which you wish to work. These configurations are extremely important when trying to help a client find the most opportune time to act and this is especially true when there seems to be no good time to act. **You can always find something to help your client by digging a little deeper.**

T-squares are important when it comes to filling in the missing link. For example:

Libra is the missing link in this T-square and when a transit crosses the missing point it activates the other planets involved. The missing link is where impetus may come from.

Diane (figure 19) has a T-square with Mars, Uranus and Chiron. Mars is in Sagittarius in the sixth house of health square Uranus in Virgo in the fourth house of home and foundation and also squaring Chiron in Pisces in the tenth house of career. This suggests a link with foundational values that are both practical (as suggested by Virgo) and an unusual approach (suggested by Uranus in the fourth house). A lot of energy and drive in work is suggested by Mars in the sixth house. Work in an area that would fit her high personal ideals is implied by Sagittarius, as well as the freedom to work independently and with philosophy or life values as symbolized by Chiron in the tenth house. She

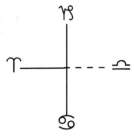

is a fundraiser and donation organizer for a major university, so her career appears to follow what is suggested in her natal chart. Also, we follow the T-square to the missing link which is 28 degrees Gemini in the twelfth house. When a transit hits this point it fills in the missing link and activates the entire T-square.

Yods are also very helpful when looking for career opportunity since they show life's purpose.

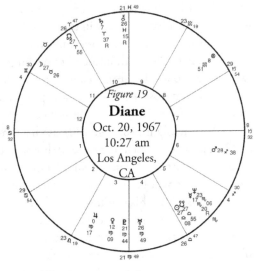

Figure 19
Diane
Oct. 20, 1967
10:27 am
Los Angeles,
CA

They are often called the "finger of fate." Again, yods are two quincunxes which are connected by a sextile. They can be planets, the Ascendant, Midheaven, Nodes, Arabic Parts, IC and Vertex.

Louisa May Alcott's chart (Figure 20) is a good example of the yod. She has her Sun in the first house. The Sun suggests where a person will

Figure 20
**Louisa May
Alcott**
Nov. 29, 1832
5:31 am
Germantown, PA

shine. Thus, the Sun placement suggests Ms. Alcott will personally shine and be recognized. She has two yods which point to how she will be able to shine. The first yod involves Mercury in her second house quincunx Mars in her seventh house, and also quincunx the North Node in her ninth house. Mercury symbolizes communication and writing. Mars symbolizes energy and action. The North Node in the ninth house of publishing and Mars in the seventh house of contracts point to Mercury in the second house and suggest communication and writing as a way to earn a living. Also, personal values are involved with a second house placement and suggest that values may be a part of what she writes, i.e., the values Ms. Alcott wrote about in her book *Little Women*. The second yod involves Mercury in the second house of money and values, the Moon in the third house of communication and writing which point to the North Node in the ninth house of publishing. Even though there are only two planets above the horizon and Saturn is in the tenth house suggesting hard work and possible obstacles along the way, both yods suggest a very strong chart for writing and publishing.

Al Gore (figure 18, page 170) also has a yod from his Aries Midheaven and Uranus in Gemini in the eleventh house both quincunx his fourth house Chiron in Scorpio. Again, because Uranus is in the eleventh house, it suggests his focus will be unusual or radical and for the good of mankind or large groups. Since his Midheaven is the cusp of his career house, his career may be geared toward this focus. It points to the fourth house of home or foundation suggesting home and foundational values will be brought into play with his career. As we know, his father was also a politician. Again, this pretty much describes the Al Gore public figure.

Diane (figure 19, page 171) has two yods, one consisting of the Sun in the fifth house and Mars in the sixth house both quincunx the Moon in the eleventh house. This suggests creativity or children (fifth house) and work toward the benefit of a large group. The other yod is the Moon in the eleventh house of groups and wishes and Chiron in the tenth house of career quincunx the Sun in the fifth house of creativity, children and speculation, which suggests creative ways of fund raising as well. This also suggests an option of working with children and with Chiron in the tenth house (Chiron can symbolize a wound that needs healing), it may mean work in the area of healing. Chiron can also symbolize higher education and Diane is working for a university.

Whenever a transit aspects a point of the yod, it is a good time to work to advance in your career.

Sarah (figure 4, page 29) has a **grand trine** between her Neptune in the fifth house and her Ascendant and Midheaven. You can see why Sarah considers her children (fifth house) as her foremost career. Although she is very good in accounting, she will probably be happier with a career in the arts or theater. If she stays in accounting, she would do quite well with programs funding the arts. She is always happier when being creative.

Arabian Parts

Arabian parts, also called Arabic points, are mathematically calculated points in the ecliptic that represent a synthesis of two or more factors and suggest the inner workings of the individual. **I look at three particular Arabic Parts when helping clients with their careers, the Part of Fortune, the Part of Sudden Advancement and the Part of Profession.** In order to calculate the Arabic parts you begin with the signs of the Zodiac and each sign is given a number starting with 0 to 11, Aries being 0 and continuing until Pisces as number 11. The numbers for the signs indicate the number of completed signs. A Sagittarius placement has eight completed signs (through Scorpio). A Taurus placement has only one completed sign (Aries), etc. The Part of Fortune (or substance) is the Ascendant+the Moon-the Sun. If your Ascendant is 10:01 Sagittarius and the Moon is 12:07 Cancer and the Sun is 03:04 Taurus, your Part of Fortune would be:

Sagittarius	8	10:01
+		
Cancer	3	12:07
	11	22:08
-		
Taurus	1	3:04
Aquarius	10	19:04

Your Part of Fortune would be 19 Aquarius 04. The Part of Sudden Advancement is calculated for the Ascendant plus the Sun minus Saturn. If you look at the planets, this calculation makes a lot of sense. The Ascendant is you personally, the Sun is where you shine, and Saturn is where you must work to establish a foundation for the future. Using the motifs of these planets would be a way to advance in your field.

The Part of Profession is calculated for Ascendant+Moon-Saturn. Rather than calculating the Arabic parts, since most of us use the major computer programs to calculate charts, I also use the program for the listing of the Arabic parts. It takes a long time to calculate a chart, midpoints, parts and so forth. Also, if you look at different books on Arabic parts, they call the parts by somewhat different names in each book. For example, the Part of Karma is often called the Part of Reincarnation; it just makes sense to use the computer program.

Sarah's Part of Fortune is 19 Virgo 12 in the fourth house, widely conjunct her Mercury and two midpoints. This suggests her strength as a homemaker and why home and family are so important to her. This is a very strong area to be activated by transit.

Midpoints and Sensitive Points

A **midpoint** is the halfway point between two points on the horoscope. The points on the horoscope can be a planet, Node, Ascendant or Descendant. **Any time a midpoint is conjunct a planet within 1 degree (or 2 degrees at most) it is a very strong point.** Sarah's Mercury/Midheaven midpoint in her sixth house is conjunct her Mars. Therefore, the Mercury in Sagittarius transit on the day she began her job is activating this midpoint and suggesting a great deal of conflict in her home, since her natal Mercury is in her fourth house. I will discuss midpoints further in this chapter and will demonstrate why this is such a strong point on Sarah's chart.

Sarah's Part of Sudden Advancement is 5 Sagittarius 38 conjunct the exact degree of Mars in her sixth house of work. It is also conjunct the Mercury/Midheaven midpoint. This is a very strong point to be activated by transit since a transit here will activate her career house (of which the Midheaven is the cusp), her home and foundation, as well as her house of work and service. This point was being activated by the Mercury in Sagittarius transit at the time she began her new job. You can see how she would go around and around between her home, work and future career. This transit is a fortunate placement with a lot of mental activity and Sarah will have a great deal of energy, with her natal Mars, to get the job done.

Sarah's Part of Profession is 29 Pisces 20 and conjunct her North Node in the eleventh house. The eleventh house indicates groups and since her Part of Profession is located in this house, it indicates she would do well working with large groups or for a large company. Her new job is for the school system, quite a large group.

The South Node symbolizes motivational factors and should be considered with regard to employment. What motivates your client to want to work at a particular job? **Anytime there is a planet conjunct the South Node, it is a very strong motivational factor** and where the South Node lies is important. If you look at Sarah's chart, her South Node is in her fifth house of creativity and conjunct her Saturn and Venus. Thus, Venus here suggests creativity and Sarah will probably do well in a creative position such as the arts, music, design, etc. Saturn suggests she will have to work very hard but will be rewarded with the Venus placement. In fact, she will want to work hard if she can be creative. Sarah is a very good accountant. If she continues in accounting, she would do well in a job which funds the arts or affords an artistic or creative atmosphere within which to work. This placement, coupled with her fourth house placements, indicates that Sarah would do very well working in the arts and working out of her home, probably in some sort of design business. This would also decrease her conflict between going to work and being there for her home and family.

The use of sensitive points and midpoints is crucial to career counseling. It is where you find help not apparent anywhere else in the chart. No matter what, you can probably find a sensitive point or midpoint to work with when your client insists on career direction.

Sensitive points are points on the astrology chart which, when activated by a transiting planet, aspect other planets, the Midheaven, Ascendant, etc. You examine these when you are trying to find a good time for a client to begin employment, change employment, move up the ladder, or obtain further education for his/her job. For example, in Sarah's chart, any time a planet transits 4 degrees Aries, it will sesquisquare her Pluto which sits next to two midpoints (of the Moon/Venus and Venus/Uranus); what appears to be a transit of no importance is actually of great importance *vis-à-vis* the third house. It can set off communications and open doors for her. Sensitive points have planetary applications just like signs and houses. They speak back and forth to each other. They are not mythical. They are astronomically correct.

Midpoints are probably my favorite to work with in counseling. They can stand alone, trigger the planets of which they are the midpoint, and, if coupled with another planet (within 1 or 2 degrees conjunct), they are incredibly strong points in a chart. **Any time a planet transits a midpoint which is conjunct a planet, either by direct transit or aspect, it is a time to act.**

Following are two examples of transits to midpoints that are conjunct planets. The transits were active on the day Sarah began her new job:

1. Neptune transiting her eighth house was trine her Mars/Uranus midpoint and the Moon/Mars midpoint, both of which are within 1 degree of her natal Mercury in house 4 (her home). The eighth house is the house of other people's money. She is an accountant for the school system (other people's money) and, again, going to work greatly disrupted her home life. The transiting Neptune also trines the Moon/Venus midpoint which is conjunct Pluto. This is also a very strong aspect which suggests emotions (the Moon) and conflict (Mars) in the home at the time she goes back to work.

2. Transiting Saturn squares the Mercury/Midheaven midpoint which is conjunct Mars in Sarah's sixth house of work. As you know, Saturn suggests restrictions and obstacles to be overcome, and this is certainly the case with Sarah going back to work (sixth house). Saturn is retrograde and transits back and forth over that point, indicating a difficult period of time.

Whenever a midpoint is hit by transit, that area of the chart will be activated, as well as the planets that are the subject of the midpoint. For example, in Sarah's chart her Mercury/Midheaven midpoint in the sixth house (on the day she began her new job) was due to be transited by Mercury within the month. It will not only transit, the midpoint but its theme also activates her fourth house (where her Mercury lies) and her Midheaven. Thus, when Mercury transits this midpoint, Sarah will likely be even more stirred up at home with a lot of talk about her new job. Also, she may already be thinking about how she can be recognized and advance to a tenth house career.

Another midpoint Sarah should watch with regard to her career is Mars/Jupiter (17 Capricorn 02) which is tied to her sixth and tenth houses. Activations of this midpoint are crucial times for Sarah to make job choices. Great energy which can be geared toward work and unusual work opportunities may arise. The same is true with the Mars/Uranus midpoint (22 Virgo 36) which is linked with the sixth and second houses. Another crucial midpoint to be activated if Sarah stays in accounting is the Mars/Midheaven midpoint at 13 Capricorn 38 which falls in her eighth house of other people's money.

Pluto in conjunction with a midpoint suggests a type of karmic ramification with a moral component. This is especially true if the midpoint involves a luminary or node, but works with any planet. Pluto conjunct a midpoint within one or two degrees suggests some type of public

prominence in help-
ing transform mores,
and involvement with
humanitarian or moral
matters. At the very
least, it is an incredibly
strong placement with
which to deal. I have
included four examples
of this.

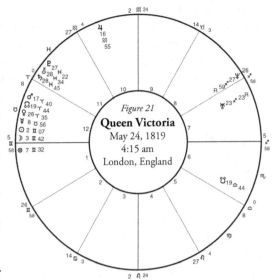

Figure 21
Queen Victoria
May 24, 1819
4:15 am
London, England

Queen Victoria
of England (Figure21)
had Pluto within one
degree of her Mercury/
Jupiter midpoint in
the eleventh house of
wishes for the future (what she would want for England and the monarchy) stemming from Jupiter in her tenth house (her reign) and Mercury
in her twelfth house (her unconscious motivations).

Princess Diana of England (Figure 22) had Pluto conjunct her Mercury/
Neptune midpoint in her eighth house of government stemming from her
seventh house of marriage (to Prince Charles) and her tenth house of career
or public prominence. She sought to make the monarchy more accessible
and humanitarian. Both
of these women had a
Mercury component so
there was a lot of com-
munication with their
ideas, and they created or
began to create a type of
moral shift.

President William
Clinton (Figure 23) has
Pluto conjunct his Mars/
North Node midpoint
within two degrees. Mars
sits in his first house and
suggests tremendous per-
sonal drive and energy;

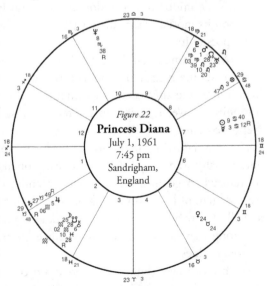

Figure 22
Princess Diana
July 1, 1961
7:45 pm
Sandrigham,
England

North Node sits in his ninth house of higher conscious philosophy and also foreign matters; and both affect his eleventh house of dreams, hopes and wishes for the future. Thus, his personal drive is coupled with his higher conscious beliefs and geared toward his dreams for the future. As President, he had major public achievement in the economy and national hu-

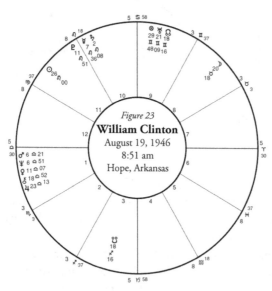

Figure 23
William Clinton
August 19, 1946
8:51 am
Hope, Arkansas

manitarianism, realizing his Mars/North Node midpoint conjunct Pluto placement. With regard to foreign matters, he was heavily involved in trying to keep peace with the Israel/Palestinian situation, and there was a precarious balance during his term as President. When his term ended and he was no longer involved in the peace process, violence erupted and increased in the area. Anyone born within a day of President Clinton would have this Pluto conjunct Mars/NorthNode midpoint and it does not necessarily mean that everyone will act upon its motifs or that their actions would be publicly prominent; it is just a possibility.

Muhammed Ali (Figure 24) has Pluto in his twelfth house (subconscious mind, behind the scenes activities, private enemies, institutions and incarceration) conjunct within just over one degree the midpoint between Jupiter in his tenth house (career and honors) and Neptune in his second house (money and personal values). He gave up his heavyweight title (tenth house) for his personal values (second house) and actually went to jail (twelfth house) for his moral convictions when he refused to go into military service and participate in the Vietnam war. A man of his status and fame would not be put in the front lines to actually fight, but his Islamic convictions against war and violence were so strong that he was willing to sacrifice his freedom and career for his personal values.

Elvis Presley (Figure 25) had Pluto conjunct his Neptune/Chiron midpoint. Chiron is in his sixth house of work, Neptune is in his ninth house of higher consciousness and Pluto is in the eighth house of government. Remember, when he first appeared on television, the T.V. cameras could only show him above the waist because of his dancing. He was one of the early performers of the rock 'n' roll era which involved a change in perception of America's strict morals. This is not to say everyone who has Elvis Presley's Pluto conjunct Neptune/

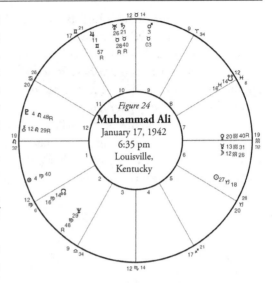

Figure 24
Muhammad Ali
January 17, 1942
6:35 pm
Louisville,
Kentucky

Chiron midpoint (these planets and Chiron move very slowly and this may be a factor for some time in charts) will have such an effect on society, but there is potential on a smaller scale, or in one's own way, to affect the lives of those around them if they take advantage of the planetary motifs. All persons with Pluto conjunct a midpoint are not going to be prominent, but this

placement does suggest strong moral and transformational potential.

Sarah has a Moon/ Venus midpoint at Pluto in her third house and a Venus/Uranus midpoint at Pluto in her third house. This ties in her creativity and personal effort along with communication skills and again indicates to me that she would work well in a creative area using her imagination while com-

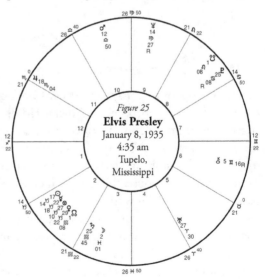

Figure 25
Elvis Presley
January 8, 1935
4:35 am
Tupelo,
Mississippi

municating to others in an area such as design or politically representing others. She has a strong potential for prominence.

When clients are at a loss as to what they really want to do with
their lives or do not feel they are very good at anything, **I look at planet
combinations for a clue**. Ebertin's *Combination of Stellar Influences* is where
I look first and usually do not have to look anywhere else. His definitions
are quirky and often "do not fit the mold" but work quite well in career
counseling. It is a very good guide.

If you look at figure 26, you will see an example of a client, Ken, who
did not seem to have a strong career chart, yet was an advertising writer.
It was the combination of planets that indicated where he could excel in
a career. He has a South Node (where motivation lies and is enhanced by

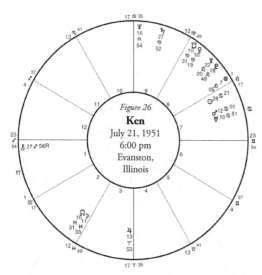

Figure 26
Ken
July 21, 1951
6:00 pm
Evanston,
Illinois

conjunctions to planets)
conjunct Venus (a benefic
conjunction) which is in
the house of other people's
money. This placement is
opposite his Moon in Pisces
which suggests intuition,
combined with Jupiter in
the third house implying
writing and communica-
tion, a persuasive person.
Thus, advertising is a very
good profession since he
is using his persuasiveness
and the sponsor's money
to put his ideas into the
media. The opposition may suggest hard work or a difficult time achieving
success. He also has Neptune conjunct his Midheaven which is a very strong
suggestion of imagination in career or a career dealing with aesthetic or
idealistic motifs. Also, Saturn rules Capricorn which is intercepted in Ken's
first house of identity and basic essence which are tied to career. Since Saturn is in the ninth house, this may include writing or publishing, and with
Saturn it suggests hard work.

Planet combinations may be crucial in indicating options a client
has. You should present options in a positive tone and express difficulties
as "caveats," something to watch for rather than something discourag-
ing. Positive thinking is crucial in career counseling. Most people are
insecure about their career moves and how much they will be able to accomplish. Clients require positive input.

Solar Arcs and Viewing Midpoints in Charts on a Dial

Solar arc direction is another good way to look at a chart at a specific time in the life. It is a form of progression based on moving all planets and points according to the arc of the Sun. Once you have the position of secondary progressed Sun for a specific time, say your client's 30th birthday, subtract the position of her progressed Sun from it, and that is the solar arc for the time of her 30th birthday. Add the solar arc to the natal position of all other planets or points and you have a solar arc directed chart for the birthday. Of course this method of direction can also be done very simply with any number of astrological software programs that are available.

Looking at a chart on a rotating dial is an easy way to spot midpoints without calculation. You can use a 360° dial, of course, but I especially like to use a 90° dial, since it is so easy to spot all of the action aspects (conjunction, square, opposition and also half-squares at a glance), as well as the midpoints. But, if you haven't used a 90° dial before, some orientation is needed. Here is a picture of a 90° dial, with glyphs drawn to mark the beginning of each of its three sections. The first section, which starts at the zero degree (arrow at the top of the dial), contains the cardinal signs: Aries, Cancer, Libra and Capricorn. The second section contains the fixed signs: Taurus, Leo, Scorpio and Aquarius. The third section contains the mutable signs: Gemini, Virgo, Sagittarius and Pisces. This means that signs that are normally square or opposite each other are now piled on top of each other.

Figure 27

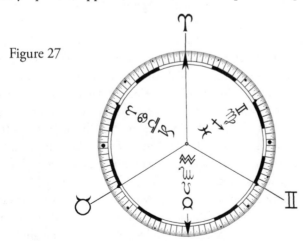

When you turn the dial so that its arrow points to a planet, you can immediately see not only what other planets or points are conjunct to it, but also which ones are square or opposite, since they will be close together on the pointer. Semi-squares and sesquiquadrates will be directly opposite. These hard aspects are most likely to represent action, and thus are very important.

It's easy to spot midpoints when you use a dial. Just turn the dial to point its arrow at any planet and then look to see which planets are equidistant from the pointer arrow on either side. Obviously, the planets on either side form a midpoint to the planet on the pointer.

Once you have a natal chart set up in dial format, you can then also enter transiting, progressed or solar arc positions, too, for quick viewing of how they relate to the natal chart and to each other. You could set up concentric wheels for this, or you could simply use a different color marker for each type of factor, such as natal chart in black, transits in blue, solar arc in green, etc. I will use the concentric wheel method to show you an example of using the dial to look at Sarah's chart with her solar arcs and transits for the day she began her new job.

Solar Arc for Sarah's New Job

On the illustration shown (Figure 28), the inner wheel is Sarah's natal chart, the second (middle) wheel shows her solar arc directed chart and the outer wheel shows the transits for the day she started her new job. I always use Reinhold Ebertin's *Combination of Stellar Influences* when delineating the combinations of planets I see on the dial. I find his interpretations are almost always germane to a client's situation. I use a 2 degree orb for solar arc (or 3 degrees to see the onset of a problem). As an aside, I always use the exact degree for life threatening conditions.

When I look at Sarah's dial chart, I notice Moon at 2° is conjunct Uranus at 2°, which indicates Sarah will have success and change in her life, as well as time of stress because of the disruptive influence of Uranus on her emotions, represented by Moon. This combination can also indicate a desire for more personal independence and freedom. Her work gave her more independence, but less freedom to do as she pleased during the day (it was a double edged sword). Uranus is 1° conjunct Sun, which again indicates Sarah may have a change in life and/or a change of vocation, as well as inner tension and ego changes. Solar arc Uranus is 3° from transiting Mars, which suggests tension and aggravation *vis a vis* work. Transiting Mars has set off the Moon, Uranus and Sun conditions, and as you can see, there was a very sudden change in career, since Sarah went back to work after eight years, in spite of the fact that she has always considered her main career that of wife, mother and homemaker.

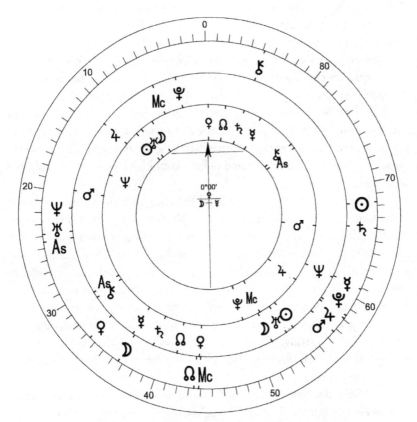

Figure 28: Sarah's Chart in 90° Dial Format
Inner Wheel: Natal Chart
Middle Wheel: Solar Arcs
Outer Wheel: Transits

Returning to work gave Sarah more confidence, thus ego changes. Although her new job turned out beneficially for her, the adjustment and emotional strain of putting her children into day care and the tension on her marriage were tremendous. Sun conjunct 2° Jupiter is a fortunate placement for going back to work after eight years of being a homemaker, and suggests the tenacity to persist in both her career and as a good homemaker. This placement is personally lucky for Sarah, and helps her overcome obstacles.

However, solar arc Pluto is conjunct natal Moon by 2°. This indicates emotional upheaval and impulsive action with long term effects. Her impulsive action was to call someone from her past for emotional support, and had he been available, she probably would have begun to see him and may have dissolved her marriage at that time. The Mars transit 2° from solar arc Sun indicates that she will be successful in her career, but it also denotes some irritability. There is a tendency for quarrels. This is a somewhat explosive placement, but knowing Sarah's disposition, she would not explode (though her spouse might). Although Sarah achieved success on the job, there were upsets and quarrels at home because of her new role as the "working Mom." The Mars transit 2° to natal Jupiter (which suggests expansion) manifested as expansion of Sarah personally, within her new job, rather than cause tension at home (which could have become an explosive situation).

The Pluto transit is 1° to natal Jupiter, which indicates a desire for something more spiritual, and this is an obvious desire, given her circumstances. This is also true in light of Saturn's 1° transit to natal Mars, which often indicates harshness and mental or emotional pain, as well as frustration in undertaking new tasks. Sarah is in obvious need of spiritual activities at this time to help her overcome the frustration of her new circumstances. In fact, she should be encouraged to find a spiritaul outlet, just a strongly as she is encouraged to seek someone with whom to talk—both will relieve tension.

The transiting Moon is conjunct solar arc Mercury, suggesting changes in mind set, obviously brought on by being a working, rather than stay at home mother.

Solar arc Mars is within 1° Neptune, which can mean irritability, lack of energy, but also inspired thoughts, with both being ramifications of the new job. The caveat here is not to use drugs and alcohol as an escape or aa a means to cope.

Transiting Midheaven and North Node are conjunct solar ard Venus. This is such a help in a difficult time. There is genuine friendshp developing with those at work, which helps the tension at home.

Solar arc Neptune and transiting Mercury are at the same degree, perhaps manifesting in subconscious disturbances and a lack of clarity in thought. There is a need for spirituality to overcome faulty judgment. This situation is improved by the transiting North Node and Midheaven conjunct the solar art Venus (discussed previously).

Natal Mars is conjunct transiting Saturn. This is perhaps the most difficult placement, relating to lack of energy, the resistance to what Sarah wants, disputes and a tendency to rush around too much and perhaps cause an accident because of the rushing. Lack of focus caused by fights at home can also cause accident situations.

Natal Saturn is conjunct transiting Chiron, suggesting feelings of great obstacles and a need for healing. There is a feeling of being trapped. This is the second difficult Saturn placement, suggesting that there are obvious karmic lessons to be learned.

Sarah's natal Moon and solar arc Midheaven are within 1°, indicating changes in objectives leading to alterations in life. Midheaven is 2° from Uranus, which often indicates advancement in one's career or a change of occupation. For Sarah, this was an overall readjustment of her circumstances. I feel that if she was able to find more time for spirituality, she would have had a far more easy time of adjustment than she had. Had I analyzed her chart prior to, rather than after the fact, I would have tried to convince her to make time for spirituality for her own sanity, no matter what else was occurring. Almost five years later, the stress of that time is still felt, and will continue to be a source of trouble in her home life. This is the type of situation in which we, as astrologers, must stress the need for selfish time out and selfish acts, as well as to seek a professional for counseling. The client must have a spiritual "time out." Someone in Sarah's state will be hard pressed to perform well on her job, without some time for herself—some time for spiritual endeavors. Even those who do feel they are "spiritual people" should be encouraged to take up hobbies such as music or art as a form of release.

Recapitulation

The following is an outline of the steps in total, effective career counseling:

    I.   Interpret the whole chart as described in previous chapters with a view toward career.

    II.   Use the "at least 3 charts" method, using transits and aspects.

    III. Use the following:

        A. Transiting Jupiter and Saturn

        B. Unaspected planets

        C. Stellium of planets

        D. Grand Crosses, T-Squares, Grand Trines, and Yods

        E. Sensitive Points

        F. Midpoints

        G. South Node as a Motivational Factor

        H. Arabic Parts and

        I. Combinations of Planets.

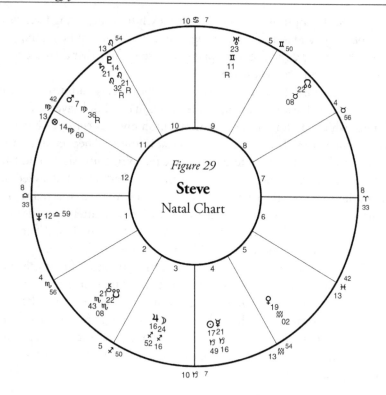

Figure 29

Steve

Natal Chart

Steve
A Man Following His Career Potential

See figure 29 above for Steve's chart. I am combining the "at least three charts" method with advanced methods to show how it all fits together in this chapter. For this example, I will add transits to the houses as I come to them, as well as aspects discussed in the advanced methods chapter. You will see a complete picture of career potential.

Steve joined the Marine Corps immediately after high school graduation. He enlisted specifically to go to Vietnam. He received an "early out" of the Marine Corps and joined the police force of a large city.

He sounds very much like the ultimate "man's man." In reality he is very soft spoken and there are no hard edges. He is very fair and even. He has a very quick mind and a good sense of humor. He handles administrative duties with ease, and if you just met him, you would never guess he is a police officer.

Steve was given the task of aiding in the investigation of members of his own police department for violation of civil rights, planting evidence, keeping evidence for personal use, and the like, and writing an initial report of his findings. He was a part of an investigation wherein everyone was investigating everyone else. He was to aid in the investigation of one particular unit of the criminal division. As a result of this investigation (which is ongoing at the time of writing this chapter) several known criminals have been released from jail and it is expected as many as 300 more persons may be released or, at the very least, their cases will be reviewed. At the time I finished this chapter, there were news reports almost daily regarding the investigation. There was a report which cited poor field supervision, lack of standards in recruitment, lack of discipline, and much more, as part of the problems. Top officials were pointing at each other and trying to pass blame. The police chief and the mayor were coming under attack. A federal investigation into civil rights was implemented. The investigation was uncovering probably one of the worst cases of wrongdoing in a city's police force. Eventually, the entire unit of the task force had been disbanded and another unit appointed containing no one from the previous unit. Crime was up at least 38% in the city. Although I did not know of further activity other than the initial report, Steve's work in the investigation was one factor that helped cause a major shake-up in the police department.

Steve's Natal Chart

Since this involves a police investigation, I left out birth data and any other confidential information.

As I delineate Steve's charts, there will be repetition of **many** points and characteristics. That is because the characteristics and patterns are repeated throughout his natal, solar return and lunar return charts. It is this constant pattern that shows Steve's direction as it pertains to his career. I am also only discussing placements which I feel are pertinent to his career or any personal turmoil which may be directly or proximately caused by career situations.

How in the world did this fourth house Sun in Capricorn get placed in the position of such an investigation? In fact, Steve has a Sun and Mercury in Capricorn. At first glance he should be an accountant. He has no planets in his sixth or tenth houses—he should be an accountant in the background of a very large firm.

Now, look closer at Steve's chart. We must view his entire chart and delineate the chart just as you would any natal chart with a view toward career. His occupation will begin to make sense as you look at the Ascendant and first house.

When looking at Steve's (or anyone's) career, the first thing I look at is the Ascendant to see what his personal direction may be and how others perceive him. Steve has a Libra Ascendant and true to his rising sign he is fair and balanced, weighing one thing against another for a just solution. Libra represents justice. The area of law within which Steve chooses to work is police work. Like any good Libra, Steve is always courteous, polite and can be charming. He also does not appear to be a "tough" cop. He is altruistic, compassionate and still very much like the idealistic kid who joined the Marine Corps to save the world. Who better to help expose corruption in a police department?

Steve has also found a way to incorporate his Libra nature with its love of beauty and art. His wife is an artist and their home is filled with her work. They socialize very little with other police families. When Steve comes home, the aesthetic side of Libra is fulfilled.

Neptune in Libra in Steve's first house suggests Steve has keen insight and intuition into the direction to search for the corruption. Neptune here also deals with the philosophy of law enforcement, and suggests there could be some danger from some type of clandestine plotting which Steve must watch out for. (This will appear in other areas of the chart as well.) Also, Neptune rules Pisces which is on the cusp of the sixth house of work and service, bringing his first house direction into this house of work. Steve feels it is his duty to "protect and serve" for the good of society.

Both Steve's Part of Fortune and Part of Sudden Advancement are at 2 Scorpio in the first house conjunct his second house cusp. This suggests Steve will put forth a lot of personal effort, based on his personal values. He will create his own fortune and seek his own opportunity for advancement.

The second house is not only money and possessions but the house of your personal value system. Steve has Scorpio on the cusp of this house and the co-rulers of Scorpio, Pluto and Mars, are both in the eleventh house which, among other things, denotes large groups. His values deal with what is "good for the whole" of society. Steve has the Scorpio characteristics of fearlessness (good for police work), tenacity, energy and thoughtfulness. But remember, Scorpio also has a dark side including suspicion and shrewdness, a person attracted to the underworld and the dark side of human nature. What could be a more positive outlet for this other side of Steve than working in an environment which exposes him to the dark side of human nature and uses his positive traits to deal with the problems associated with this dark side of humanity? This is Steve's Libra Ascendant working with the positive traits of Scorpio in his personal value system while he can still acknowledge the negative traits of Scorpio. The Scorpio also suggests success due to Steve's perseverance, tenacity and courage. Scorpios are the natural detectives of the zodiac. While Libra is mellow, Scorpio helps Steve to be a better police officer by providing drive and tenacity.

There is a midpoint between the eleventh house Mars and the second house Chiron at 14 degrees Libra 39 which is conjunct within 2 degrees to the first house Neptune. Remember, where a planet sits conjunct a midpoint is a very strong point on the chart. Thus, a transit to Neptune will transit the midpoint as well and will activate the first house, the second house (personal values), and the eleventh house (hopes for the future). Venus was transiting this point when Steve was given his assignment. Given Steve's personal value system of fairness and justice, he was willing to take this most difficult assignment. This assignment may affect his eleventh house of hopes and wishes in that he may get a promotion or some form of recognition from his work. This assignment is far reaching in that it is beginning to clean up the city's police force.

There is also a grand cross in Steve's natal chart; Venus, Chiron, the North Node and Saturn tie together the second house of personal values and money, the eighth house of government (the police system in this case), the fifth house of creativity and the eleventh house of groups and goals (namely a better city and a better police department). This grand cross was triggered when Venus transited Neptune since it also transited the Mars/Chiron midpoint discussed above. The Chiron part of the midpoint would in turn affect the other points of the grand cross. You can see from this example how, if you dig deeper, transits affect so many areas of the chart.

If we look at the third house which is, among other things, the house of conscious mind and how Steve communicates, we see Sagittarius on the cusp. Sagittarius is the idealist and the humanitarian. In need of personal freedom, he can appear aloof. Steve needs this detachment for his current assignment. Jupiter in this house suggests Steve has an ease in speech and writing. He has very good communication skills and would be a good PR person. The Moon here suggests some unfinished education and Steve may feel that if he had further education in his field, he would have gone further. However, the Moon trines Saturn in the eleventh house and suggests Steve knows who he is and what he wants for the future. The Moon in Sagittarius suggests that although Steve can be emotional in thought, he does not show it. Steve will hide whatever emotions this assignment brings.

There is a mystic rectangle (linking trines, sextiles and oppositions) between Venus, Uranus, Jupiter and Saturn bringing together communication (Jupiter in the third house) with creativity (fifth house), his higher consciousness or personal philosophies (ninth house) and work for the good of the whole (eleventh house). **This is actually a very strong chart for a progressive approach to police work.**

There are two yods in Steve's natal chart. **The yod is the "finger of fate" and indicates life's purpose.** Steve's two yods are very important when viewing his career. There is a yod between Mercury in his fourth house (which represents his foundation, where he is coming from), Saturn in the eleventh house (his wishes for the future and also groups of people) and Uranus in the ninth house which is his philosophy. You can see Steve's life's purpose points toward his foundation from higher conscious philosophies of working for the good of the whole of humanity. There is also a yod between Chiron in his house of personal values and Mercury in his fourth house representing his foundation, to Uranus in Steve's house of philosophies. Again, Steve's personal values point toward a ninth house idealistic pursuit. Steve could have just as easily been a law school professor or a public defender were it not for something in his foundation and his upbringing. If I looked at Steve's chart without knowing he is a police officer, at first glance, I honestly would have thought he was a civil rights attorney, a public defender or perhaps a business or economics professor. I have not discussed Steve's parental influence with him, but I feel his father had a lot to do with his choice of career.

This assignment took place over a period of a few weeks so I cannot pinpoint a specific day of transits but looked at the transits over that period of time. The Sun was transiting Steve's first house when he began working on this assignment. The Sun transit sextiled Jupiter in the third house (communication and writing) when the situation started to become public. Jupiter in the third house is in Sagittarius and is the natural ruler of Sagittarius. Jupiter symbolizes expansion and the Sun transiting Jupiter further expanded communications dealing with this assignment. No wonder this investigation came to the public forefront as quickly as it did (in a matter of a few weeks). Also, the Venus/Neptune midpoint sits on Jupiter and this is a very strong point in Steve's chart to be hit by transit. This may bring great changes for him personally along with the potential changes it will bring to the police force. Sagittarius also represents idealism which must be applied to the situation of one officer investigating his fellow officers. Fortunately, the Sun/Jupiter is benevolent and Steve should be able to keep his Libra traits of humor and charm throughout this whole assignment.

The natal Sun in the fourth house suggests that as Steve gets older his wishes will be fulfilled. He will receive honors. Although Steve is only in his fifties, he is doing what fulfills him and is recognized for his abilities. I feel that he will receive some sort of recognition when the assignment ends. The location of the Sun (in the fourth house) shows where Steve's life's energy will be directed. In Steve's case, what he does, his direction, is based again on his foundation and "upbringing." Mercury, also in the fourth house, trines the North Node in his eighth house, bringing together his foundation and government.

The Sun and Mercury are in Capricorn suggesting a steady, methodical, plodding worker. This brings stability to Neptune in Libra in the first house, implying a person with a great analytical, as well as intuitive, mind—perfect for investigation.

The Sun in Capricorn is ruled by Saturn in the eleventh house suggesting that Steve's hopes and wishes, based on his values and ideals, will come to fruition.

True to the Capricorn Sun and Mercury (the plodding, steady worker with the analytical mind), before Steve received his current assignment, he worked implementing a computer system for the police department.

Steve's Part of Profession is 11 Aquarius in his fourth house. This suggests his foundational influence plays a large part in any profession he would choose. His paternal influence is probably very important to his choice of profession.

Venus in Steve's fifth house in Aquarius is somewhat at odds with both his personal value system (since it squares Chiron in his second house) and his government position (since it squares the North Node in his eighth house). Steve would probably like to be more free socially than his obligations allow him to be. This could also suggest financial pressures. Venus here suggests success in love and happiness through children. Venus rules his eighth house of government suggesting he may be very creative in his work. Also, Venus here suggests that his family support helps give Steve peace of mind when he goes to work—they are a support system for him.

Pisces is on the cusp of his sixth house of work and service. There are no planets in this house but Pisces is ruled by Neptune in the first house in Libra, again bringing law and justice together with work and service.

Uranus is in the ninth house of higher conscious philosophy and is in Gemini. Gemini is ruled by Mercury which is in Steve's fourth house. This leads me to the conclusion that Steve's home and family life, his foundation and how he was raised, are important with regard to his ideals today. Uranus is ruled by Aquarius. There is Aquarius in Steve's fourth house further reinforcing his foundation as the basis for his higher consciousness and ideals. There is also Aquarius in Steve's fifth house of speculation. In order to promote his ideals and higher conscious philosophies, he may take risks or gamble with his actions. He should be careful to not take too many chances in this investigation. His thinking is very versatile and his ideas are much more conventional than meet the eye. Some people may feel he is going too far.

This assignment was a challenge to his personal value system. It was a turning point. The matters at hand could have gone either way. This was a test for Steve and what he really believes in. Was he willing to sacrifice and do what was right, what his moral compass told him to do, or would he take the easy out and look the other way at wrongdoing? This test of his values corresponds to the ninth house reorganization behind the scenes at work. His values passed the test and he was a part of the catalyst for certain reform in the police department.

Cancer is on the cusp of the tenth house (the Midheaven) and is ruled by the Moon in the third house of communication and conscious mind. This is very important for Steve's career. The ruler of the tenth house in the third house can suggest government commissions, i.e., the appointment by his department for the investigation. It also suggests communication is a strong asset for Steve in light of his career. Communication is also evidenced by Steve's previous assignment with the computer system. Cancer here affords Steve a lot of insight in his career. In other words, he has good "cop instincts."

Since Cancer is ruled by the Moon in Sagittarius in the third house, Steve must be given freedom of thought in his career and his career must support his ideals.

It is interesting to note that more planets are in houses 1 through 6 than in houses 7 through 12, suggesting a more private person. Steve was working behind the scenes just as he did with the computer system. Before the computer assignment, he was in a central command post which was literally underground. His work was behind the scenes, but his work had great impact.

Saturn is in the eleventh house in Leo. Saturn in the eleventh house can operate for the good of social or human causes. In Steve's case, his career to protect and serve is just that. I always look at Saturn and Jupiter as keys to career counseling. Here Saturn is at its peak working steadily to influence the structure of our society in a positive way. Saturn in the fire sign Leo suggests tremendous energy to keep steadily working towards goals. Since Saturn traits include working alone and managerial work, the computer system and this investigation appear ideal for Steve. Saturn here suggests hard work to initiate reform, to work for the greater good of society. Saturn suggests an unyielding person who does not bend the rules, and expects others to follow suit. Those who do bend the rules will be rooted out, as was the case with the corrupt officers on the force. Saturn in the eleventh house indicates that prestige may come with championing the right cause. Saturn suggests a desire for order, not chaos. Saturn also implies a separatist from group identity. Steve works for the common good of the group, but will not lose personal identification and values.

Saturn in Leo is ruled by the Sun in the fourth house and this again goes back to foundation. It suggests that how Steve works is very much related to how he was raised.

Saturn is also one point of the mystic rectangle connecting Steve's life work and purpose, groups, conscious mind and superconscious philosophies, and risk-taking to produce desired results. The fulfillment of this mystic rectangle comes from the first house Libra Ascendant and the second house Scorpio values and suggests the result is Steve's choice of police work. This is also quite a placement for an investigator. He will "leave no stone unturned" in seeking the truth and justice. Saturn tends to stabilize the boldness of Leo which is very important in police work.

Pluto in the eleventh house suggests group dynamics and working for the good of the whole. Since Pluto is the planet of reorganization and is far reaching, it suggests that the ramifications of the investigation should be felt far into the future. As stated, within a short period of time, there were articles in the front section of the newspaper that discussed "finger pointing" by top city officials, the chief of police and the county district attorney trying to blame others for the appalling situation with this specific corrupt group. Shortly thereafter it was announced that the city district attorney was appointing many more prosecutors for police corruption. A few weeks after that, a federal investigation was announced. Finally the unit was disbanded, and a whole new unit appointed.

Mars in the eleventh house suggests unpopularity or disagreement with others. It goes without saying that this investigation created a great deal of unpopularity with many police officers. Mars in Virgo symbolizes an active mind and good analytical skills. In Virgo, it can denote working, although vigorously, quietly and alone. Mars in the eleventh house can also indicate violence linked to friends, and, in the case of a police officer, this is not difficult to understand. Mars here can also indicate that friends can be a problem. With this investigation, it is also easy to understand how some friends on the police force could be a problem.

The twelfth house is the house of subconscious mind and has Virgo on the cusp. Virgo is ruled by Mercury which is in the fourth house. Again, Steve's foundation and upbringing play a crucial role in his subconscious motivations. He felt compelled to take his current assignment even if he did not consciously think the decision through.

The most important points for Steve are his two yods. Since yods represent life's purpose, I feel we should take another look at Steve's two yods. Both add up to the same thing: work for the common good of humanity derived from personal philosophy, personal value system, and his foundation and upbringing. Mercury is at the apex of one yod with Uranus and Saturn as the other points. Mercury is the foundation (fourth house) combined with Uranus and higher philosophy (ninth house) and Saturn (eleventh house) indicating hard work for the good of the group or whole.

The other yod is Uranus at the apex (ninth house—higher consciousness and philosophy) with Chiron (second house—personal values) and Mercury (fourth house—foundation). This suggests Steve can really only work with something that promotes his ideals, personal values, and the values instilled in him by home and his foundation.

If ever a person was to rise to his life's work, it was Steve with his investigation assignment.

Probably during the week that Steve wrote his initial report, a few transits really stand out. Transiting Mercury was conjunct Chiron in the second house, setting off the Chiron/Mercury/Uranus yod. The transiting Moon was also conjunct Chiron setting off this yod and, as you know, the Moon can signify change or fluctuation. This investigation was certainly going to help change the police department. **Remember, Uranus (the point of the yod) is in the ninth house which is the twelfth house to Steve's tenth (or behind the scenes of his career). Thus, this is the yod that represents working behind the scenes to change the police department.** These transits that set into motion Steve's behind-the-scenes investigation.

The Saturn transit in the eighth house opposed Chiron in the second house, indicating obstacles and difficulties for Steve. He had to work very hard to uncover the facts he needed for his report. Remember that Saturn is one of the planets to consider with regard to career. Wherever Saturn sits is where hard work and lessons occur. Transiting Saturn resides in the eighth house of government (the police department).

Another important transit was Uranus on the cusp of the fifth house and opposite Pluto in the eleventh house. According to Ebertin, the Uranus/Pluto combination is a process of transformation, a collapse of the old order of things. This suggests bringing new ideals and actions into a corrupt atmosphere. However, this combination can also suggest violence or "subversive" activities. Steve, and everyone else involved in the investigation had to be very careful. This was the beginning of police reform and the end of turning a blind eye to certain activities. It was not popular with everyone. When Uranus hit exactly 14 Aquarius and was exactly opposing Pluto, some of the prisoners who had been "set up" by the police were released.

As stated above, I could have just as easily pulled attorney or public defender (the opposite of the police who prosecute the law), or law professor from this chart. It appears to me that Steve's choice of police and military has to do with the home, foundation and early childhood influence (his sense of duty so to speak).

When this assignment came to fruition, the Sun was transiting Steve's second house of personal values and money, suggesting this assignment could also lead to promotion and more money. Again, when the Sun transited Chiron, it hit a point of Steve's natal yod of Chiron/Mercury and Uranus. This yod concerns his personal values, foundation and philosophy. Thus, it suggests Steve would very much like to correct this bad situation. **This Sun transit reinforces the Mercury transit.**

In November, transiting Venus in Libra was conjunct Neptune in Steve's first house. Libra represents justice and the justice during this transit was suggested by the release of the first prisoners.

Going into December, Mars opposed Saturn and Pluto in the eleventh house. This is the combination Ebertin ascribes to death, and there could easily have been riots, increased gang activity and retaliation for what was coming out in the press. It was a very crucial time.

In December, Mercury was conjunct Jupiter in the third house. This transit suggests that wrongdoing will be brought out into the open. This was when the correction of wrongdoing started as the criminal releases began. This placement suggests success in a mission that is talked about. Mercury/Jupiter represents public awareness of the situation.

Transits to Midpoints Relating to Steve's Career

The following midpoints are connected to Steve's career. Any planetary transits of these midpoints should be considered.

Pluto in the eleventh house at 14 Leo 21 is conjunct the midpoint (at 15 Leo 52) of Uranus (in the ninth house) and the Ascendant. Any time a planet transits any one of these points, Steve's ideals, personal values and humanitarian concepts are activated.

Saturn (21 Leo 32 in eleventh house) conjuncts the Chiron/North Node midpoint (at 21 Leo 55) again bringing into play Steve's personal value system, government, work for the good of the whole, and the hard work suggested by Saturn.

Mars (7 Virgo 36) in the eleventh house is conjunct the Uranus/Chiron Midpoint (at 7 Virgo 27)—again bringing in Steve's personal value system from the second house and personal philosophies from the ninth house into the energy of Mars and working for the good of the whole (eleventh house). Mars energy is very strong when enhanced by a midpoint.

The Saturn/Chiron midpoint is 6 Libra 37 and Steve's Ascendant is 8 Libra 33. This again brings Steve's personal value system (Chiron in the second house), humanitarianism (the eleventh house) and life pattern (Ascendant) into play.

The Venus/Saturn midpoint at 20 Scorpio 17 is conjunct Chiron in House 2 (21 Scorpio 42). Any time that point is transited, Steve's personal values, work for the whole, and taking a risk for his values come into the picture.

The Venus/Neptune midpoint is 16 Sagittarius 0 and conjunct Jupiter (at 16 Sagittarius 52) in the third house. Any time one of these points is triggered by a transit, you can be sure that whatever Steve is working on will be communicated, and he will be personally recognized for his work.

With the fact that there are two yods in Steve's chart, which suggest work based on a very strong personal value system, behind the scenes activity and work for the good of the whole, Steve's assignment seemed to fit his life's purpose. Even more startling is the fact that there is a yod in his solar return chart for the year, which again emphasizes his life's purpose and strongly suggests that at least a large part of why he is a police officer will be fulfilled this year.

Steve's Solar Arcs

I prepared Steve's solar arc chart for the data that the task force was set up to investigate the police scandal. On the 90° dial illustration (Figure 29a), look at the first 30 degrees in the solar arc (outer wheel) chart which surrounds Steven's natal chart (inner wheel). You will see a lot of activity there, but the second 30° has the most telling placement for this investigation.

In the first 30° degrees, the natal Ascendant (As) and Midheaven (Mc) are close to the same degree as Solar Arc Venus (1). Since Venus is a benevolent planet, it's connection to the Ascendant brings personal protection to Steve at this difficult time, and helps him professionally, since Venus is in close aspect to his Midheaven. These are fortunate placements for Steve as he proceeds with his investigation.

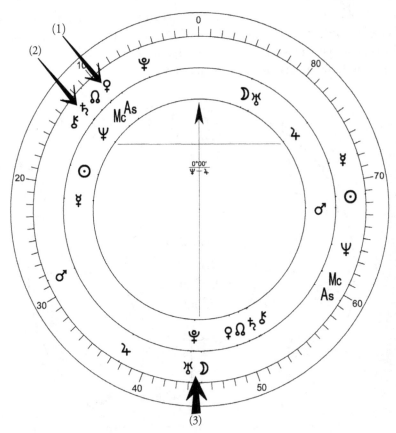

Figure 29a
Steve's Chart in 90° Dial Format
Inner wheel—Natal chart; Outer Wheel —Solar Arcs

Also in the first 30° natal Neptune is conjunct solar arc Saturn (2),
which lends itelf to a mathematical execution of plans to bring out that
which is hidden, or the fact that deceptive matters are brought to the forefront through hard work. Since Saturn is also conjunct solar arc Chiron,
there is a situation in need of great healing, and it will be a difficult road to
get through the healing process. This sounds pretty much like the difficulty
Steve would have investigating the hidden and deceptive practices in the
police department, and its need to heal and move forward after the scandal
is made public.

The most telling placement is in the next 30 degrees with natal Pluto
conjunct Solar Arc Uranus and the Solar Arc Moon (3). Pluto/Uranus may
manifest in acts of violence, subversive activities, or acts which would feel

like "holding a gun to someone's head." This sounds very much like the police activities Steve was investigating. When combining the Pluto/Uranus placement with a conjunction to the Moon, there would be the start of a new condition or change in the police department.

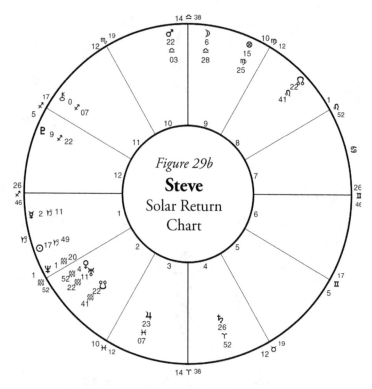

Figure 29b
Steve
Solar Return Chart

Steve's Solar Return Chart

When looking at Steve's solar return chart (above), you can see that this was certainly a year for Steve to come to prominence. What a way to do it—helping with a behind-the-scenes investigation bringing police corruption to the forefront!

The first thing I noticed in Steve's solar return chart was a yod with Mars in the tenth house and the North Node in the eighth house pointing to Jupiter in the third house. This yod in his solar return chart clearly suggested Steve's direction for the year. It was from his tenth and eighth houses (profession and government) to his third house of communication. Note that Mars was in Libra (justice and the law) in the tenth house of careers and honors. This project brought commendation and probably more notoriety than Steve wanted. Jupiter in the third house of communication suggested there was no way that this project could be covered up, and the corruption would come out. The North Node was in the eighth house (government and, in this case, the police). Both Mars and Jupiter suggested a great deal of communication with Jupiter in the third house. This was a very beneficial assignment for Steve. Mars indicated he had a great deal of energy which he needed since this assignment was in addition to his regular duties. Mars squared the Sun in Steve's first house and suggested a great deal of tension with this assignment. Mars opposed Saturn in the fourth house and suggested Steve also had tension from home (his wife did not like the extra work of the assignment). Mars sextiled the North Node and suggested the job would flow smoothly. At the time of the assignment, the transiting Sun was in Libra and conjunct Mars in the tenth house. This transiting luminary combined with the Mars energy suggested Steve could come to the forefront in his career. He may not be personally known to those involved in the corruption or to the public, but his superiors will recognize his work. What a difficult placement for a behind-the-scenes job! The point of the yod being transited by Jupiter in the third house of communication suggested that the whole scandal would be brought out. There seemed no way to keep it under wraps. The transiting Sun was conjunct Mars which is part of the yod and part of Steve's life direction for this year. This yod is also a reflection of the two yods in Steve's natal chart. **The yods suggest how far-reaching and very important this assignment was.** This was the start of major police reform and suggests a more humanitarian police department in the 21st century.

There is a grand trine with Saturn, the North Node and the Ascendant. The North Node again is in the eighth house (government/police work) and the Ascendant represents Steve's personal effort and personal recognition for the job. Saturn suggests very hard work and, in the fourth house, is based on Steve's foundation and upbringing, to do what is right. Saturn in the fourth house suggests Steve's psychological roots. He must be the overachiever. He must do something meaningful. Saturn is in a cardinal sign and implies a great deal of ambition and determination. Steve is persistent. He may feel a need to prove himself to his father. Saturn in a fire sign suggests breaking out of the rigidity associated with Saturn, and Steve had to think of more creative ways to achieve his goals. The Aries drive and the Saturn organization are perfect for executive work. Aries energy takes away the Saturn anxiety. However, Saturn suggests work alone, which is how Steve completed this assignment.

The solar return chart is a road map for the upcoming year. **A yod in the solar return chart is a map which has been marked and is ready to go.**

With most of the planets in the solar return in houses ten through three, Steve's frame of reference was very personal and he would not look the other way at what he perceived to be wrongdoing.

Steve had five cardinal planets in his solar return, which suggested a tremendous amount of activity. He was probably torn between what he wanted and needed to do. He had to be very organized and watch being too impulsive. However, as stated above, Saturn in Aries helped control the fire sign energy.

Steve had five air planets in his solar return chart. This suggested an emphasis on rational thought and a lack of emotional thought (especially true with only one water planet). This was a good time for organization and objectivity, and indicates the perfect mental state for an in-depth investigation. With only one water planet, Steve could have had the "macho man" attitude and been very self-sufficient. It was a good time to work alone.

The Sun in the first house suggested Steve would use personal effort and have personal success this year. According to Mary Shea in *Planets in Solar Returns*, the Sun in an angular house suggests a focus on new situations and correcting old ones. This was a time for a career push through personal effort and/or a new project. This certainly sounds like Steve's assignment of correcting police activities, and when the transits moved into January and February he should have received recognition at work.

The solar return Sun squared Mars in the tenth house, suggesting that Steve would have to work hard. Personal effort was the key. This was a very difficult aspect personally, just as this assignment was personally very difficult for Steve. It was a time for professional achievement, but it would only happen through very hard work at a very difficult time. Steve's Part of Sudden Advancement is in the first house suggesting Steve will personally take responsibility for any advancement in career this year.

The Moon reflects change in a solar return chart. The house in which the Moon sits suggests the area of change. Steve's Moon was in his ninth house. This indicated a change in his higher philosophies, or possibly higher education or travel to a foreign country. However, with regard to career, remember that the ninth house is the derivative twelfth house to the tenth house of career. The Moon here suggested a shake-up behind the scenes at work. This shake-up may have affected or altered Steve's higher conscious philosophy, but the change for Steve was his involvement in the shake-up in the police department. Since the Moon was in Libra, the suggested change probably deals with justice.

The Moon represents unconscious thought. With the Sun and Mercury in the first house, Steve is integrating higher philosophy and consciousness into personal action. This is an interesting placement for an investigation. Of course, Steve could not look the other way regarding the actions of his fellow officers. His own conscience would not let him do so; he had to actually take personal action with regard to the situation.

The Moon trine Neptune suggested Steve would intuitively know where to direct the investigation. The Moon also trined Venus in the second house and suggested a connection between higher conscious philosophy and personal values. The Moon in the ninth house implied work behind the scenes (since the ninth house is the derivative twelfth house to the career house). The Moon also suggested the work would be rewarded with financial gain or promotion (or both) since it was trine the second house of money. The Moon in Libra in the ninth house indicates that Steve went back and forth, over and over again, evaluating the issues at hand. This may have been a very emotional time for Steve while he was dealing with Libra issues of justice and the law. Remember, other placements suggested a lack of emotion, so whatever he was feeling, he probably kept to himself.

Transiting Venus went from the eighth to the ninth house during the first week of the investigation. since Venus is pleasure-oriented, that suggested Steve would have some protection and peace of mind during this most difficult time. The Venus in Virgo transit to the eighth house of government was very significant during the week of the investigation. It squared Pluto in Sagittarius in the twelfth house just as it left the eighth house. Since Sagittarius suggests idealism and Pluto suggests reorganization and reformation, Steve's situation seemed to be that of the idealistic man trying to help reform the police department from behind the scenes, but the square aspect indicated that this was a very difficult job. Transiting Venus was trine to Mercury in the first house, suggesting a great deal of thought and personal activity for Steve.

When the transiting Moon was conjunct Neptune at the end of the first week of the investigation, it trined the ninth house Moon and suggested the changes and shake-ups behind the scenes of work at the very time Steve was probably writing his report. The Moon trine the Moon seemed to represent the changes which immediately followed the report.

With Mercury in an angular house and in a cardinal sign, Steve was probably overscheduling and trying to do too many things at once. It suggested he was stressed by demands. If Mercury were not in Capricorn, Steve could have been really out of control, but Capricorn suggests organization, and that Steve could handle the situation at this time.

Mercury trined Saturn, albeit out of sign, but in this case I think it works, suggesting seriousness and structure in thought. What Steve finally decided should go into his report, along with the entire investigation itself, certainly had serious consequences. This was the start of prisoner release, review of over 300 cases, the hiring of more prosecutors for police misconduct, the politicians and police higher-ups pointing fingers at each other, and so forth.

Mercury square the Moon in the ninth house suggested again that Steve was going back and forth over the issues. It must have been very difficult, and a very emotional issue, to think of investigating fellow officers.

Venus can symbolize relationships and finances for the coming year and Venus had all good aspects in Steve's chart. Venus in the second house was trining the Moon, suggesting a change in jobs or possibly a salary increase. Venus here also suggested dealing with moral or ethical issues, which was certainly the case this year for Steve.

Steve's Part of Fortune is in the third house of communication suggesting the communication to the public of the police department's wrongdoing. Although this may be difficult, it may be fortunate for Steve. Communication and reports are strongly favored this year.

Steve's Part of Profession is in the sixth house at 6 Gemini suggesting that Steve's work is very important this year.

Mars shows us where energy is expended. In Steve's case, Mars in the tenth house suggested lots of energy geared toward production, self motivation, independent action and new projects. In other words, a majority of Steve's energy this year would be spent on career. Mars was quincunx Jupiter which indicates verbal flare-ups at work or, in this case, negative remarks to the press. Mars was sextile the North Node in the eighth house of government which can be good for promotion and new assignments.

More importantly, Mars in Libra is ruled by Venus in the second house suggesting moral issues and personal values were involved with Steve's potential promotion and/or pay raise. Again, Steve's assignment definitely dealt with moral issues and values.

Mars in opposition to Saturn in the fourth house suggested trouble from home. Again, Steve's wife did not like this assignment as it involved additional hours and possibly some danger for Steve.

Mars was semisquare Pluto in the twelfth house. Per Ebertin, this suggests extraordinary vigor and self-confidence but also injury through assault. This investigation had the potential of being dangerous and the danger could have come from some of the officers involved in the wrongdoing. This danger was also suggested in Steve's natal chart, and he needed to be warned to watch out without sounding too loud an alarm. This is one of those situations where you must try to help your client but do so tactfully. Warnings should be expressed as caveats.

Per Ebertin, the Mars/Pluto/Saturn aspects indicate a person who leaves no stone unturned, an obvious plus for this assignment.

Mars in the tenth house suggests much initiative and individual work. There is a lot of drive to get the job done. Transiting Mars was on the Ascendant and conjunct Mercury in the first house. Again, here was the personal drive and energy. This is a very strong transit when coupled with Mars in the tenth house of the solar return chart. Steve was totally driven at this time.

Jupiter is often beneficial to the house in which it is located in the solar return chart. Jupiter symbolizes expansion. In a water sign, the expansion may be overwhelming. In Steve's case, Jupiter was in the third house of conscious mind and communication. Jupiter here suggested a tremendous amount of activity. Concentration was very important. It was a time during which the mind wanted to expand. Jupiter here also implied that Steve would be involved with ethical questions. It suggested difficult decisions. This was certainly true in light of Steve's investigation.

Remember Jupiter is the point of the finger of the yod between Mars and the North Node combining philosophy, moral decisions and career. These are the only aspects to Jupiter other than a square to the Ascendant which suggests personal soul-searching and moral questioning. Can you imagine how difficult this year and this assignment in particular had come to be?

Saturn suggests the harshness of reality. In the solar return, Saturn shows our limitations and the areas upon which we must work in order to grow. With Saturn in the fourth house, Steve came face to face with his foundation and who he is. Was he one of the guys, or would his principles take over? Could he investigate fairly? This appears to be the harsh reality with which he was dealing. Saturn suggested acceptance of responsibility and difficult consequences.

One positive aspect is Saturn trine both the North Node and Ascendant. With this trine, personal effort and hard work are usually rewarded. According to Ebertin, the Saturn and North Node aspect indicates that personal effort will be rewarded, but also can indicate feelings of isolation. This assignment was definitely isolating.

Uranus suggests upheaval, and change is not easy. You throw things up in the air and the pieces fall where they may. Conditions in the house in which Uranus is located change significantly over the year. You may or may not seek change, but change will occur. Uranus suggests a period of detachment and separation.

Uranus in the second house suggests a change in earning power and finances (major or minor). Change could have been negative or positive. In Steve's case with Venus here, the suggested change should have been positive. Also morals and values were being reviewed and changed. For Steve, this placement suggested a change in the values of the police department. Uranus could mean Steve would have to defend his report to his fellow officers. In other words, there would be dissension, and he would have to defend himself and his standards.

Uranus was trine the Moon and conjunct Venus. As discussed, the Moon was in the ninth house of higher philosophy and Venus was in the second house of values, suggesting the pulling together of values and personal philosophy into a time of self-definition. Uranus was also sextile Pluto in the twelfth house and trine the Midheaven (the cusp of the career house). Transiting Uranus was also interesting in that it sat in the second house of personal values and was trine Mars in the tenth house of career. The large number of aspects and transits in this solar return chart indicated the importance of Steve's investigation, based on his personal values and philosophies, and the shake-up it would cause, as well as the potential benefit financially with a promotion for Steve. However, the most important thing was the long-term (the Pluto sextile) changes the investigation would cause in the police department based on a strong set of personal values, philosophy, and a good foundation.

In a natal chart, Neptune represents generational attributes; in a solar return chart, it becomes more of a personal planet. Thus, here it suggests personal beliefs, spirituality or personal ideals. Since Neptune in Steve's chart is in the first house which represents personal traits, this suggestion is intensified. Neptune here implies commitment to something much larger than oneself based upon strong personal principles. He was obviously disillusioned by uncovering the activities of his fellow police officers. He was seeking the higher values of his profession. As an individual, Steve was insignificant in the overall picture, and working for the good of the whole. Neptune here also suggested that Steve should be aware of the possibility that others might try to deceive him.

Neptune was trining the Moon in the ninth house suggesting a very emotional time when dealing with higher issues. It was conjunct Venus (which represents personal values) and sat in the second house of personal values. This conjunction was very positive. These aspects were very important to the investigation.

Neptune was also square Saturn; Steve had to work very hard at this time and stay balanced between reality (Saturn) and illusion (Neptune).

Pluto was in the twelfth house and is very much at home there. There were probably things going on with the investigation and behind the scenes that even Steve did not know about.

Saturn was part of the grand trine. This trine was from the Ascendant to Saturn and the North Node in the eighth house of government. This again pointed to Steve's personal effort (Ascendant), based on his foundation and personal values and to the government (in his case, the police department). As you know, the eighth house represents taxes, government, insurance and other people's money. The reason I feel you must know a little about your client's circumstances is to see which of these definitions is pertinent to the situation at hand. At this point in Steve's life, the eighth house seemed to be representing the government .

Pluto suggests the understanding of complex issues—the bad cops and Steve's efforts to bring the situation to light. Pluto in the twelfth house was not the most opportune time to bring matters to light, but, because of the press, keeping the investigation from the public was impossible. With Jupiter in the third house of communication at the point of the yod, this investigation came out.

Pluto is sextile Uranus indicating transformation and collapse of an old order. Uranus is chaotic. Once this investigation started, the impetus of the investigation carried it along. When all is finally said and done, there should be new values and a new order in this particular division. After the first two months of the new year, and only four months after the initial report, great changes occurred. Over twenty officers were suspended; over forty convictions were overturned. A federal investigation into civil rights violations was ordered. There seemed no end in sight.

Pluto/Uranus (according to Ebertin in his *Combination of Stellar Influences*) may also indicate acts of violence. There was a real possibility of urban unrest because of this scandal, as well as violence within the department itself. This was yet another aspect combination indicating potential violence. Pluto was semisquare Mars in the tenth house and Mars was part of the yod. This transformation of the police force was very difficult (the semisquare) and again the problems were brought out into the open (tenth house Mars as part of the yod). Mars/Pluto (according to Ebertin) can also

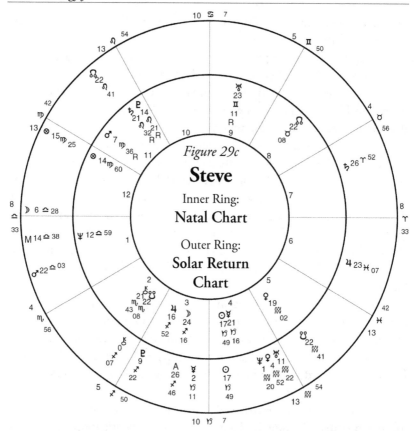

Figure 29c

Steve

Inner Ring:
Natal Chart

Outer Ring:
Solar Return Chart

mean violence. Again, Steve had to watch for violence, and the city could have had to deal with urban unrest as a result of the findings.

In figure 27c, I have placed Steve's natal chart as the inner wheel and the solar return chart as the outer wheel. Wherever the solar return house cusp sits well within the natal chart can suggest conflict between the two houses. It is interesting to note that the only houses that do not have another house cusp sitting well within them are the sixth house (work and service) and the twelfth house (subconscious motivation and hidden matters). Obviously, no matter how conflicted Steve may be with his assignment, deep down in his soul there is no real conflict between his unconscious motivations and his work.

When placing the planets of the solar return chart around the natal chart, you will note that the Midheaven (the cusp of the tenth career house) sits in the first house, bringing a great deal of personal effort into Steve's career this year. Mars sits in the first house suggesting a great deal of drive and energy.

The solar return Midheaven squares the natal Sun in the fourth house and sextiles natal Pluto in the eleventh house. Again, as in other areas of the charts that have been discussed, there is a conflict between career, personal efforts for the good of something greater than himself, and the home or foundation.

Solar return Pluto sits in the natal third house of communication and represents reorganization of thought. It also suggests that the reorganization going on will be communicated to the public. Since Pluto is associated with the masses and/or the whole, this will be a reorganization of procedure, supervision and attitude within the department. Only a few months after the initial report, there were many news reports on television, as well as front section articles in the newspaper. Solar return Pluto conjunct natal Jupiter can lead to roles of leadership, which in this case is leadership for reform.

The solar return Ascendant is conjunct the natal third house Moon (this Ascendant is also part of a grand trine). The solar return Mercury sits in the natal third as well. Although the investigation, along with the resulting shake-up and public scrutiny, is something the police department (and city officials) would like to avoid, because the Ascendant, Pluto and Mercury are sitting in the natal third house of communication, it would be almost impossible to avoid public awareness.

Neptune, Venus and Uranus in the solar return sit in the natal fourth house and oppose the tenth house. Again, this assignment was met with negativity at home. Also, the fourth house is the derivative seventh house of the tenth house and reading these planets as partners to tenth house matters, Steve must watch for deception from partners (Neptune) and also self-deception in not wanting to see what is really happening.

Solar return Jupiter is in the natal sixth house and suggests an expansion of work and duties. This is also part of the finger of fate yod with solar return Mars (first house) and solar return North Node (eleventh house). As you can see, the solar return yod is pointing directly to the natal house of work and service, showing potential havoc at work.

Solar return Saturn sits in the natal seventh house. It is part of the grand trine which sits in the natal eleventh house and natal third house. The eleventh house is associated with groups and hopes for the future, and the third house is communication, another suggestion that the scandal will come out. Saturn is also opposing Steve's natal first house. Since Saturn is the area within which Steve must work and in which there may be obstacles, his personal efforts will probably be blocked by partners in the department, and he must work very hard for reform. Again, this also suggests that his marriage partner is not happy with this assignment.

The solar return North Node (part of the solar return grand trine) is conjunct natal Saturn in the natal eleventh house (remember solar return Saturn is part of that grand trine and is giving the grand trine a double dose of Saturn obstacles and lessons, as well as hard work). However, I feel Saturn is a good place to look since this is where progress is important. The lessons of this Saturn are reform of the group and good of the whole. This is the beginning of reform in departmental attitudes and activities even though these Saturn lessons are hard to learn.

The solar return Moon is in the twelfth and is conjunct the natal Ascendant. This is a very emotional time for Steve. It is a difficult assignment. With the Moon sitting in the natal twelfth house, he will keep his emotions hidden, but they are very deep. He probably could use some counseling at this time to get through this most difficult task. **This is one of those times when, if you are not a trained counselor or therapist, you should really encourage your client to seek short-term professional help to get through a difficult situation.**

When delineating Steve's chart, I find it is the combination of planets and their aspects, and the houses within which they sit, more than the signs the planets are in, that truly tells the story.

Solar Return Midpoints

Remember, in natal charts, prominence with a moral component is suggested when Pluto is conjunct a midpoint within 1 degree or 2 degrees at the very most. The same is true to some extent in solar return charts. At least there is a suggestion of prominence and moral or ethical transformation for the solar return year. In Steve's solar return chart, the midpoint of his ninth house Moon and second house Uranus is conjunct his twelfth house Pluto within one degree. Also the Venus/Midheaven midpoint is conjunct Pluto within 1 degree in the twelfth house. Since this is a sign of prominence, no matter how internal and behind the scenes the investigation was, there was a very strong possibility it would be brought to the forefront. Also, the twelfth house is the derivative third house of communication to the career house, so this Pluto midpoint combination suggests communication to the public.

Although there are several midpoints conjunct planets in the solar return chart, the Moon/Uranus midpoint stands out in relation to Steve's career because the ninth house Moon (changes behind the scenes of the career) and Uranus (which represents chaos and is in Steve's personal value house) are combined with Pluto (long-reaching reform and reorganization). The Venus/Midheaven midpoint just adds to the strength of this point and also tends to be beneficial for Steve in his career. The Moon is in Libra (the sign of justice). The results of this investigation will be very progressive and human rights will benefit greatly. In fact, this investigation has already been described by one top official as a "life-altering experience" for the department.

If you are having difficulty in helping a client find a time to move forward with his/her career, **an extension of the above discussed solar return midpoint** is a useful method. Place the solar return planets around your client's natal chart; when a solar return midpoint sits conjunct a natal planet within one or two degrees it also creates a very strong point with which to work.

Steve's Lunar Return

See figure 29c on page 210. Steve's assignment to help with an initial report on police corruption lasted over a short period of time and I will delineate the lunar return chart for the month the report was finished.

The Moon, the most important planet in a lunar return chart, is in the third house of thought, communication and writing, so it would stand to reason Steve's report would initiate change and reform, and would be communicated to the public this month. Steve has only two planets above the horizon and the rest of his lunar return planets are below the horizon, suggesting he will work behind the scenes or his work will be more private, even though later it will be communicated to the public.

Steve has a lunar return Virgo Ascendant suggesting a practical, competent and discreet approach to work this month. Venus in Libra in the first house suggests charm and the ability to handle people, which would be good for this assignment. Libra suggests a balanced approach to the law.

The Sun in the second house suggests Steve may be feeling compromised by his position when writing this report. The Sun here suggests a lot of energy put into personal values, and he must report what is right regardless of consequences or the animosity of his peers. The Sun here suggests that his self-worth is more important to him than compromising his principles. The Sun is part of a T-square with Uranus and Saturn suggesting the difficulty Steve will experience when acting on his personal standards, and the shake-up that is coming with Uranus in Aquarius. Uranus sits in the fifth house suggesting a creative approach. In Aquarius, it suggests that visionary and far-reaching reform may stem from this initial report. The point of the T-square without a planet, or the missing part of the T-square, is thirteen degrees Leo in the eleventh house of dreams and wishes, indicating Steve's wish for the future of the police department or a better police department with this assignment.

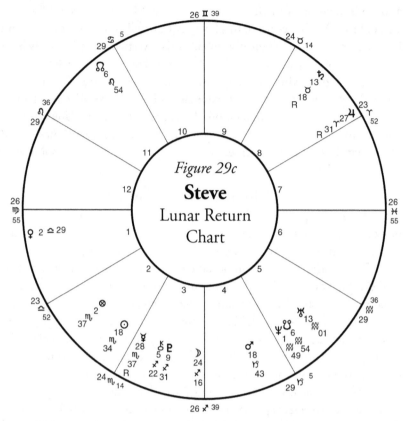

Figure 29c
Steve
Lunar Return
Chart

There is a lot of activity in the third house of communication and conscious thought. Steve will be very stirred up mentally with Mercury, Pluto and the Moon there.

Steve has two yods in this chart or two "fingers of fate." The first yod is Jupiter and the Midheaven pointing to Mercury in the third house. This yod alone suggests Steve's current assignment with Mercury, the writing of the report, and brings in Jupiter in the eighth house of government (the police department) and the Midheaven which is the cusp of Steve's career house. This is the third chart that has a yod suggesting Steve's position at this time and reinforces his natal and solar return charts.

Pluto is also in the third house. Pluto suggests a time of transformation and a time to deal with difficult subjects. Pluto here is not superficial thoughts. Pluto is in Sagittarius suggesting idealism. Pluto suggests mental power games and also investigation. Thus, Pluto also suggests this investigation and report, and in the house of communication, that the report will come out. Pluto in the third house suggests transformation through communication. Pluto is conjunct the Moon/Mercury midpoint suggesting communication with emotions will be involved in the transformation. Pluto is conjunct the Venus/Uranus midpoint suggesting a shake-up (Uranus motif) of some kind. This described Steve's work on the initial report which became public and caused a major shake-up. Pluto is also conjunct the Moon/Mercury midpoint in the third house, the Moon suggesting change, Pluto suggesting transformation and Mercury suggesting writing and communication. This describes the result of Steve's report.

The Moon is also in the third house, suggesting this may be an emotional time. In Sagittarius, Moon suggests Steve's ideals are in the forefront of his mind, and his report should reflect his feelings and thoughts. The Moon is part of a T-square with Ascendant and Midheaven, bringing personal effort and career into play. Thus, Steve's personal actions, emotions and the ideals he is communicating through this report and career are tied together. With the T-square, this month could be difficult for Steve.

Mars in the fourth house indicates there may be tension at home. However, Mars trines Saturn in the eighth house of government suggesting energy for hard work this month in Steve's job in the police department.

Neptune and Uranus are both in the fifth house in Aquarius suggesting an unusual, creative approach and a shake-up as well. Neptune square Jupiter in the eighth house of government suggests insight but difficulty, and challenges around visions, ideals and ethics, while Jupiter suggests expansion and opportunity. Uranus is sesqui-square the Ascendant and Midheaven suggesting this assignment may be personally chaotic, as well as causing a shake-up in career. Both Uranus and Neptune are in Aquarius suggesting idealism and reform. This is Steve's derivative twelfth house to his sixth house of work and service suggesting a shake-up and confusion behind the scenes at work and, of course, his assignment was to be done behind the scenes.

Aquarius is on the cusp of Steve's sixth house of work and is ruled by Uranus in the fifth house. Again, the fifth house is the "behind the scenes" house of work, so work will be done in the background and Aquarius suggests visionary and far reaching reform.

Steve's Part of Sudden Advancement is 16 Pisces in the sixth house of work, suggesting advancement in work this month.

There are two planets in the eighth house. The eighth house, among other things, is government, and in Steve's case, the police department. Both Jupiter and Saturn sit here, and these are two of the planets that I look at closely in career counseling. Jupiter here suggests expansion and opportunity. Jupiter in Aries suggests high ethical standards and the en-

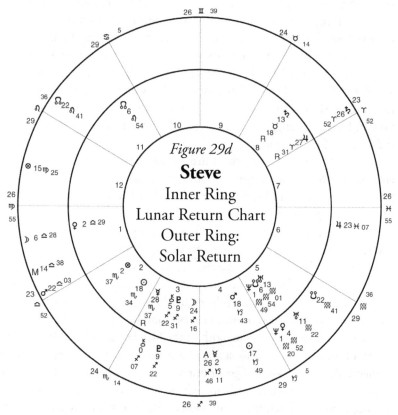

Figure 29d
Steve
Inner Ring
Lunar Return Chart
Outer Ring:
Solar Return

ergy to push forward toward your ideals. Saturn in Taurus here suggests hard, down-to-earth work and a great deal of responsibility. With this placement, Steve may see the best but also the worst in his fellow officers. Saturn's placement suggests an area where hard work of the past is rewarded or, if work has not been done properly, it will come back to haunt you. It may also suggest the beginning of hard work toward something new and better. In Steve's case, the Jupiter/Saturn placements this month really describe his assignment and initial report on police corruption. The eighth house police department's past actions came back to haunt them "big time." Jupiter suggests opportunity and growth in the police department. Saturn suggests that, although the wrongdoing of the past will come out, there is a beginning of hard work toward a better police department.

Jupiter is in Aries and Aries is ruled by Mars in the fourth house. This suggests Steve's foundational values will come into play. Saturn in Taurus is ruled by Venus in the first house and suggests personal responsibility and hard work for Steve. Saturn is trine Mars suggesting a lot of energy expended toward work this month. Jupiter is trine the Moon suggesting emotions. Since the Moon is in the third house, it suggests a lot of communication as well as emotional issues. Jupiter is part of the yod with Mercury in the third house of communication and the Ascendant, so Steve will have personal input and there will be a great deal of communication. It is also part of the yod with Mercury and the Midheaven. This one placement totally suggests Steve's actions regarding the report and its effect, both personally and on his career, as well as its effect on the police department this month.

Steve's Part of Profession is 7 Taurus in the eighth house of government (police department) suggesting this month is very important to Steve in his profession.

Gemini is on the cusp of the tenth house of career. This suggests possibly two jobs or doing more than your usual job, as was the case with the extra work on the report. It also suggests a lot of mental activity. Gemini is ruled by Mercury in the third house of communication and writing. For Steve, the communication and writing came out in his career house in the form of the report that was made public. Mercury is in Scorpio and is co-ruled by Pluto. Pluto is also in the third house suggesting Steve's report may begin a process of transformation.

Steve's Part of Fortune is in the eleventh house of dreams, hopes and wishes for the future, suggesting he will be able to make a difference; his wishes for a better police department should come to fruition in the future, based on work started this month.

As you can see, Steve's lunar return reinforces the delineation of his solar return and natal charts. The themes that are repeated again and again in each chart are very strong indications of work, career opportunity and change this month. Because Steve has yods in all charts, his career opportunity is quite apparent. It is unusual to find so many yods throughout multiple charts. At this point in time, his career is very important both to Steve and to the police department.

When placing the solar return planets around the lunar return chart, (see Figure 29d on the previous page) we can see how the year's forecast compares and enhances this month's forecast. The Moon suggests changes. In the solar return chart, the Moon sits conjunct the solar return Midheaven which is widely conjunct Mars, all of which sit in Steve's lunar return first house. This suggests Steve's personal efforts and energies may create change in career since the Midheaven is the cusp of the career house. Mars suggests a lot of energy expended. The solar return Moon conjunct lunar return Venus in Libra in the first house suggests Steve will have good mental balance even in emotional situations. The solar return Moon trines lunar return Uranus in the fifth house suggesting radical and unexpected change, and it trines Neptune suggesting insight and intuition. It is sextile lunar return Pluto in the third house of communication and again suggests change created by Steve's report.

Solar return Mercury trines lunar return Jupiter suggesting communication along with opportunity at the police department but Mercury is opposite the lunar return's tenth house of career suggesting this is a mentally difficult assignment for Steve. In fact, solar return Ascendant, Mercury and Sun all sit in Steve's lunar return fourth house of foundation and oppose the tenth house of career, suggesting a difficult time with this assignment this month. It appears he would prefer to hide at home rather than have to write this report. Also, it suggests conflict between home and career and, as stated previously, his wife was not particularly fond of this assignment. Also, his foundational values would be opposed to what has been going on at his place of his work and career.

Steve's solar return Venus is in the lunar return fifth house suggesting charm and balance to deal with radical changes behind the scenes at work and it is trine solar return Venus in the first house giving some ease to this personally difficult assignment.

Steve's solar return Jupiter is in the lunar return sixth house suggesting expansion and opportunity at work.

Perhaps the second most telling placement is solar return Saturn within a one-degree conjunction with lunar return Jupiter in the eighth house of government. This brings the Saturn/Jupiter motif of the police department discussed above to a very close and strong conjunction, and suggests opportunity for a new direction which, through hard work, should create a better police department.

Thus, the solar return planets sitting in the first, third, fifth, sixth and eighth lunar return houses reinforce the delineation of the natal and solar return charts.

Solar return Saturn now sits conjunct Jupiter which is a part of the Mercury, Jupiter, Midheaven and Jupiter, Mercury and Ascendant yods. This placement is the key to the report coming out this month. Saturn is indeed suggesting that the wrongdoing of the police in the past will come out, and also is suggesting a start for a new and better police department in the 21st Century. This appears to be the month the report should come out, and also the month the report should start a transformational process for the future.

As you can see, although Steve has no planets in his tenth house and only two planets above the horizon on his lunar return chart, by looking at the entire chart we have strong career potential this year and this month. Solar return planets sitting in the first, third and eighth houses of the lunar return chart and lunar return planets in these houses as well are very important to career potential. As stated before, I feel you must know your client's circumstances to delineate effectively. It helps to know that Steve is a police officer since this fact steered me into looking at the eighth house of government for career insight. Also, in the lunar return chart Uranus and Neptune sit in the fifth house. I could suggest problems with a child, and that may very well be the case along with career implications, but knowing Steve is a police officer and seeing the eighth house, this Neptune/Uranus placement strongly suggests, coupled with natal and solar return charts, changes behind the scenes at work, as well as dealing with egotists.

Conclusion

The "at least three charts" method enables you to develop a very clear picture of the motifs and career potential suggested in your clients' astrology charts. As you can see from the examples of Sarah, John and Carole, each of their charts either enhance or add to the motifs suggested in their other charts. It is the repetition of the motifs which will guide you in career counseling. When you add the advanced methods into the three charts delineation, you will be able delve even more deeply into analysis of the charts, drawing career potential from less obvious or somewhat obscure parts of the astrology chart. Steve's chart is a very good example of in-depth delineation with a view toward career.

**Thank you for considering the
"at least three charts" method in
career counseling and
best wishes for success in all
of your astrological endeavors.**

Reference Books

Astrology at a Glance,
Barbara Hawkins and Gayle Lakin-Geffner,
Hawkins Press, 1986.

A-Z Horoscope Maker, Llewellyn George,
Llewellyn Publications, 1978.

Combination of Stellar Influences, Reinhold Ebertin,
Ebertin-Verlag, 1972

Dial Detective: Investigation with the 90° Dial
Maria Kay Simms
Cosmic Muse Publications 2001, an imprint of Starcrafts LLC

Planets in Solar Returns, Mary Shea,
ACS Publications, 1992

Planets in Transit, Rober Hand,
Whitford Press, a division of Schiffer Publishing, inc. 1987

Rulership Book, Rex E. Bills,
American Federation of Astrologers, 1991

Transits, Reinhold Ebertin,
American Federation of Astrologers, 1971

Yod, Miss Dee,
American Federation of Astrologers, 1989

Chart data for public figures and celebrities are taken form Lois
Rodden's AstroDataBank,
currently accessed through Astrodienst
www.astro.com

About the Author

Gayle Geffner has been an astrologer for over thirty-five years. She has published articles in *Aspect Magazine* (USA), *The Regulus Ebertin Newsletter* (Australia), *Today's Astrologer*, published by the American Federation of Astrologers (USA) and *Baltimore, Maryland Chapter of NCGR Newsletter*, *NCGR's Memberletter* (international) and *NCGR's Geocosmic Journal* (international). Gayle has authored an  earlier version of this book, *Pathways to Success: Discover Your Career Potential with Astrology*, published by ACS Publications in San Diego, and she is also author of the book, *Creative Step-Parenting*, published by American Federation of Astrologers. She is co-author, with Barbara Hawkins, *Astrology At A Glance: A Guide for Astrological Delineation* published by American Federation of Astrologers, which is a classroom guide.

Gayle's academic degres include a BA in History from California State University, and two paralegal certificates from University of West Los Angeles School of Law (in corporations and in litigation). She currently lives in Los Angles, CA.

To contact the author, write to:
Gayle Geffner
c/o ACS Publications, Starcrafts LLC
334-A Calef Highway
Epping, NH 03042

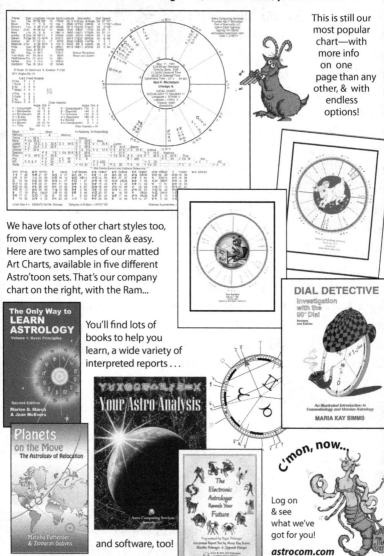

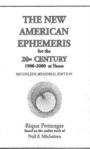
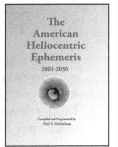
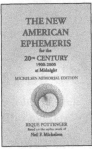
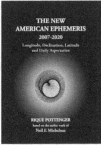

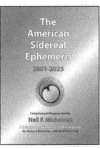

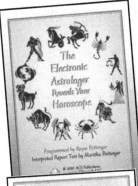